THE TRUTH OF IMAGINATION

Some Uncollected Reviews and Essays by

EDWIN MUIR

AUP titles of related interest

THE HISTORY OF SCOTTISH LITERATURE
general editor Cairns Craig

Volume 1 Medieval and Renaissance *editor R D S Jack*
Volume 2 1660 to 1800 *editor Andrew Hook*
Volume 3 Nineteenth Century *editor Douglas Gifford*
Volume 4 Twentieth Century *editor Cairns Craig*

TEN MODERN SCOTTISH NOVELS
Isobel Murray and Bob Tait

A BLASPHEMER AND REFORMER
a study of James Leslie Mitchell/Lewis Grassic Gibbon
William Malcolm

LITERATURE OF THE NORTH
edited by David Hewitt and Michael Spiller

POPULAR LITERATURE IN VICTORIAN SCOTLAND
Language, fiction and the press
William Donaldson

LANDSCAPE AND LIGHT
Essays by *Neil M Gunn*
edited by Alistair McCleery

A BIBLIOGRAPHY OF THE WORKS OF NEIL M GUNN
C J L Stokoe

GRAMPIAN HAIRST
an anthology of Northeast prose
edited by William Donaldson and Douglas Young

FROM THE CLYDE TO CALIFORNIA
Robert Louis Stevenson
edited and introduced by Andrew Noble

THE LAIRD OF DRAMMOCHDYLE
William Alexander
Introduction by William Donaldson

THE TRUTH OF IMAGINATION

Some Uncollected Reviews and Essays

by

EDWIN MUIR

edited and introduced by

P H BUTTER

ABERDEEN UNIVERSITY PRESS

First Published 1988
Aberdeen University Press
A member of the Pergamon Group

The Publisher acknowledges subsidy from the Scottish Arts Council towards the publication of this volume.

British Library Cataloguing in Publication Data

Muir, Edwin, *1887-1959*
The truth of imagination: some uncollected reviews and essays
1. Literature, ca 1800-1950. Critical studies
I. Title II. Butter, P. H. (Peter Herbert), 1921-
809'.03

ISBN 0 08 036392 X

Printed in Great Britain
The University Press
Aberdeen

CONTENTS

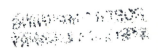

PREFACE

Muir's criticism 'was of the best of our time', wrote T S Eliot. Most of it was contributed as essays and reviews to periodicals. His wit and discrimination sustained over long periods of reviewing three or more books a fortnight were extraordinary. Most of the best of the essays were collected in *Latitudes* (1924), *Transition* (1926) and *Essays on Literature and Society* (1949, enlarged 1965); and the best of his contributions on Scottish literature are available in *Edwin Muir: Uncollected Scottish Criticism,* ed Noble (1982). This volume is a selection from the mass of criticism (dozens of essays, about a thousand reviews) that has not yet been collected.

There is no point in reading about books one has not read and never will. So most of my selections concern writers who are still well known. Those which deal with writers who are not much read now are chosen with the hope of leading some to make discoveries, and are naturally all favourable; one does not dig up the dead only to bury them. They should not give the impression that Muir was weakly indulgent; they are assessments of only a few of the several thousand books he reviewed. Though a sheep-spotter rather than a goat-slayer he discriminated firmly between the excellent, the good and the mediocre.

In order to cover a fair range of writers I have omitted many interesting reviews of books by authors whom he wrote of several times; and have listed some of these in the notes. Those who wish to explore further should refer to Elgin W Mellown's *Bibliography of the Writings of Edwin Muir* (Nicholas Vane, 1964; revised 1966) and his *Supplement to Bibliography of the Writings of Edwin Muir* (University of Alabama Press, 1970).

In the Chapter headings 'English' refers to writings, other than by Americans, in the English language. Where a writer, because of appearing with another in a review which cannot be divided, appears in the wrong chapter, this is indicated by an asterisk in the table of contents.

I gratefully acknowledge the help of Mr Mellown for his bibliographies; of Mr Gavin Muir, the copyright-holder; and of the staffs of many libraries, especially of Glasgow University Library, Manchester Central Library, the Mitchell Library, Glasgow and the National Library of Scotland.

I

ENGLISH

E M FORSTER   A Passage to India

The Nation (New York) CXIX,
8 October 1924, 379–80

Mr E M Forster stands apart from the main movements of present-day English literature. He has a striking lack of eagerness for doing the things which other writers do, a striking freedom from the mob instinct in a region where it is today strongest, among writers and artists. He is inclined toward the ironical school of which Mr Lytton Strachey is the instructor, but he differs from Mr Strachey's pupils in an important respect: they underline their inclination until they succeed in making it resemble Mr Strachey's as closely as possible, but Mr Forster lets his remain where it is, supported on itself. His work is a work of inclinations, adroitly balanced, and rarely slipping into the faux pas of a decision. With great tact he knows how to go half-way in any given direction, and his talent consists in knowing exactly where the half-way point is. This knowledge implies a great deal of experience in reserve behind it, and there is no doubt that that experience is real. Mr Forster gives his reservations the weight of categories which everybody would be more intelligent by accepting; and no doubt they would, though Mr Forster attaches too much importance to intelligence. He writes always as a man who knows better than any one else while not insisting on the fact. And he writes thus because he is, first, a capable man, and, secondly, a man of taste. He knows where he stands; he has found his place, and there is a note of assurance, accordingly, in all he says. But although his utterance is genuine as that of few of his contemporaries is, one doubts whether it is profound. The intellect is not exercised to its utmost in going half-way in all directions. Practical expedience, intelligence of a rare kind, may be shown in doing that; but hardly wisdom, not the passion for truth which animates great art. Mr Forster does not possess these qualities; on the other hand, he has an intelligence of greater force and purity than that of any other imaginative writer today. That intelligence is a scrupulously truthful one; but its distinguishing character is its refusal to pursue truth beyond a certain point. This is why his books, in spite of their skill, produce a total effect which is not decisive.

A Passage to India is a very accomplished novel. It is the kind of novel which could be written only by a very cultivated man, but it shows Mr Forster's cultivation more clearly than it does his intuition. He does not convince one that he understands his characters; he convinces one only that he understands their misunderstandings, that he knows where they are wrong. His theme is the antagonism, founded largely upon misapprehension, between a colony of Anglo-Indians in a little Indian town and the natives; but although he never shirks the subject he never gets to close grips with it. His picture of mutual misunderstanding is consummate. He presents English people and Indians speaking together, the Indians at a word flying off at an incomprehensible tangent, the English blankly amazed. Nothing could be better than his account of the party at Fielding's, where some English people and two Indians, chatting amiably, find themselves, without knowing why, moving poles asunder. There is the most exquisite artifice in this economically managed scene. The trial, too, is beautifully rendered, and the riot after it is wonderfully neat, a little too neat. Mr Forster always says the right word, selects the significant detail; yet his art is essentially a kind of impressionism. Miss Quested, the open-minded young Englishwoman who comes to India resolved to know it and refusing to be put off with 'a frieze of Indians', gets little more than that in the end, nor do we; for Mr Forster's Indians have the coldness of a procession, and if more delicately exact than Mr Kipling's, they have less personality. The author gives us glimpses of their psychology, but he does not understand that psychology, and cannot explain it to us. It is here that a reader who wants to pursue one path until he comes to the end will rebel against Mr Forster's intelligent resolve to go only half the way. There is no end, Mr Forster would no doubt reply. Here is a picture of the muddle: if you try to probe it farther it will only become more baffling. At any rate, his picture is wonderfully drawn. He holds the balance evenly between the Anglo-Indians and the natives, without a hint of prejudice, idealistic or imperialist, and with no fear of the opinions of the English public. He is above the quarrel, and without much hope for its issue. It required courage of a rare kind to write the book.

The story is simple. Mrs Moore and Miss Quested, the prospective fiancée of Mrs Moore's son, come to India, and are at first repelled by the English official attitude to the Indians. When they suggest a more sympathetic attitude they are always told from the height of a ten or twenty years' experience, 'That is not the point'; and baffled by the English, they turn to the Indians. But by these they are baffled in a different way: they find good-will, even gratitude, but they are misunderstood at every turn. Their sympathy eventually involves them in an adventure in which the younger woman is sexually assaulted, or thinks she is (the point is not clear), in a cave to which a young Moslem doctor has conducted her. The doctor, who is innocent, is arrested and tried; there is a prodigious racial fuss raised by the English, and hysterical indignation among the natives. In the end the doctor is acquitted by the testimony of the woman who accused him, who comes to the conclusion that she was suffering from hallucination. For letting them down she is forthwith ostracised by the Anglo-

Indians. A tumult follows the legal decision, and the English fear violence, but the riot passes into a farce. The novel, one feels, should have ended here; but Mr Forster adds a final section portraying, with an unconvincing irony, an aspect of Indian religious life. It is the only feeble part of the novel, and, seeing that it is the end, the part which could least suffer to be feeble. But, apart from it, the book is executed with rare scrupulousness. The writing, when it does not slip into fine writing, as it does once or twice, is a continuous delight. The novel is a triumph of the humanistic spirit over material difficult to humanise. It is this first of all, it is also a work of art exquisite rather than profound. Last of all it is a peculiarly valuable picture of the state of India seen through a very unembarrassed and courageous intelligence.

D H LAWRENCE St. Mawr, together with *The Princess*

Nation and Athenaeum XXXVII, 30 May 1924, 270-1

In *St Mawr* Mr Lawrence seems to have reached a very dangerous stage in his development as a writer. Never before has he been so patchy, so sure of himself and so unsure of his theme, so confident and at the same time so unconvincing. His inspiration fails again and again, but he flings the second-rate and the palpably histrionic at his reader with the same conviction as he shows when he is at his best. Has his note of conviction become a habit, meaning always less than it seems to mean; or, while intensely in earnest, is he really unsure of both the things he is trying to convey: his revelation of life as an artist, and his philosophy? At any rate, his philosophy is obscure—he has never yet formulated it clearly, which means that he has never comprehended it clearly; and his intuitions, so profound once, seem to have become falsified. The characters in *St Mawr* are little better than mouthpieces for the author's hopes and despairs about modern life. His women talk as only he himself writes in the more didactic pages of his books. The situations are frankly distorted to put in the wrong everything in which he disbelieves. Rico, the artist, intended to represent one thing which Mr Lawrence definitely dislikes—the 'emancipated,' uprooted, tolerant, sceptical type of intellectual who is to be found in all great cities—is portrayed with an unfairness which deprives him of every attribute of emancipation, toleration, or scepticism, leaving nothing in him for us to react against, or to make Mr Lawrence's excessive reaction comprehensible. In spite of all the hard things said about him, the villain turns out to be only a fool: a figure to be laughed at or pitied, but unworthy of hatred. Yet Mr Lawrence hates him, and tacitly admits him as an equal; and that is a measure of the gross lack of proportion in the story. The only explanation one can think of is that Mr Lawrence takes his theories so seriously now that he cannot take seriously enough the objective problem from which his theories started. And his grip on his technique has weakened with his grip on reality. *St Mawr* is short—a novelette of 180 pages—yet it is formless; the development loose and arbitrary, the ending insignificant, showing a weakening of power. There are, of course, a few marvellously vivid scenes which remind us that Mr Lawrence is a writer of genius; and the minor characters, Mrs Witt, the groom Lewis, and, above all, the horse, St Mawr, are crammed with vitality. But the main conflict between the protagonists, Rico and Lou, is intellectual melodrama; it fails completely. And, except for a few descriptive passages in the author's best style, the short second story, *The Princess* fails also. It is an unrestrained exercise in the romantic.

ARNOLD BENNETT

Calendar of Modern Letters I No 4,
June 1925, 290-6

The three representative novelists of the age which ceased so suddenly and so completely with the beginning of the War were undoubtedly Mr Wells, Mr Galsworthy, and Mr Bennett. Twelve years ago Mr Bennett would have been generally considered the least conspicuous of the three; today he is, on the whole, the most conspicuous. In a world alien to his way of thought he is respected; and our respect for him is, perhaps, chiefly a tribute to his personality. For he has immense vitality; he is never daunted; he gives always, and takes delight in giving a sense of capability. These are qualities which equally in a confident and optimistic era such as that which preceded the War, and in a doubting and pessimistic one such as we live in now, would be bound to be welcomed. They increase our sense of power if we feel strong, and temper our sense of impotence if we feel weak. They are biologically useful; they inspire confidence. The question whether Mr Bennett's vitality is the artist's vitality, his courage the artist's courage, and his competence the artist's competence, has been generally overlooked in the satisfaction which his positive qualities, artistic or not, have given us. Yet it is an important question. The competence of the practical man to deal with the section of life which his will encounters is something quite different from the competence of the artist to deal with experience imaginatively. To the man of action this practical competence is so real that its reality is nearly unconditional; it is the ground, conscious and unconscious, of his actions; it is axiomatic. To the artist, on the other hand, it is largely an illusion; he sees that it is based on negative as well as on postive qualities; that, for example, it implies a limitation of vision, useful biologically, but injurious to the artist; that it starts with all theutilitarian illusions from which art alone, now that religion is in a state of suspended animation, can give us freedom. A book written by a man of practical capacity, if that capacity extends to the art of writing, will be always interesting. But its virtues will be the virtues of a practical personality, not those of art. Whether Mr Bennett's novels belong to this category is the main critical question that can be asked concerning them. Provisionally let us hazard the judgement that he is a practical man who has chosen to express himself through the art of the novel; that he is an imaginative writer whose imagination is limited to such intuitions as can come to one who is determined to master the machinery of life rather than to see.

Take, for instance, Mr Bennett's indomitable sense of his capability. It is disquieting that this is hardly to be paralleled in literature. Balzac, it is true, had some of it, but we recognise it in Balzac not as a virtue, but rather as a defect of his qualties, as his chief illusion about himself, the touch of vanity which falsifies his work. Now in Mr Bennett this invariable competence to deal with all sorts of situations and all classes of experience on an excessive note of confidence is not a defect of his qualities; it is his characteristic quality. And we become conscious that this competence is simply the *savoir faire* of the practical man who *must* master the situation, and to do so must see no more in the situation than he can master, rather than the courage of the artist, who must see the situation in itself, whether it can be practically mastered or not. How clear and definite Mr Bennett is when he is describing states of mind which his characters as successful people will remember later with profit; and how vague and incompetent when he writes about states of mind which will be of no conceivable utilitarian value to them! As Hilda Lessways led Sarah Gailey home from the scene of the attempted suicide,

> She was not extremely surprised. But she was shocked into a most solemn awe as she pressed the arm of the poor tragic woman who, but for an accident, might have plunged off the end of the groin into water deep enough for drowning. She did really feel humble before this creature who had deliberately invited death; she in no way criticised her; she did not even presume to condescend towards the hasty clumsiness of Sarah Gailey's scheme to die. She was overwhelmed by the woman's utterly unconscious impressiveness, which exceeded that of a criminal reprieved on the scaffold, for the woman had dared an experience that only the fierce and sublime courage of desperation can affront. She had a feeling that she ought to apologise profoundly to Sarah Gailey for all that Sarah must have suffered.

This is admirable; it describes the reaction of a practical young woman to an experience she has never encountered before. We see her cataloguing her sensations; she will learn from them; they will make her in some way more competent. But then follows her imaginative reaction:

> And as she heard the ceaseless, cruel play of the water amid the dark jungle of ironwork under the pier, and the soft creeping of the foam-curves behind, and the vague stirrings of the night-wind round about—these phenomena combined mysteriously with the immensity of the dome above and with the baffling strangeness of the town, and with the grandeur of the beaten woman by her side; and communicated to Hilda a thrill that was divine in its unexampled poignancy.

The transition is astonishing. The situation passes from the intensely practical, where Mr Bennett's mastery is complete into the intensely human; and at once his mastery falls from him; he takes refuge in the vaguest of rhetoric. The moment which Hilda will remember all her life, when the sea, the sky, the city before her and the woman by her side, are changed, and become part of one universal experience—this moment Mr Bennett cannot describe; he can only make us feel that he is impressed by it, a little theatrically. He is vague here, as every practical man is when he is faced by something on which his will cannot operate.

The predominance of the practical in Mr Bennett's novels is shown still more strikingly in their descriptive passages. There have been few writers who have described so fully as he, and yet have avoided describing visually. Conrad, perhaps an equal slave to description, used all his powers to make the scene visual; Mr Bennett uses his to tell us all about it. Conrad does sometimes make us see what he wishes us to see; Mr Bennett, at his best, describes something which, if we happened to see it, we should recognise. His directions are like those of a man in the street who tells us how many turns we must take to reach a certain place, and by what signs we may recognise a shop there which we wish to find. We should have to pass through a street under repair, and then he would proceed to say that the gas main had burst a week before, and dozens of windows had been smashed. But after passing the street we should come to a square, and he would say that one side of this square was blocked, and why, and soon we should be well into the middle of a history of the square. Nevertheless, we must ignore the square and turn to the left into a short narrow street, and the shop would be the fifth on our right; there would be three stone steps leading down into it. All these things, because they had a bearing on practice, would interest our guide, and finally we should find the shop. And in Mr Bennett's novels we always find the shop; but we do not go into it to see it, but always for a different purpose, and the consequence is that we never see it, we only know what is in it. We begin to have a sense, perhaps, that here a whole drama of buying and selling, of tear and wear, of credit and cash, is being worked out, and as practical men we are thrilled. We feel at last that if we chose we could run the shop; for the practical man likes to think there is nothing he cannot manage, and that is the secret of his curiosity about all practical undertakings, even when they are outside his scope.

Thus in Mr Bennett's novels we are always brought back to the illusions of the practical man. The mass of machinery which keeps urban civilisation going, the means of transport, of profit, and of pleasure; our chairs, our fireplaces, our baths; the beds we sleep in and the bells we ring; all these are of supreme interest to the practical man, because to him they are not merely pieces of dead convenience, but instruments upon which he impresses his power. They are of supreme interest, too, to Mr Bennett. They are not merely the environment amid which his characters live; they are the *media* through which his characters express themselves. They bring people together; they become integral parts of friendship and of love. In this benevolent working of the mysteries of machinery Mr Bennett finds a certain romance which to the less practically-minded will for ever seem a little naive. A mechanical part of our environment, a telephone or a tramcar, heralds a love affair, or becomes part of one. Is it not marvellous? Mr Bennett seems always to be saying; but we are never quite sure that it is marvellous. Hilda Lessways is about to meet Edwin Clayhanger after a long absence.

> When she was going down the stairs, she discovered that she held the *Signal* in her hand. She had no recollection of picking it up, and there was no object in taking it to the breakfast room! She thought; 'What a state I must be in!'

So a newspaper reveals Hilda's state of feeling, and so furniture, houses, property, clothes, express the minds, morals, and passions of Mr Bennett's characters.

This mode of presentation is, of course, perfectly valid, for obviously the accessories of modern life are enormous in their sheer weight, and obviously they have become part of our expression as well as of our experience. But obviously, too, they are not such a great part of experience as Mr Bennett implies. He tries to make his environments do too much; he over-emphasises them, and gives them a false impressiveness—a sign, perhaps, that his conscience is not without a suspicion of guilt. In the unnecessary description of St Andrew's Church in *Riceyman Steps*—unnecessary, for the church appears only to be described, and disappears after that—we can see Mr Bennett's style in acute distress, becoming embarrassed, and sinking into journalese, in an attempt to conceal the fact that the church is really unimportant. He begins self-consciously:

> St Andrew's Church, of yellow bricks with freestone dressings, a blue slate roof, and a red coping, was designed and erected in the brilliant

> reign of William IV, whose Government, under Lord Grey, had a pious habit, since lost by governments, of building additional churches in populous parishes at its own expense. Unfortunately its taste in architecture was less laudable than its practical interest in the inculcation among the lowly of the Christian doctrine about the wisdom and propriety of turning the other cheek. St Andrew's, of a considerably mixed Gothic character, had architecturally nothing whatever to recommend it. Its general proportions, its arched windows, its mullions, its finials, its crosses, its spire, and its buttresses, were all and in every detail utterly silly and offensive.

That, it must be admitted, is Mr Bennett at his worst. Yet the emptiness and calculated verbosity of the second sentence tell us a great deal about him; they always appear when the inspiration fails. They fall like a judgment on Mr Bennett when he is writing about the artistically irrelevant, when he is padding. Perhaps it is an uneasy conscience which makes him pad the style at the same time, and leads him into the bad taste of periphrases like 'in the inculcation among the lowly of the Christian docrine about'.

There is more padding in Mr Bennett's later novels than in his earlier. The plots are constructed, one might almost think, to make the padding necessary. In *Riceyman Steps*, the hero is the owner of a second-hand bookshop; he is also an antiquarian interested in the streets and history of Clerkenwell; and, in addition, he is a miser. In other words, his interest, his passion, is for things, not for people. *Elsie and the Child* shows us still more clearly the limitations of the practical and capable view of life. What a mass of machinery, of hotels and yachts, what a disproportionate interest by all the characters in the furnishings of existence, what a poverty and difficulty of human reaction amid this waste of machinery! In perusing Mr Bennett's optimistic pages, a weariness of the spirt sometimes falls on one; one is saddened by the pleasure which these characters have in using that vast mass of machinery, which to most is not a means of pleasure at all, but a bleak necessity.

It is his delight in all the properties of modern life that fixes for us Mr Bennett's spiritual era. That era is Late Victorian; it comprises the few decades which saw the complete triumph of machinery and had not yet realised the barrenness of that triumph. The fight against machinery, waged by Carlyle, Ruskin, and Arnold, was over; the time of weariness in the midst of machinery had not come. Meanwhile, the industrialisation of England had marvellously increased one thing which, more than the growth of knowledge or the decay of religion, was modifying everyday life: it had marvellously increased property. Mr Bennett would be inconceivable in an age which did not believe religiously in property, either as a thing bringing happiness, or as a thing which will being happiness in the future, through a more equitable distribution of its resources. He would be equally inconceivable in any age when property was relatively scarce; in

England before the industrial revolution. He is the representative of an era of almost universal and absolutely naive optimism, which is now past. And more than any other writer of that era, he has its limitations and its simplicities. His work as a novelist is dated. But the qualities which make him an anomaly as an artist make him also a very interesting and original literary personality. He has brought into literature qualities which are seldom found there, qualities which perhaps should not be found there, but qualities which, nevertheless, are interesting as well as admirable. They marshal themselves into a unity, and we see behind them a character of weight and integrity, and of a thoroughness which once more takes us back to the happy times of Victoria. And it is perhaps the possession of this character, this personality, which makes Mr Bennett so interesting to the present generation.

F M FORD No More Parades

Nation and Athenaeum,
31 October 1925, 186

Mr Ford is a competent craftsman; his eye runs over the task and sees at once what is needed; his powers of execution do not fail him; and finally—a rare quality—he hardly ever adds a touch more than is necessary. *No More Parades* is admirable, then, as a piece of technique; but it is also something more, for Mr Ford has genuinely felt his theme, and his imagination has accordingly been hard at work. He has, moreover, taken a great deal of pains with his hero, Tietjens, not merely 'catching' him impressionistically, but thinking him out, and attempting—what only writers of the first rank succeed in doing—to make him real and credible on all the planes of human reality. The greatest masters of the novel do this with all their characters, as it were naturally and involuntarily; and it is this that gives such fullness to *The Brothers Karamazov* and *War and Peace*, so that there is no weakening of reality, no relief from this world so much more intense than any our experience can show us. Yet to succeed in this way with one character in a novel would be an extraordinary distinction, and one feels that Mr Ford has just missed doing so. In the first scene at the military base, Tietjens as patriot, man of action, stoic, is built up with admirable solidity; he seems to be unassailable. But when in the next scene he is introduced into the dining-room of a hotel to meet his wife, somehow the environment at once makes him false; and he has to be built up again. Mr Ford does build him up again; the figure becomes more solid, credible, real; his completeness smiles at us once more. The catastrophe comes in his wife's bedroom. We simply cannot envisage him in it, so intrenched has he become by this time in the camp and the hotel, so real has he become there, but there exclusively. It is a curious defect in a figure so solidly constructed; it is almost as if Mr Ford had tried to create out of elements of one quality a figure which should belong completely to another. Tietjens, we feel, has been imagined in this situation and in that; but he has not been imagined in himself; outside the situation he does not exist, and the situation in part creates him. Intellectually and morally he is convincing, but his emotions are only adumbrated, and his relations with Sylvia are therefore unaccountable. The presence of a man of Tietjens' intellectual and moral constitution in Sylvia's bedroom should have been extraordinary, like Prince Myshkin's encounters with Nastasya; but Mr Ford treats it as an ordinary if belated marital contingency, accepting the conventional situation where he should have given us the psychological reality. The other scenes are admirable.

OLIVER ONIONS and L H MYERS *Whom God Hath Sundered* and *The Spite of Heaven; The Clio*

Nation and Athenaeum XXXVIII,
14 November 1925, 262

The reason why of two novels apparently of the same degree of mediocrity one should become a best-seller and the other fall flat remains a mystery, but three volumes in this list might lead one to imagine that serious reputations, books that can be judged by purely critical standards, sometimes present the same difficulty. *Whom God Hath Sundered*, a trilogy written by Mr Onions before the war and now reprinted in one volume, belongs to the same literary generation as the works of Mr Bennett and Mr Galsworthy; it is, moreover, of the same order, or very nearly so; yet while Mr Bennett and Mr Galsworthy are universally known, Mr Onions has almost been ignored. The result may partly, perhaps, be set down to a certain subtle eccentricity of temperament which transpires through Mr Onions' work. It is almost a necessary condition of novel-writing, even at its best, that through it the author should establish a sympathetic communication with the reader. Fielding and Thackeray did this directly—in intimate parentheses, in confidential apologies for the characters. Scott and Dickens did it unconsciously and all the time; their pulses moved with those of their public; they had no need of explanations. Mr Bennett does it too, more subtly, perhaps, but never—and that is essential—too subtly. This is the reason why, admirable and honest as his novels are, they are read by a large public. Now it is precisely this ability to establish sympathetic communication that Mr Onions lacks. His knowledge of life is wide; his skill in presentation equal to it; but his temperament—because it is more original, if one likes, than Mr Bennett's—puts an obstacle between him and the reader. His work is in some ways very like Mr Bennett's. There is the same consuming interest in all the modes of life in the modern world; the same competence in rendering them; the same occupation with the machinery of existence, with institutions, business, furniture; and even the same tendency towards melodrama which seems to go with all these. But it is characteristic that while Mr Bennett puts his realism in one set of novels and his melodrama in another, Mr Onions presents them together—a combination which neither the educated nor the illiterate reader will have. He gives the impression that he is resolved to take his own road rather than the beaten track of the realistic novel; he is in some indefinable way too personal, almost opinionated. There are three suicides and one murder in his trilogy, and although they are imaginatively conceivable, and excellently handled, one feels that the book would be more convincing without them. The author may, of course, be right, and the reader wrong; it is here, at any rate, that a coldness begins to appear between them. Yet in his delineation of character Mr Onions is even better than Mr Bennett. Louie Causton is a more living character than Hilda Lessways, and the lesser figures, the inimitable Mr Mackie, Weston, Merridew, Kitty Windus, could hardly be better. Mr Onions' latest novel, *The Spite of Heaven*, is not nearly so good. There are excellent scenes in it, and the pompous Italian art patron is detestably real; but everything is a little too fussily done, and the melodramatic finish is not a legitimate effect so much as a shock. Yet it would be difficult to think of more than six contemporary novelists whose work has more fundamental literary merit than Mr Onions'.

The other book which makes one wonder on what principle reputations are apportioned is Mr Myers's *The Clio*. The author's first novel, *The Orissers*, was given more enthusiastic reviews than any other volume which had appeared for years. To quote the critics, it had 'a conviction and an intensity of imagination that mark if off from other novels and link it . . . with *Moby Dick* and *Wuthering Heights'*. It was 'a work conceived and executed on the grand scale.' It was 'a great book'. Yet Mr Myers's name is certainly less well known, even to the better public, than those of Mr Waugh, for instance, and Mr Arlen. This is quite incomprehensible. *The Clio* is a brilliant, enticing, witty, and profound work. Ostensibly it is a record of a cruise up the

Amazon. Many things happen by the way, most of them fantastic; but the author succeeds brilliantly in his central task, that of presenting a party of rich, civilised, and sophisticated people against the background of nature, primitive, indifferent, and inhuman. It is obvious that the book might very easily have developed into a sermon against civilisation, or against our illusions about nature, or about the transitoriness and triviality of existence. It never does so; we emerge from the story conscious that we have been given a remarkably just and complete, above all an undeviatingly intelligent, appraisement of human values. Civilisation, and what must for ever underlie it, are shown in their interaction; are shown not merely with justice, but with wit; and we are left not with anything so inadequate as a point of view, pessimistic or optimistic, but with the enigma itself, the enigma which, if it is not completely satisfying, is more satisfying, than anything else. Because he has a sense of values, because the intensity of his thought gives him objectivity, Mr Myers has achieved in this story what Mr Huxley has often attempted but never yet quite achieved: a true evocation of the disillusioned and pessimistic spirit of the age. In wit he is Mr Huxley's equal; in intellect he is immensely his superior. There are signs of immaturity still in his style, but even his faults are full of originality; and his thought is so fascinating and profound, and has such resources behind it, that it is a continuous delight. The characters are never, perhaps, quite real, but in the world in which they move they are exquisitely characterised. They are creatures partly of the world and partly of Mr Myers's speculation; they are figures, at any rate, in a philosophic comedy which is in the highest degree interesting.

D H LAWRENCE The Plumed Serpent

Nation and Athenaeum XXXVIII,
20 February 1926, 719

The Plumed Serpent is surely the most garrulous book Mr Lawrence has ever written. His chief fault as an executant, indeed, has always been garrulity. He perpetually turns back, repeats himself, feels, perhaps, that he has not said something quite as he wished to say it, and hammers on until finally it is either not said at last, or said magnificently. This we have come to accept, with resignation, as his customary technique; but in the present book his wastefulness of attack is still greater, for apparently he has never decided what to do. He wishes to convey an impression of Mexico, he wishes to write a story about Kate and her relations with two men, he wishes finally to provide the age with a myth and a gospel. But he rarely succeeds in combining the three. His descriptions of Mexico are travel impressions; his account of Kate is fiction of the same kind as *Women in Love* and *Aaron's Rod*; and when he describes the ritual and creates the hymns of the resurrected god Quetzalcoatl, he is a theorist, a visionary, living in a world which contains neither Kate nor Mexico. In all three genres, and especially in the last, he occasionally excels. Some of the earlier hymns to Quetzalcoatl are profound and beautiful. But even in these he finally slips into that 'vain repetition' which, there is the best authority for believing, is acceptable to God as little as to the readers of a book. All this raises the question whether Mr Lawrence is indeed so sincere as he seems to be. The closest parallel in modern literature to his hymns to Quetzalcoatl is 'Also Sprach Zarathustra'; but would we have believed that Nietzsche was in earnest about his gospel if he had incorporated it in a novel and accompanied it with a guide to the Riviera? Mr Lawrence is an original personality, perhaps a great writer, and his message to the age must needs, therefore, be important and should be able to stand by itself. But that he should muffle it up in a modern novel makes us feel that he doubts its validity; and that he should accompany it with political animadversions on contemporary Mexico and bursts of exasperation at white races and Indians makes us think that it is only of ordinary importance to him. The moments of inspiration in *The Plumed Serpent* seem to have hardly more significance for him than the moments of futile indignation. And even his denunciations are slipshod; they weary us finally because very rarely do they grip upon the definite evil. Mr Lawrence curses largely, but he curses carelessly; and if a curse is to be of power it must be exact. He describes the feelings which the evil of the world arouses in him; we recognize that these feelings are vivid; but the evil itself is obscured behind the emotional storm it awakens. In some of the earlier hymns to Quetzalcoatl there is greater profundity, perhaps, than Mr Lawrence has ever shown before. The new religion is made credible by the sheer loftiness of inspiration. But not even the new religion is sustained; it falls away as fatally as the book itself. Still a 'Thus Spake Quetzalcoatl', a collection of some of the hymns in this volume, with perhaps a few more, might have been magnificent. But as it stands the book is an outpouring of anything and everything; it does not so much lose, as defeat, its effect.

GEORGE BERNARD SHAW
Translations and Tomfooleries

Nation and Athenaeum XL,
4 December 1926, 341-2

In this volume we have the unaccustomed spectacle of Mr Shaw writing without any deliberate moral aim, and enforcing no lesson. He says in a note, it is true, that 'irresponsible laughter is salutary in small quantities', and this may be construed as a justification, though none was needed. But the truth, one imagines, is that Mr Shaw was simply enjoying himself in writing the more farcical pieces collected here. These include 'The Admirable Bashville', 'Press Cuttings', 'Passion, Poison, and Petrifaction', and 'The Fascinating Foundling'; all of them probably known already to a number of his readers. Undoubtedly, as he claims, they belong to the genre 'which amuses [playwrights] and their audiences harmlessly'. But it is curious how little of the quality which we think of when we think of Mr Shaw is in them. 'One throws off these things,' he says, 'as Beethoven threw off a few bagatelles, and Mozart a few senseless bravura pieces for friends and mere violinists.' But there is in the trifles thrown off by Beethoven and Mozart much more of themselves, of the personality which they expressed in their more serious works, than there is of Mr Shaw's public personality in these trifles of his. One sees more clearly than before that it is not imagination nor power to create character that makes him a good dramatist, but moral enthusiasm and suppleness of mind. When he is not exercising these he is merely a shadow of himself. His wit shines only when it is illuminating the moral issues which chiefly interest him; its light is almost lost when it is applied to incidents of actual life. There is, of course, excellent farce in 'The Admirable Bashville' and 'Press Cuttings', as there is in his more serious plays; but in the latter it is full of vitality, while here, because the invention is neither enriched with fancy nor pointed towards a moral end, it gives forth a rather empty sound.

The volume makes one realise, indeed, how much of Mr Shaw's best work depends for its effectiveness on his farcical gift. Mitchener and Balsquith are pure figures of farce, and Mr Shaw hardly needed to tell us that the former 'is not the late Lord Kitchener': he is obviously a vaudeville stock character, and excellent of his kind; he is made for the music-hall stage, and would be inconceivable off it. The interesting thing is how much he resembles other characters of Mr Shaw. The main originality of these, one can see, is that they are real figures (as Mitchener and Balsquith are not) distorted into terms of intellectual farce. Mr Shaw's Caesar pleases us (if he does please us), not because he is more true than the Caesars of other dramatists, but because he is turned into a subtle and credible farcical figure. Mr Shaw's Napoleon, Cleopatra, and Joan are so original because he has not tried to interpret them at all, but has conceived them quite arbitrarily in terms of farce, as nobody else would have thought of doing. They are not seen through the eyes of comedy merely, retaining the essential qualities with which legend and time have endowed them. They are completely transposed: Caesar becomes someone whom we know not to be Caesar at all, Joan someone who could not have faintly resembled Joan; and the drama through which Mr Shaw conducts them is a serious burlesque. The dramatic effectiveness of this burlesque, its wit and ingenuity, are beyond question; but there always comes a moment, generally a sentimental one, when the author, finding that burlesque will not express all he desires to express, treats it as if it were an actual representation of life; what should be a poignant note is struck; and everything suddenly rings false. In the one serious piece in the present volume that note is struck very loudly. This is 'The Glimpse of Reality', a short play showing how a wastrel finds his soul on seeing death in front of him. 'There is nothing like a good look into the face of death: close up: right on you: for showing you how little you really believe and how little you really are.' How easily Mr Shaw's characters begin to preach at such and less poignant moments! How ready they are to whip out the lesson, and how often that lesson is one which the author has forced them to commit to memory! But usually the burlesque is so witty that it survives these heart-to-heart indiscretions. There are few of them in this volume.

The longest piece in the book is 'Jitta's Atonement', a three-act play by Herr Siegfried Trebitsch, the Austrian writer who has translated Mr Shaw's plays into German. In rendering it into English and slightly altering it, Mr Shaw informs us that he is repaying a debt of gratitude. But for the play itself there is nothing to be said.

T F POWYS Mr Weston's Good Wine

Nation and Athenaeum XLII,
24 December 1927, 488-9

In fullness of conception and sustained imagination 'Mr Weston's Good Wine' is probably the best story Mr Powys has yet written. It is also by far the most balanced and satisfying. All Mr Powys's stories have suggested allegory. They do not describe actual life, but rather evoke a dream image more simple than the reality, in which good and evil are seen more clearly confronted than the realistic imagination sees them. In the present story Mr Powys openly adopts the allegory and employs it with great effect. Mr Weston is a name for God, and his wines, of two kinds, are Love and Death. He comes at seven o'clock one evening to an English village; all the clocks stop, time is changed to eternity, and various strange things happen to the villagers. The rector begins to believe in God, and dies in peace, Mrs Vosper is carried down to Hell, water is turned into wine, and a young girl has intercourse with an angel of whom she has dreamt. Once more in this story, in short, the author is exclusively concerned with the realities of good and evil, and the world he describes is not the actual one in which these things are inextricably mixed, but a simple, schematic, intense world in which they are separated and set in clear opposition, a world which contains heaven and hell, and contains nothing much between them. But if Mr Powys's statement of the problem is simplified, so are his terms. Goodness is a simple thing to him, evil, too, a simple thing; and it is their very obviousness, their immediacy, that gives us such an intense awareness of them in this story. For a simplification such as Mr Powys's seems to wipe away all the inessentials which stand between us and this particular kind of truth; we feel that he brings us into the presence of powers which the generality of writers refuse to see. This is Mr Powys's great virtue; his great fault is that he does not see those things objectively at all, but through a violently idiosyncratic temperament; and the truth of his portraiture is confused beneath an habitual and sometimes absurd over-emphasis. There is another limitation inherent in an imagination so simple as Mr Powys's: that it cannot admit of much variety of invention in the author. If people are simply good or bad, the writer cannot do much more than set them in a few typical situations to which their response is already half-known; he will inevitably tend to repeat those situations. Consequently, even in the present story, the most various he has written, the author has not been able to avoid an occasional monotony. But his virtues by far outweigh his faults; there are beautiful and inimitable pages in 'Mr Weston's Good Wine'; the whole is executed with skill and power; and the quality of the imagination, though exaggerated, is profound.

VIRGINIA WOOLF

Bookman (New York) LXXIV,
December 1931, 362-7

Mrs Woolf's first novel was *The Voyage Out; The Waves* is her latest. There is little in common between those two books, one is tempted to say, except the sea, which is in them both. The sea indeed is in all Mrs Woolf's books, either as a background or a memory, and not even the walls of London can keep it out. Her mind appears loath to travel quite beyond sight or sound of it, and she employs it by preference as a reservoir of similes and metaphors. It appears in the opening page of *Mrs Dalloway*, which is a novel whose very theme is London, and one remembers also that other passage describing the heroine sewing a silk green dress. She 'collected the green folds together and attached them, very lightly, to the belt. So on a summer's day waves collect, overbalance, and fall.' The simile is recondite and yet strangely apt; it could have occurred only to a writer who thought often about the sea, so often that it came to hold more and more unexpected and abstruse correspondences. In *To the Lighthouse* the sea has actually grown dangerous, becoming something very like a symbol, a fact which may help explain the occasional unreality of that book. It may help to explain also why in *The Waves* one of the characters damns symbolism so heartily. There is no symbolism, however, in *The Waves*; there is, on the contrary, something in comparison with which symbolism appears a mere makeshift.

But without trying to discover what the sea is a symbol for in Mrs Woolf's books, it is clear enough that it stands for something in her imagination, and it is this something that connects her first book with her latest, and at the same time, taking advantage of the privilege of an ocean, explains the great distance between them. *The Voyage Out* was at least innocently symbolical; it was at once a very remarkable first novel in the conventional style of the time, owing a little to Chekhov, as most good novels did just then, and also a first voyage out over unknown seas where, at least as a possibility, lay the islands which Mrs Woolf later discovered.

There is, for instance, in *The Voyage Out* as in its immediate successor *Night and Day*, that sense of a confusion of categories, of tragedy and comedy coexisting in the same situation, which she found such original ways of expressing in her later books. At first she conveyed this mixture of comedy and tragedy as certain of the English novelists had done before her; Sterne in particular, the supreme master in this style; and Scott, a writer whose name recurs persistently in her books, almost like a refrain; but she did not permit herself their whole-hearted resignation to a shamelessly luxurious emotion; it brought her troubled thought rather than carefree effusion. In this she complied with the spirit of the age. For one reason or another—perhaps it is the spread of a more scientific way of regarding everything, including our emotions, perhaps it is merely that the emphatically unemphatic code of the public schools is extending everywhere—a novelist nowadays who values his or her intelligence is reluctant to deal in tears, far less therefore in tears and laughter in the same breath. We are so much more austere in such matters than our ancestors that scenes which were to them an opportunity for people of sensibility to evince the delicacy of their feelings now disgust us by their indelicacy. We are repelled indeed by quite a number of things in these half-comic, half-pathetic scenes: by the unnecessary piling on the agony, the almost nonsensical clash between two zones of emotion, two worlds of emotion, and by the conduct of the novelist, who makes not the slightest effort to square them, but instead is transparently pleased at having arrived at such a happy sentimental conjuncture, and wishes us to admire him for his punctuality.

Tears are a solvent, laughter is a catharsis, but in an age when people analyse their emotional responses, these particular ones too must lose something of their authority, until it becomes doubtful whether they can claim even to be legitimate. So the sort of emotional complex which once evoked them, either singly or simultaneously, and in doing so apparently resolved itself, nowadays continues to burden the writer's mind, which in turn has to work at high pressure to resolve it and get rid of it. In other words the art of fiction has become more intellectual. So that what was a glorious opportunity a hundred or even fifty years ago has turned into a tormenting problem, which, sometimes much against his will, leads the novelist on through a whole series of questions. How can such contrasts coexist? What are tragedy and comedy? What is experience? and finally, Why am I asking all these questions at all, seeing that I know there is no answer to them? Mrs Woolf's questions begin, I think, from this problem of the coexistence of comedy and tragedy, at any rate from a perceived fundamental ambiguity in life, to which laughter and tears, even in solution, are not a sufficient or even an apposite reply. Starting from this problem, and it is formulated in her first two books, the progressive development of Mrs Woolf's art, up to its crown in her latest book, is quite comprehensible.

Yet in spite of that her first two books are very unlike their successors. In them she conscientiously accepted the novel as it was; she treated its limitations with solicitous respect; she seemed resolved above all to avoid the characteristic virtues which we recognise now as hers: she refused to take any short cuts, and she eschewed not only lightness, but the very appearance of it. Parts of *Night and Day* are actually dull, and not with a naturally outpouring dullness, but with the more deadly sort secreted by a writer resolved to concentrate on her job and carry it out according to given rules whatever the spectator may think; it is a kind of dullness that may almost be called disinterested, even self-sacrificing. From the writing of *Night and Day* Mrs Woolf must have learned a very great deal, but apart from that the book is a fine one; if the mould did not suit the author's genius, what she poured into it was entirely her own. There are scenes in it which persistently linger in the memory: the meeting between Denham and Rodney on the Embankment, and Katherine's wanderings through London on the evening that she broke her appointment. There is also that exquisite interior, the Hilbery household, and the delightful Mrs Hilbery. The strange thing about *Night and Day* as about *The Voyage Out* is the general not displeasing grayness as of a winter's day in London; the light which irradiates every scene she touched later is quite absent.

It began to tinge her work as soon as she entered on what may be called her experimental stage. There is a glimmer of it in *Monday or Tuesday*, a small volume of sketches; it flickers brilliantly but fitfully in *Jacob's Room*, shines steadily in *Mrs Dalloway*, fades considerably in *To the Lighthouse*, but in *The Waves* gives a more intense light than ever before, a light from which veil after veil has fallen. *The Waves* is so greatly superior to anything else of Mrs Woolf's that one is tempted to consider the rest of her work, even the exquisite *Mrs Dalloway*, as irrelevant, and to take this as the sole measure of her genius.

But that would be unjust, for Mrs Woolf is one of those writers whose very failures and half-successes are valuable as marking a line of development. So *Jacob's Room* and *To the Lighthouse* with their hesitancies, their occasional dullnesses, their traces of falsity, are more to be admired than the easy success of *Orlando*. *Orlando* is a charming and unreal trifle; a little too deliberately charming, perhaps, and a little irritatingly unreal, for it is never quite unreal. But it is difficult for Mrs Woolf to rid herself of all seriousness when Time is her theme; it is the problem that has occupied her ever since *Jacob's Room*. The idea of *Orlando* was a witty one; a character who survives for several centuries, maintaining his identity, but changing his attributes so radically that, beginning as the hero of the story he ends as its heroine: this was an admirable invention for incarnating the impartiality of Time's mutations. Yet as Mrs Woolf cannot take such things merely wittily or merely fancifully, the wit is less detached than wit should be, and the fancy has never quite the freedom of fancy. The book is a success in an illegitimate style; the comparative failures of *Jacob's Room* and *To the Lighthouse* are worth a score of such triumphs.

In *Jacob's Room* Mrs Woolf recreated a character through memories and associations, and gathered the limbs of Osiris imbedded in various strata of time and space. The separate limbs are exquisitely articulated, but one has the impression that some have not been retrieved, and that the others have been assembled somewhat haphazardly. The book is fragmentary. In *To the Lighthouse* she strove rather to evoke Time itself, both directly and through the characters. The book consists of three parts. The first describes a summer's day in the Hebrides; it is followed by a short section called "Time Passes"; then there is another summer's day several years later in the same, now changed, setting. As a single achievement the middle section of this book is perhaps the best thing Mrs Woolf wrote before *The Waves*. It describes the gradual dilapidation of the house where the action has passed and will pass again. The house is beset by countless great and little forces, by wind, rain, mice, dust, neglect, its own age. A very powerful sense of time is conveyed in this way. But when Mrs Woolf writes about time she is carried away; the middle section of *To the Lighthouse* is consequently far too strong for the other two: it did not need all this, one feels, to make a few characters a few years older. The time she evokes has hardly anything to do with individual human life at all, except accidentally, like evolution, for example; it is so much too powerful that it seems to have no effect at all, like an electric charge which, multiplied a thousand times, passes through one's body without one's feeling it, whereas, reduced to the right voltage, it would act devastatingly.

Mrs Dalloway, which came between *Jacob's Room* and *To the Lighthouse*, is more perfect than either. In it, instead of scattering her characters through time, Mrs Woolf gathers them into a single summer's day in London, and in doing so gathers time there too, thus producing for us another of its ambiguous facets. Everything in this book is steeped in time, either as a memory or a property of this one day, so that it is difficult to tell what the figures are which move about in it, whether they are mere aspects of a day, or human characters who would be as solid in sullen and foggy weather. There is something more dreamlike, one imagines, than the author intended, in those figures whose names one forgets so soon, while remembering their little mechanical gestures, and the bright rooms and streets, the sounds of bells and traffic that surround them. But if they are more than commonly perishable it is at least partly the author's almost clairvoyant sense of time that makes them so; they fade when subjected to it as certain colours do in an intense light. So that all the undoubtedly deft characterisation which Mrs Woolf lavishes on them seems wasted, and is sometimes tiresome; it is as if she were trying to characterise eleven o'clock in the morning, or four in the afternoon, for the characters might almost have been called after the hours. As parts of the changing moods of one day they are charming, they are even real; it is when the author tries to give them the attributes of independent entities that everything becomes false. Her characterisation is skilful, understanding, sensitive, and the only thing that keeps it from being masterly is that it is not applied to characters; there are none in the book.

Mrs Woolf quite discards characterisation in the ordinary sense in *The Waves*, and her vision of life at last stands out clearly. She seems no longer concerned with temporal attributes in this book, but with permanent things: the problem of time which she has pursued for so long has yielded her here a resolution. The six figures whose monologues make it up are being freed from the illusions of time. They stand beyond time and see themselves within it; they incarnate something in the spirit which in the midst of change is not deceived. They have been blamed for not being characters, and very ignorantly; for to such beings character is merely a costume they put on, and have to put on, before they go on the temporal stage to play their parts. If they are to be called characters at all, then they are characters who have awakened.

It is difficult to find any parallels in literature for these six figures, or for the dimension in which they move. One may be reminded now and then of Pirandello's much overpraised *Six Characters in Search of an Author*; but the resemblance is only a surface one. For Pirandello merely presents schematically a few aspects of illusion, whereas Mrs Woolf has pierced to something deeper, to that part of us which refuses to be deceived. Is there a part of us which refuses to be deveived? If there is, it exists where consciousness is most intense, alert and magnanimous. It exists also at a level where laughter and tears, whether singly or simultaneously, are no longer apposite responses. These six figures are something new in literature, so new that a critic may legitimately refuse to try to find a formula for it. The book is a continuous revelation on a level rarely touched by the novelist.

In conception, however, it is quite simple. Six characters, three men and three women, tell in alternate monologue their stories from childhood to middle age. The whole is written in the present tense, the response of the monologist accompanying every event as it happens, the awake character who regards and the somnambulist character who acts being indissolubly attached and yet separate. Seen by this passionate observer all action, all emotion, all change becomes a series of pictures. 'There is a hill striped with houses. A man crosses a bridge with a dog at his heels. Now the red boy begins firing at the pheasant. The blue boy shoves him aside. "My uncle is the best shot in England. My cousin is Master of Foxhounds."' 'The cart grows gradually larger as it comes along the road. The sheep gather in the middle of the field. The birds gather in the middle of the road—they need not fly yet. The wood smoke rises. The starkness of the dawn is going out of it.' In a stream the pictures follow one another. 'And when evening comes and the lamps are lit they make a yellow fire in the ivy.' 'A child playing—a summer evening—doors will open and shut, will keep opening and shutting, through which I see sights that make me weep. For they cannot be imparted. Hence our loneliness; hence our desolation. I turn to that spot in my mind and find it empty.' 'There is the puddle, and I cannot cross it. I hear the rush of the great grindstone within an inch of my head. Its wind roars in my face. All palpable forms of life have failed me. Unless I can stretch and touch something hard, I shall be blown down the eternal corridors forever. What, then, can I touch? What brick, what stone? and so draw myself across the enormous gulf into my body safely?' 'It was only for a moment, catching sight of myself before I had time to prepare myself as I always prepare myself for the sight of myself, that I quailed. It is true; I am not young.' 'So I went out. I saw the first morning he would never see—the sparrows were like toys dangled from a string by a child.' Why are all those pictures so strangely vivid, like windows violently broken in the closed wall of experience? Because they are seen not by the acting character, but by his other self who watches him from beyond time. 'All these things,' one of the six says, 'happen in one second and last forever.' Such sufferings and pleasures are like those of bound spirits to whom has been left the liberty to look and judge.

Mrs Woolf's conception of life in this book is a pessimistic one lightened only by the supersensual pleasures of the contemplating self. 'All these things happen in a second and last forever.' 'If there are no stories, what end can there be, or what beginning? Life is not susceptible perhaps to the treatment we give it when we try to tell it.' (Incidentally this has not prevented her from trying to tell it.) 'But now I made the contribution of maturity to childhood's intuitions—satiety and doom; the sense of what is unescapable in our lot; death; the knowledge of limitations; how life is more obdurate than one had thought it.' And in a description of a meeting of all the six figures: 'We saw for a moment laid out among us the body of the complete human being whom we have failed to be, but at the same time, cannot forget.' It is in intellectual formulations such as these that the grief of Mrs Woolf's ideal observers finds its keenest edge. That grief is very keen, but it is not a grief that can be solved by tears; it is hostile to them.

Nothing is stranger in modern literature, and nothing probably could tell us more about it, than this hostility to tears, the mark at which once even the greatest writers aimed. All that one can do is to note it. The modern writer, no matter how passionately or deeply he may feel, is never concerned with the tears in things. D H Lawrence was a man who felt and wrote with conspicuous passion; George Eliot, let us say, was a women who felt and wrote not with conspicuous passion; yet in her calm way she tapped the fount of tears, whereas D H Lawrence, while arousing many emotions in our breasts, quite ignored this immemorial source of relief. In spite of all his anti-intellectualism he was more penetrated by what he himself called the virus of intellect than George Eliot, though she was as powerfully resolved to be intellectual, as he to be 'instinctive'. Indeed almost all modern novelists are more intellectual in a certain sense than any of their predecessors of fifty years ago: in the sense that the intellect conditions their emotional responses more decisively, making those responses less naive and immediately satisfying. More deliberate and unsure also, however; for it is difficult to achieve, where the intellect is in part control, any effect possessing the simple inevitability of a burst of tears. This may partly account for the sense of emotional frustration, of indefinite postponement, which so many modern novels produce. It may account, for instance, for Lawrence's equivocal operation on us. The old catharsis was definitely impossible; the new one was difficult to find. In *The Waves* a new catharsis has been found. Its art is at once modern and complete.

The great step forward that Mrs Woolf made in *The Waves* is reflected also in the style. *Mrs Dalloway* was a wonderful piece of writing, but its grace had a touch of hesitation, even of fussiness, with all those clauses and sentences ending in 'ing'. But the passage describing Clarissa sewing the silk dress is one of the finest in the book, and may serve for a test of comparison:

> So on a summer's day waves collect, overbalance, and fall; collect and fall; and the whole world seems to be saying 'that is all' more and more ponderously, until even the heart in the body which lies in the sun on the beach says too, That is all. Fear no more, says the heart. Fear no more, says the heart, committing its burden to some sea, which sighs collectively for all sorrows, and renews, begins, collects, lets fall. And the body alone listens to the passing bee; the wave breaking; the dog barking, far away barking and barking.

How different the rhythm of that is from that of the passages I have quoted from *The Waves*. It is a fluttering rhythm, a rhythm in which a thousand almost imperceptible hesitations are concealed. In *The Waves* this prose has put away all hesitation, and cuts out images and thoughts in one sweep. It is impatiently, almost violently immediate. What it recalls most strongly is Rilke's superb prose, which was a sort of inspired shorthand. And one imagines that it has changed in this astonishing way because Mrs Woolf is dealing directly now with immediate and essential truths of experience. The result is an authentic and unique masterpiece, which is bound to have an influence on the mind of this generation.

D H LAWRENCE, PETER QUENNELL and JAMES JOYCE
The Lovely Lady; Sympathy and other Stories; Two Tales of Shem and Shawn

Listener IX, 8 February 1933, 232

These three volumes show surprisingly—surprisingly, for one is always apt to forget it—in what a variety of ways the short story may be used. No prose form can so quickly become mechanical and lifeless, as the popular magazines show; yet on the other hand it gives a writer a handier means of fixing a novel impression, sustaining a novel attitude, than a full-length story can do, where the normal stuff of experience soon asserts its rights. The real vice of the modern short story is that it is very often likely to belong to what people call the literature of escape. It generally 'opens windows'—but if one asks on to what, it is very difficult sometimes to give an answer. If the window were to remain open long enough, through the course, for example, of an average-sized novel, we should perhaps be able to judge whether the country it shows us is that of wish-fulfilment or of actual experience. As it is we cannot always tell; we hope and doubt. That is why such stories are so stimulating to the imagination, and why the results of that stimulation are so often unsatisfactory, ending in some unexpectedly barren prospect. Such stories incite us to continue the original escape for a little longer by ourselves, and as the desire presently encounters a check, they deject after encouraging us. Stories that are intended simply for our delight—the supreme examples being those in *The Arabian Nights*—are quite different; their operation on our wishes ends with themselves; the escape stops where the story stops. Mr Joyce's two short tales seem to be of this kind, though I cannot pretend to understand them, except here and there. Lawrence's last collection of stories are mainly in the modern window-opening style, with one or two that are semi-allegorical. Mr Quennell's have less of unresolved desire in them, and a firmer sense that in life certain factors are sooner or later bound to come into play, shutting a whole row of windows. Consequently of these three books his leaves the least dissatisfaction behind it, and is the most steadily faithful to experience; though it is without the brilliant bursts of illumination that light up Lawrence's uneven work.

It has become a literary canon that Lawrence is at his best in his short stories. Yet if he had written nothing but them we should have a very inadequate idea of his powers. His long novels, it is true, are full of outrageous faults; his vision of life as he sees it almost always becomes confused at a certain point with his vision of life as he would like it to be; his characters turn into symbols; he remodels them quite arbitrarily without waiting for experience to do it for him; it is as if he were suddenly impatient with life and could no longer endure the drudgery of describing it, seeing that it might have been so different and so much more beautiful. So, except, perhaps, for *The Rainbow*, every one of his novels, while rich in separate beauties, misses beauty as a whole, for before it can achieve that, an adventitious beauty, frailer than that which would have been won by accepting life as it is to the end, is impatiently superimposed. Yet only the long novel could have given him scope for the flow of his genius, or for the 'flow' that he mentioned so often and that seemed so necessary to him; and if at one point or another it seemed fated to deviate from reality and lose itself among chaotic symbols, the reader had at least the pleasure of watching the splendid spectacle while it lasted. His short stories represent at most a short spurt of that impetuous energy. They have always a hasty impatient movement, as of one trying to set down experience in shorthand. That was immensely effective in certain of the stories in *England, My England*, but the present volume shows the method exaggerated almost to the point of self-caricature. The description of Mrs Attenburgh in the first story is an example:

> Her niece Cecilia was perhaps the only person in the world who was aware of the invisible little wire which connected Pauline's eye-wrinkles with Pauline's will-power. Only Cecilia *consciously* watched the eyes go haggard and old and tired, and remain so, for hours; until Robert came home. Then ping!—the mysterious little wire that worked between Pauline's will and her face went taut, the weary, haggard, prominent eyes suddenly began to gleam, the eyelids arched, the queer curved eyebrows which floated in such frail arches on Pauline's forehead began to gather a mocking significance, and you had the *real* lovely lady in all her charm.

That is a remarkable description, but one feels it is a little wrong, and that an imagination which could see a human being in such automatic terms must itself have had something automatic. Is it possible that the 'flow', left to its own devices, may become in course of time a little automatic? Here is another description, this time of an elderly Armenian:

> His thick, fine white hair, which stood up on his head like a soft brush, was curiously virile. And his curious small hands, of the same soft dull paste, had a peculiar, fat, soft masculine breeding of their own. And his dull brown eye could glint with the subtlety of serpents under the white brush of eyelash. He was tired, but he was not defeated.

Here again a voluntary human character is reduced to an instinctive automaton. And there is something automatic in the mere writing of these stories: in the helpless reiteration of words like 'rather', which are involuntarily question-begging, and in the frequency of epithets such as 'curious', 'queer', 'strange' and 'peculiar'. One story, 'The Overtone', contains magnificent writing; in it there are several pages of Lawrence at his best, pages which no living writer could equal. But there is a make-believe quality in many of the others; the characters are conducted with only a perfunctory regard for probability to a denouement fixed from the beginning by the author's idiosyncrasies of thought rather than by his imagination. The book is well worth reading, for it is by Lawrence; but his genius burns fitfully and smokily in it.

The first thing that strikes one in Mr Quennell's stories is the felicitous exactitude of the style. It responds with equal success to whatever the author is treating. For instance the sea: 'Bridget was alone upon the deck, looking out over a vast expanse, silken grey (pale clouds were stretched across the sun) which billowed with a soft continuous movement as though muscles beneath the skin of oily light were swelling and subsiding in the waves.' Or a face: 'She might have been twenty-seven or twenty-eight, but long experience had somehow flayed her features, reducing them to an expressionless white core, in which the eyes were independent of the smile.' One could go on quoting, for the writing is almost uniformly of the excellence shown in these extracts. The atmosphere in which the various events happen in these stories is one of extraordinary quietude, a tense and almost strained quietude, in which the slightest movement seems a little violent, giving the effect of an inaudible detonation. It is as if the actions were mines carefully prepared, and sprung upon us, in the silence imposed by Mr Quennell's style, at exactly the dreaded and expected moment. This gives an undue deliberation, a somewhat artificial emphasis, to many of the story endings. But the first and longest story in the book, 'Travellers 1', is quite exempt from this peculiarity; it traces the development of a very elusive and yet real conflict of wills between two women with the most exquisite finesse and understanding. It is as nearly perfect, one feels, as it could possibly have been. None of the other stories is quite so excellent; but all of them are the work of a man of original and exact imagination. They acquire a unity by leaving their characters at a moment of disillusionment in which some idle or deep-rooted desire is given its quietus. It might be objected that the shutting of windows is no more an ideal end to a short story than the opening of them, but Mr Quennell is at liberty to claim that it is in accordance with the plan of his book, and that any book is necessarily a limited thing. In any case this volume is a most distinguished one.

The difficulty of writing about Mr Joyce's little volume is that it is not amenable to any of the methods of literary criticism known thus far—

that is, for several thousands of years. It obviously requires a new kind of reading to be understood. The difficulties it presents have no resemblance whatever to those presented by the harder passages in Shakespeare, or by the later work of such a writer as Rimbaud. So it would be disingenuous for anyone, without having learned this new art of reading, or knowing whether it can be learned, to appraise the book. 'The Ondt was a weltall fellow, raumybult and abelboobied, bynear saw altitudinous wee a schelling in kopfers.' There is no possibility of criticising that by any standards set by Shakespeare and Goethe, of both of whose languages the passage is a mixture. The only question of any interest is whether human speech, which has lasted for several thousands of years, and is at bottom, in spite of its many and baffling variations, so essentially subject to the same laws, the same logic, that any one language can be translated into another—whether such a thing can be reversed or set aside by any writer, even if he should be a man of genius like Mr Joyce. And that is really not a question at all. The work in progress of which this volume is a small excerpt may turn out to be a curiosity of great interest, and of possible value, but one cannot imagine that it will have any effect on language, or consequently on literature.

J C POWYS A Glastonbury Romance

Listener X, 12 July 1933, 76

This book is between 400,000 and 500,000 words in length, that is, the size of five average novels; it describes the life of a whole town and takes us into the most intimate secrets of about forty characters; it evokes the environment within which these characters live—hills, valleys, moors, streams, churches, houses, hovels, shops, streets, lanes; and finally it tries to relate all these people and things, animate and inanimate (if Mr Powys will allow the latter term to apply to anything at all) to a First Cause beyond the silences of the uttermost stellar systems. An attempt so comprehensive and so tremendous deserves more than the normal attention that a novel receives, and on the dust cover there are tributes from six writers, one of whom places the book on a level with the greatest works of fiction ever written. Mr Hamish Miles finds it 'enormous, in the very strictest sense of the word'. Miss Eleanor Farjeon regards it as the greatest work of 'the greatest living writer of fiction'. 'With the single exception of Thomas Hardy,' says Mr Hugh Walpole, 'no English novelist of the last thirty years has evoked the very stuff of the English ground with the power and the poetry which Mr Powys has at command.' 'In breadth, rhythm, and intensity,' says Mr Gerald Barry, '*A Glastonbury Romance* has something of the mighty pantheism of Rubens.' Mr C S Forester regards the book as 'one of the most significant and notable of the century'; while Mr J D Beresford makes the extraordinary act of faith: 'I believe that *A Glastonbury Romance* is one of the greatest novels in the world, to be classed with Tolstoy's *War and Peace*.'

Such superlative praise, coming from critics of such experience, makes one chary of saying anything in depreciation of the book. Besides, it is certainly impressive as well as enormous—an excellently chosen epithet; and it is the work of a man of unusual originality of imagination. The best proof of this is that he has created in the book a whole world, complete in itself. He does not merely describe a milieu, as so many contemporary writers, even the better ones, have sunk to doing; he evokes. It is solely about what he evokes that one may have some doubts; the evocatory power is there in abundance. In a note at the beginning he himself says: 'Not a single scene, or situation, or character, or episode in this book has been drawn in any respect, or in any sense whatever, from real life. All is pure invention; and the author is absolutely unacquainted with any living individual or with any existing industry in the Glastonbury of our time.'

That is a challenge, but it is also the first criticism that is likely to occur to anyone. The characters are obviously drawn too largely from Mr Powys' imagination and too little from nature; the world they make up is clearly a world hatched in his mind and then projected and given a local habitation in Glastonbury. But the highest flights of the imagination seem to rise from a union of these two processes, of intuition and observation, and when the first quite dispenses with the second it is likely to go astray now and then and produce creatures that, though perhaps impressive in their way, are sometimes monstrous, or even absurd. Mr Powys by his own admission has taken this risk on a grand scale, and the result is a disconcerting mixture of profound truth and sheer psychological melodrama in which it is hard to discover where reality ends and make-believe begins. The London of Dickens was an imaginary structure supported by a diabolically sharp power of observation. Mr Powys' Glastonbury is also an imaginary structure; but one can never be quite certain whether it is real or merely some town in some English Ruritania; or rather one is certain one moment and uncertain the next. There is this constant ebb and flow in the story; one feels in touch with reality at a deep level, and on the next page one may be reading what seems like wild fantasy or even bombast. And Mr Powys infuses as much energy into the one as into the other.

The characters are equally mixed. A few are splendid. Geard of Glastonbury, ex-servant, ex-preacher, sensual mystic and mayor of the town, is, making all allowances for the extravagant powers that Mr Powys claims for him (they include restoring the dead to life), a justly apprehended and superbly portrayed figure. He gives us the feeling, so rare in fiction, that we know everything about him, not merely his outward appearance and his thoughts, but his most secret impulses, his very nature. Mat Dekker, the vicar of Glastonbury, and his son Sam are also excellently drawn, and the Welsh Mr Evans, though tinged deep with melodrama, is a powerful portrait of a tortured sadist. But when Mr Powys comes to his madmen and madwomen the whole action seems to flare up into a fantastic nightmare. And the action itself, if unusual, would be imaginatively convincing if it were not for those periodical atmospheric commotions. It turns on the struggle between Geard the mystic and Philip Crow the materialist for the soul of Glastonbury. Crow wants to industrialise it and bring it 'into line with modern development', Geard to awaken the old religious potencies that once made it a place of pilgrimage. Geard joins forces with a group of improbable communists (who would have been better had they been taken from real life); communal workshops are set up, miracles happen, and Philip Crow is brought to the verge of ruin. Finally a flood sweeps over the town and Geard voluntarily takes leave of life after having rescued his rival. The plot is one that requires a considerable suspension of one's incredulity, but it is excellently handled. It certainly would never have occurred, however, to the author of *War and Peace*.

Where Mr Powys does resemble Tolstoy is in the direct and motionless attention that he gives to each of his characters in turn. They all have their private lives which on examination prove to be interesting, and the resulting sense of busy human diversity is what gives the book its peculiar rich fullness. Mr Powys' imagination is extraordinarily open and receptive to all forms of human experience; indeed, receptive is far too colourless a term for the ecstatic zest with which he embraces all the manifestations of life that the nerves can feel or the imagination conceive. This zest is the secret of his power, but it is also the source of his weaknesses; for he ends by trying to embrace things, such as the First Cause, that are too unwieldy for him, and consequently by reducing them, necessarily but arbitrarily, to more manageable dimensions. So while we read him on the First Cause that exists beyond the uttermost stellar systems we cannot help feeling that he is speaking of a very watered down and indeed almost private entity. Besides, he speaks of it both dogmatically and vaguely, as when he says in his first sentence: 'At the striking of noon on a certain fifth of March there occurred within a causal radius of Brandon railway-station and yet beyond the deepest pools of emptiness between the uttermost stellar systems one of those infinitesimal ripples in the creative silence of the First Cause which always occur when an exceptional stir of heightened consciousness agitates any living organism in this astronomical universe.' That tells us very little in a great many words and does nothing to create that 'nobly timeless' quality which Mr Miles rightly finds in the book. That quality flows from a very different and more valid cause: from Mr Powys' vision of human life; and the timelessness would have been enhanced, not destroyed, had the rhapsodies on the cosmos, the sun influences and the earth vibrations been left out. They overlay without explaining those things. They vulgarise, in the vain hope of achieving an impossible completeness, a sincerely religious vision of the world with an imaginative completeness of its own.

It is in his style that Mr Powys' uncertainty of inspiration comes out most clearly. It is consistently verbose, occasionally archaic in a picturesque way, and sometimes inflated in a journalistic way, as in the sentence already quoted; and it reads at its worst like a cross between Jeremy Taylor and Mr James Douglas. The book is full not merely of bad writing but, what is far worse, of bad fine writing. It can be meaninglessly metaphorical: 'A new girl was a new world to Mr Barker and his sluggish East Anglian senses stirred in their fen-peat depths, like great crocodiles heaving up out of sun-baked mud, to meet this new world.' Or turgid: 'But the maniacal and obsessional element in his design soon began to run away with the practical element.' Or merely absurd: 'This tendency of Lady Rachel's to nestle up very close to anyone she trusted, to touch them with her warm body, to yield herself to them, was it a sign that the child in her was not yet absorbed or subsumed in the young woman?' No natural thought could be expressed in this style, which tends to reappear whenever Mr Powys remembers the First Cause, directly or indirectly. On the other hand, when he comes to real things such as Sam Dekker's religious struggles or John Geard's mystical trances he sloughs it off and writes simply and immediately. But it lies sometimes like a smothering weight on the story.

These faults are very serious ones: the proof of the book's vitality is that it easily survives them. It creates its own world; it has the self-subsistent quality of a work of imagination. The imagination is mixed: sometimes quite pure, sometimes gratingly false, sometimes pretentious. Mr Powys makes us feel at times that he is a man of genuine original power playing at being a genius. But much must be forgiven a man of original power, and anyone who is interested in more than the passing mode should not miss this book.

GEORGE BARKER Alanna Autumnal

Listener X, 8 November 1933, 728

Sincerity is an ambiguous term that no reviewer can dispense with to cover a recurrent something in contemporary novels. It stands for a very common quality in current fiction, good, bad and indifferent alike, and it has the involuntary drawback of being frequently double-edged, much less pleasing to the writer about whom it is used than to the reviewer who uses it—calling up in his mind, probably, an image of dull, Dobbin-like honesty. It is a term that is applied comprehensively to all plain accounts of facts to which people usually shut their eyes; such as the life of the poor, or the faults of some national institution (like the public school) about which people have pleasing ideas, or even the vices of the very rich, but here unjustifiably, for these vices only acquire a more fascinating dinginess the more they are written about, and remain universally charming by virtue of the fact that they are luxurious. A sincere writer in this sense is one who refuses to deny the evidence of his eyes and insists on publishing what they tell him, no matter what the consequences may be; and that is a course which obviously requires considerable force of character. But it does not necessarily imply the possession of any great literary ability, nor does it even imply sincerity in the literary sense. A writer on the sufferings of the poor obviously cannot stop to analyse nicely the sincerity of his subjective response to those sufferings; he is concerned to show them in their dreadful actuality to an indifferent or case-hardened public; and the more exclusively he succeeds in that the more salutary will be the effect of his work. A writer of this kind deserves the thanks of the community itself rather than of literature. But there is another kind of sincerity, which consists rather in following with perfect honesty one's inward response to experience, distinguishing true from false sentiment, individually felt emotions from those suggested by the mass; and expressing these in some organic form with the utmost liveliness and exactitude. The first kind of sincerity is a social virtue and often a high one; the other is both that and something else which it is difficult and perhaps impossible to define; but it is in any case a literary virtue. It implies both sincerity towards the outer world and knowledge of the nature of one's own individual response to it; and that combination, it seems to me, is one of the marks of an original writer. The first book on this list, though it is in many ways immature, and is also difficult from the general reader's point of view, has this unmistakable and rare virtue.

Alanna Autumnal is not a story in any accepted sense. There are two characters, a brother and a sister, who are bound together by deep instinctive ties. Alanna, the sister, marries and is very happy. Then her husband loses his job and goes away to search for work, leaving her in her parents' house, where she presently discovers that she is pregnant. Edward, the brother, is also fettered there by inward indecision, lack of money, and pity for his sister. Forsaken by her husband, Alanna's mind is clouded by incestuous fantasies of which her brother becomes aware. This part of the book is in all probability too outspoken for some readers; but only complacency or prurience could take any actual objection to it on moral grounds. The sister dies in giving birth to her child, and the brother leaves the house.

The book consists of alternating extracts from diaries kept by brother and sister, and these describe indirectly the gradual change in their relation to each other. As both are occupied in searching their own minds, and are unusually self-conscious and capable of describing their states with vividness and exactitude, the result is as different as it could be from a realistic presentation of life. The events in the story, which are perfectly simple, exist merely for the sake of the more intense drama to which they act as contributory causes. The author is really concerned with states of mind and spiritual problems. His story occasionally flares up into melodrama, and then one feels his lack of experience; but there is a fine truth and passion in it, nevertheless, which can be felt almost continuously in the thought, the imagery and the style. The quality of such a book can be shown only by quotation; here are a few passages: 'And then one day we had no money . . . and the little room in which we lived contracted and grew dark; and the bed sagged repulsively; and the water pipes which ran around the kitchen walls circled so fast we lost our senses.' 'When the handle of the door turned, I knew who it was: who turned that circle of guilt and desperation.' 'And here she reclines, breathing away her dancing and singing and walking and swimming and leaping and being.' The book is written throughout in this vital and living style, which is poetic in the sense that it invents new equivalents for the things it describes, instead of accepting the approved counters of ordinary prose. The author's originality can be felt in every phrase he uses; it is not a matter of occasional flashes, but of the whole texture of his style and thought; and this actually makes a first reading of the book somewhat difficult. There is continuously active thought, it is obvious behind the few short passages already quoted. The following three give some idea of the quality of the thought itself as it occurs in the more reflective pages of the diaries. 'I only ask for the trick all men have, of making danger look safe' (from the sister's diary). 'Why, after all, should I try to arrange or secure my life? Has not a hand larger and more lovely than mine done so, thousands of years back in time?' 'Securely and unchangeably I am possessed by the men of my nation, like a museum or war memorial.' It is not the rightness or wrongness of such thoughts that matters in a work of imagination like this, but the understanding of life that they display, and such deep understanding in a writer of twenty is remarkable. *Alanna Autumnal* will not appeal, it is certain, to a wide public; it will irritate many people on a first reading; but on the other hand it is one of the few books that should be read more than once, and it is, as I have found by experience, even better on a second than a first reading. It is certainly the work of a writer of great talent.

D H LAWRENCE The Tales of D H Lawrence

Listener XI, 4 April 1934, 596

This collection of Lawrence's tales contains all the short stories and short novels of Lawrence already issued by Messrs Secker, and they range in length from *St Mawr*, which is virtually a novel, to stories of a few pages. The stories are arranged in chronological order, running from 'The Prussian Officer', published in 1914, to 'The Man Who Died', which appeared in 1931 after Lawrence's death, and thus give us not only a great representative body of his most excellent work in prose, but also a bird's-eye view of his development as a writer. The only fault that might be found with the book is that the dates of publication of the various stories are not given. That would have been illuminating and also have enabled one to tell more accurately when the change set in that caused the great difference between the later stories and the earlier ones.

That difference is enormous and might roughly be described by saying that in his earlier stories Lawrence was concerned with life and in his later ones with his dreams about life. The three short novels which make up the volume called *The Ladybird* seem to form a convenient landmark between these two phases of his production. One of them, 'The Fox', is almost entirely in his early style, and is one of the best stories he ever wrote, but the other two, 'The Ladybird' and 'The Captain's Doll', already contain the seeds of such future fantasies as 'The Woman Who Rode Away', 'The Princess' and 'The Man Who Died', which are less interesting as works of art than for the light they throw on Lawrence's state of mind. Already in these two stories his dreams of possible modes of living are confused with the simple and intense perception of actual living which gave such depth to his first work; characters are made to feel as he wishes them to feel or thinks they should feel, and sensations fall into categories or degenerate into *clichés*. The seeds of this change were, no doubt, innate though quiescent even in his earliest work; one can guess at them in a turn of phrase, a twist of imagination; but in 'The Ladybird' they begin to sprout, and in 'The Woman Who Rode Away' and 'The Man Who Died' they flourish wild. There seems no doubt that as he grew older Lawrence lost more and more the intense interest in life which he had as a young man and which made his response to it that of a great artist; and 'The Man Who Died', melancholy reading as it is compared with the stories in 'The Prussian Officer', is interesting for the indirect proof it provides of this. Lawrence's own voice can be heard throughout the story under the thinnest disguise:

> He could move if he wanted: he knew that. But he did not want. Who would want to come back from the dead? A deep, deep nausea stirred in him, at the premonition of movement. He resented already the fact of the strange, incalculable moving that had already taken place in him: the moving back into consciousness. He had not wished it. He had wanted to stay outside, in the place where even memory is stone dead.

All the first part of the story has this intense sadness, this almost post-mortem sorrow, relieved only by outbursts of ineffectual anger, the retrospective anger of someone who is no longer in the world:

> So always he must move on, for if he stayed, his neighbours wound the strangling of their fear and bullying round him. There was nothing he could touch, for all, in a mad assertion of the ego, wanted to put a compulsion on him, and violate his intrinsic solitude. It was the mania of cities and societies and hosts, to lay a compulsion upon a man, upon all men. For men and women alike were mad with the egoistic fear of their own nothingness. And he thought of his own mission, how he had tried to lay the compulsion of love on all men. And the old nausea came back on him.

But the hope realised of the second part of the story is even sadder, and the sacrament of love that is to make life new again is as ghostly as some encounter in the kingdom of the shades. Lawrence's hope no longer lay in this world but in a dream within his mind.

From what quality or defect this change in Lawrence's later work sprang cannot be guessed at with certainty, but there was always a great deal of self-will in his genius: he saw intensely but wilfully. This can be seen even in an early story like 'The Prussian Officer':

> But it was only the outside of the orderly's body that was obeying so humbly and mechanically. Inside had gradually accumulated a core into which all the energy of that young life was compact and concentrated.

There, in the middle of a story filled with superb imagination, we all at once come upon a bald dogmatic assertion, and all Lawrence's work, even his earliest and best, is strewn with these sudden little dogmatic assertions; it is as if the man of imagination had withdrawn for a moment and another, pragmatic and pushing, had taken his place. In his first stories these assertions are assertions about the feelings and inward workings of the characters; but in his later ones they are widened to embrace the most comprehensive generalisations on all sorts of things, while still essentially remaining as self-willed and personal as they were at the beginning:

> With sudden horror she realised that she must be in the Marne country, the ghastly Marne country, century after century digging the corpses of frustrated men into the soil. The border country, where the Latin races and the Germanic neutralise one another into horrid ash.

The last sentence illustrates two of the worst faults of his later style. He attributes feelings which only he himself would have to his characters; and then he exalts those feelings into a statement of general validity. One of the results is that at such moments his style, at its best so close and vivid, becomes uneasily melodramatic:

> And dimly she realised that behind all the ashy pallor and sulphur of our civilisation, lurks the great blood-creature waiting, implacable and eternal, ready at last to crush our white brittleness and let the shadowy blood move erect once more, in a new implacable pride and strength.

That is the same kind of fault as: 'Inside had gradually accumulated a core into which all the energy of that young life was compact and concentrated', but grown so rank and intellectually monstrous that it twisted Lawrence's whole view of life. There were two men in him: one great and one small. The great one, the man of imagination, never interfered with what he was describing, but devoted to it an intense and single attention unexampled in his generation. The other, subdued at first, ended by interfering with everything. The interferer was a man of immense eccentric talent, sometimes wise, sometimes tiresomely facetious, sometimes splenetic, occasionally a bore, but always, at least when he interrupted or distracted or put out the man of imagination, a spoil-sport and a leveller. He never quite got the better of the man of genius, however, and there are a few stories in the latter part of this volume, such as 'In Love' and 'None of That', which are nearly as good as almost all of them are at the beginning. The book gives a new sense of Lawrence's fecundity of imagination and of the power and essential strangeness of his genius. It contains an impressive body of his best and most concentrated prose work.

KATHLEEN FREEMAN The Huge Shipwreck

Listener XII, 3 October 1934, 590

Miss Freeman is a writer whose gifts have never been recognised at their true worth, and *The Huge Shipwreck* seems to me to be the finest novel that she has yet written. Her style is so transparent that what she says always seems to be simple; but actually she is concerned with the subtlest of themes: the secret windings and deviations of passion. Had she treated this subject less calmly and surely her reputation would stand higher now, and her art lower. It is not that she is not intensely concerned with her theme; but she is never involved in it, never swept round in the gyrations of the passion she describes, as so many novelists seem to think it their duty to be. The spectacle of an author being carried away often carries the reader away too by sympathy; the result is a form of popularity. Miss Freeman does not carry us away; she helps to bring us back to ourselves. She clears a space where we can stand and see everything unrolling before us, and have a clear and undisturbed view. She does this by virtue of a passion quite different from that which she is describing: a passion of contemplation that fulfils itself in something which might almost be mistaken for passionlessness.

The Huge Shipwreck is a story of conflicting fidelities which work themselves out in the lives of the characters from childhood to womanhood (for Miss Freeman is mainly concerned with women). Estella, who is the chief figure, forms a deep attachment while still a child to an older girl, Veronica, and this influences the rest of her life. The two girls are sent to the same school, where Estella meets Sadie, a friend of Veronica, by whom she is both repelled and attracted so powerfully that this too influences the rest of her life. Sadie is madly in love with Toby Ungerville, who is in love with Veronica. Toby and Veronica become engaged, but at the last moment Veronica throws him over for the man she really loves, and Sadie gets him to herself, as she had always said she would. But their life is unhappy, and in a fit of despair Sadie at last leaves him, and he falls to Estella. With her he seems to be happy for a while, but then one night he shoots himself. The central figure in the drama is Veronica, who, while herself unmoved and carefree, ruins the lives of the three people who in different ways depended on her. The plot gives very little idea of the story, for the really remarkable thing in the book is the beautiful fidelity, the exquisite sense of proportion with which the relations between the characters are traced. These relations are in the last resort indefinable, so Miss Freeman does not analyse them, she merely indicates them; but her art is so measured and just that the effect is one of perfect clarity. All her women characters are beautifully drawn, Sadie being perhaps the best of them all. The men are not nearly so good, and Toby, the most important of them, is little better than a romantic lay figure. But it is the women that matter (Toby is an excuse), and in describing their lives Miss Freeman gives an intense feeling of forces moving behind the events, that is to say of design and meaning, which is rarely found in contemporary novels. This feeling of design does not spring from any underlying dogma, but from intuition: it is part of a vision of life which sees the subtlest movements of passion and simultaneously the whole as it will work itself out. The structure, the style and the temper of this remarkable novel are all fine and all of a piece.

WILLIAM GERHARDI Resurrection

Listener XII, 17 October 1934, 670

Resurrection is a work so comprehensive in plan and so various in quality that in a short review one is likely to do less than justice to its virtues and ignore some of its defects. It sets out to demonstrate the immortality of the soul. Mr Gerhardi bases his proof of this on an experience of his own (he is himself the hero of the story, and the events with which he deals are actual events); and he calls in to support him Mr J W Dunne's *An Experiment with Time*, Proust's theory of the vases 'suspended at the height of our years', a poem by Goethe, and finally his own life as it exists in his memory. His theory is that after death our life is resurrected, not in the order in which we lived it, that is the order of Time, but at will, by the mere process of recollecting it. Nothing is until it is ended, and we shall only possess our lives in their resurrection beyond Time. Mr Gerhardi's personal evidence for this theory is an experience he had outside his body. Taking this as the basis of his proof of immortality, he builds up an argument to which he applies all his powers of intellect and imagination. The result is a book which is easily the best he has written, and also, I think, one of the most remarkable that have appeared in our time.

The plan of the book reminds one in different ways of Sterne, Proust and Gide. It is a novel about a novelist writing a novel (a class of which Sterne was the father), and probably no better form could have been devised for the author's purpose, which is to concentrate every argument he can think of, from experience, memory, reason and past literature on the theory which he is trying to establish, while at the same time allowing for the objections of the other characters with whom he discusses it. These discussions are, I think, the weakest part of the book; Mr Gerhardi cannot help seeing his objectors satirically; and although the result is sometimes good social comedy, the method obviously prejudices the argument. It mixes up two kinds of dialogue, so that the book sometimes reads like a spirited collaboration between Plato and Chekhov. This probably exaggerates the fault somewhat, and the dialogue also shifts so often from the one level to the other that it is sometimes difficult to see where the emphasis is unfair. These dialogues are essential to the plan of the book, and they are brilliantly sustained, but they do not form the chief part of it. The main aim of the story is imaginatively to resurrect the hero's past life in its perfection, out of Time, a task which Mr Gerhardi holds is also man's chief end. There are the most beautiful and strange things in this evocation of the past, as well as excellent comedy; and though uneven, the whole is held together by the author's unswerving purpose. Nevertheless, the unevenness of his work is occasionally disconcerting, as in the following passage:

> The important thing about presenting travel—I said as an aside in my book—is that it should be felt to be bits of comedy in a dream which is within another larger dream. It's the colour of the sky, the new feeling contained in a dream that matters. Note that. Action is merely the vehicle, the mechanical contrivance for conveying these dreams. Unless the cells of action release their living prisoner they are dead stones. The prisoner is released, but he escapes and none can find him. No one remembers his name. But he must exist. He is hiding in another field. In a higher-dimensional field, immune from our laws of Time. There one day we shall find him.
>
> Oh, the dust! Our emotions all choked with dust—let's clean them. Resurrection in the form of restoration? Cleansed Antiques repaired: mellowness of time, however, preserved.

The first paragraph is a good example of Mr Gerhardi's style at its best, the second of what he occasionally falls to. As a whole, however, the book is brilliantly written, in a light and supple rhythm which is not retarded by the most difficult obstacles and is of delightful ingenuity and resource. Mr Gerhardi stages his demonstration at a London party, where many people well known in the newspaper columns are present. This setting produces an effect of incongruity which is probably intended, but is not, I think, artistically effective. When Mr Gerhardi applies himself to his form of comedy he uses only the surface of his mind; and if it is true, as he says, that life creates itself only in memory, then it is clear that his memory of these scenes is too short. *Resurrection* is uneven then, and in some ways unsatisfactory, but it is an eloquent piece of philosophical imagination, and anyone who reads it once with appreciation is bound to return to it again.

CHRISTINA STEAD and LEWIS GRASSIC GIBBON Seven Poor Men of Sydney; Grey Granite

Listener, XII, 5 December 1934, 966

Miss Stead's first book, *The Salzburg Tales*, was exceptionally well received when it appeared about a year ago. In plan it somewhat resembled *The Decameron*, for it created a frame for the stories it contained, transposing them into a separate little interior world; its most arresting quality was an apparently inexhaustible invention, by turns fantastic, tragic and witty. Miss Stead's latest book is a novel; it has not been so well received as her first one; but it seems to me to be a work of incomparably greater depth and range. As Miss Stead is a writer whose quality of imagination and thought informs all that she writes and penetrates every sentence, the only way to give an idea of it is by quotation. The boy Michael Baugenault is recovering from an illness, and the following passage is from a description of a sleepless night which he spent at the window of his room:

> The river of heaven flowed wide, deep and windless, and the suffocated stars rolled slowly on their white flanks through the celestial currents. It was October; the strewn silver meteors shaken fresh from the airy crests went silting and glinting down through the signs of the Zodiac, and the hoofs of the Centaur, plunging and curvetting, beat up the dust of the Milky Way. The early morning moon in its last quarter sank gradually to the foot of the sky and entered the feathery boughs of the churchyard yews. Its sallow beam stole over the scattered trunks like bones, sunken in wet clay and smirched with mosses; it drew out the coarse grass and ivy-ends in shadows.

The next passage is from Michael's story of his own life told to his sister Catherine:

> Why is there so much darkness in the world that even the sun can only illuminate a small part of our day, at noon? . . . If you dig in the earth, it is dark within, despite the gold and fire contained there. If you penetrate beyond the diffusing envelope of air, the heavens are black; if you even look into the heart of a tree, darkness seems to rush forth as you cleave the bark; thus man goes on his way peering. The greatest occasions of life are made mysteries, such as birth, love and the adoration of God—the womb, dark and without air, the earth, the same; light is but a temporary star in our existence.

The last quotation is from a conversation between Michael and his mother:

> I remember hundreds of dreams, some of them dreamed in childhood. I would like to go on telling them all to you, it is such an ardent pleasure for me to talk about them; it is as if I were eating honey, and instead of clothes I wrapped myself in a vestment of sunlight. The veil is thin between me and the spinning chamber of the fates; when I die I will go there and dip my hands in the unwoven raw material of life, for once.

Now it seems to me that what distinguishes these three passages, apart from their strangeness, is that in them Miss Stead appears to be at once inventing and discovering the world she writes about. It is impossible, when she is at her best, to separate these two activities in her work; her inventions are living inventions, real additions to the world one's mind conceives, or, to use another analogy, a revelation of things that had been hidden or absent before. The possession of such a gift is very rare, especially in a novelist; and in Miss Stead it is united with a comprehensive and radical intellect. Her style with its large movement and exactitude of phrase is the natural vehicle for such an endowment; occasionally it might be called rhetorical, but the rhetoric is genuine, a form of eloquence proper to intense imaginative and intellectual passion.

These quotations should give some idea of the quality of Miss Stead's genius; to know its richness the reader will have to go to the book itself. It is a very unequal book, not because some of it is good and some bad (for there is hardly a page in it which can be called bad), but because it is good in half-a-dozen ways, and its virtues are sometimes merged in the most disconcerting fashion, there being too many of them in places where they are not expected, and too few of them in others where they are wanted. For instance, Miss Stead allots to one of her characters, Baruch Mendelssohn, an unlimited capacity for witty and curious speculation; but at one point in the book she gives us so much of it that it becomes almost wearisome, in spite of its brilliance. Her management of the story is equally disconcerting. She has a powerful gift of characterisation, as her preface of *The Salzburg Tales* showed; she can plant a figure on the stage with the utmost firmness. But when her characters are there she cannot set them moving naturally; they either do not move at all, like Baruch Mendelssohn, or else they move in wild fits and starts, like Michael Baugenault and his sister Catherine. To attempt a *précis* of the story would therefore be hopeless. The setting, as the title indicates, is Sydney; but though the streets of that city are vividly evoked, no reader should expect to find a picture of Australian life in the book. None of the characters is ordinary; the best idea one can give of most of them is to say that they are frustrated men and women of genius. They have so much life, and life of such a rare kind, that they do not know what to do with it. The value of the book does not depend on their reality as creatures of flesh and blood, but rather on a visionary imaginative power which turns them all into spirits. This book, with all its brilliant faults, seems to me to be a work of genius.

With *Grey Granite* Mr Grassic Gibbon rounds off his trilogy of Scottish life. It is in one way the best of the three parts: it has all the good qualities of *Sunset Song* and *Cloud Howe* and it has fewer of their defects. Mr Grassic Gibbon's main virtues as a writer seem to me to be, first, an impetuous, Rabelaisian, all-embracing humour, and, secondly, a style which rushes in full spate, carrying away with it cleanly whatever he chooses to say, however ribald or bitter. If he were to attempt a purely comic picture of Scottish life, a comic picture which would at the same time be quite serious, and exclude neither ribaldry nor the most radical satire, one imagines that he would produce something extremely powerful. In the first two volumes of his trilogy there was a great difference between his serious characters and his comic characters, a difference somewhat resembling that between Scott's heroes and heroines and his humbler creations, though, of course, not so exaggerated. Chris Guthrie and her two husbands existed on a different plane from the rest of the characters; she received preferential treatment, and that made her somewhat unconvincing; she was a picture of what the author wished woman to be, not a picture of a woman. In *Grey Granite* she becomes considerably more real; but one has only to compare her with Ma Cleghorn, a splendidly drawn portrait, to see how pale she is in comparison. The industrial town of Duncairn, with its strikers and unemployed workmen, is described so vividly that one can see and smell it; the inmates of the boarding house run by Ma Cleghorn and Chris are pinned to the wall with almost scornful ease; the account of the beating up of young Ewan Tavendale by the police is extremely powerful. But when the author conducts his heroine at the end to the scenes of her childhood and leaves her there, one feels again that he is describing what he wishes to be, not what would be. One cannot take such a thing seriously; but one can take the humour and the satire and the passion behind them with the utmost seriousness.

FREDERICK ROLFE The Desire and Pursuit of the Whole

Listener XIII, 2 January 1935, 44

The *Desire and Pursuit of the Whole*, like *Tristram Shandy*, raises the question of how a personality which would exasperate us past bound in real life can charm us so powerfully when it is expressed in fiction. Rolfe's story has no resemblance to *Tristram Shandy*, except that it has this powerful charm and reflects at the same time a personality that is displeasing. The enjoyment which we receive from his dramatisation of himself, however, is not merely malicious; for persecution mania is such a painful mental misfortune that even malice could scarcely find any pleasure in contemplating it. Yet Rolfe makes this disease, the torment of his own life, and the plague of all his friends, charming: there is no other word for it. The same thing happens with his griefs and despairs: they do not seriously move us, even though they are superbly described; they merely charm us. The vanity and malice that run an alternate race through the book, the one relieving the other, are just as harmless and turn just as inevitably into something pleasing. Vanity is probably the human failing which most quickly rouses annoyance and retaliation in other people; but when Rolfe writes of his hero, that is himself: "He read over what he had already done. It seemed to be almost as far above the ordinary as he wished it to be', we are delighted, and feel no displeasure at his presumption. And that is not merely because his work is actually far above the ordinary; in other circumstances such a consideration would not soften us. Rolfe's satire, too, savage and blistering as it has every appearance of being, produces merely an impression of comic ferocity. Take this admirable example:

> While he was speaking, the Erastian Mr Warden and his lady passed, on the way to a tardy dinner. The lady was a soured withered meagre lath of smirking female with the thinnest of pinched lips and nose-nippers, exquisitely dressed autumnally, clinking with narrow chains, famishing and parching for worshipful attention. The ghostly gentleman was meagre also, and knock-kneed: his face and head (by aid of goggles, nostrils at 45°, a flat, long upper-lip, and a thin, wide, rather abject grin) were the face and head of a skull, abnormally philoprogenitive. His gait was harassed, but obsequious. He cast a timid glance at the two English-speaking men as he went by; and would have moved, if he could have caught an eye. None was tossed his way.

How exact and apparently destructive that is, and yet how innocuous. We feel that Mr Warden and his lady, after being tossed and gored so thoroughly, are quite uninjured, indeed perfectly unconscious of their punishment; that the satire, in other words, is a purely theoretical affair in which the dreams of Rolfe's imagination are flayed and scalded with the gusto of a little girl revenging herself on her dolls for the injustices of life, but with no more pertinent effect. It is something like this that transmutes things which must in Rolfe's experience have been painful in the highest degree into pure comedy, partly conscious and partly unconscious—it is extremely difficult to put one's finger on the boundary between the two in Rolfe's work. As a stylist he was certainly more conscious of what he did than most writers: his effects were deliberate. As a portrayer of life he was perfectly sincere, with the sincerity of an incorruptible egoist. But his response to life was almost fictitious; and though most of the characters in this book are satirical portraits of actual people, they belong to the world of his fantasy, and in slaying them there he was performing a feat to which our usual responses to satire are quite unsuitable. This transmutation of reality into fantasy which gives all the ferocity of actual life a comic aspect is probably at the bottom of our enjoyment of Rolfe's work, and makes him, by virtue of what would normally be a fault, a unique writer.

If he had not been a writer of genius as well, however, he could not have performed this minor miracle. One can feel his power as a stylist in the first page, as for instance when, speaking of the manner in which Nicholas and Gilda are brought together, he says: 'A certain deftness, which I notice about things in general, causes me shrewdly to imagine that this business might have been done without devastating a pair of provinces and massacring a couple of hundred thousand Christians', which is his magniloquent way of explaining that the two lovers met as the result of an earthquake. His work is full of such delightful strokes. The descriptions of the earthquake itself and of its after-effects are worthy of a writer of the first rank; and the whole story of the adventures of Nicholas and Gilda in Venice is managed with extraordinary skill. This remarkable book was kept back from publication for several years, Mr A J A Symons says in his admirable introduction, because of its scurrilous portraits of R H Benson and various other people, which might have provided matter for libel. It tells the story of Rolfe's life in Venice a few years before his death. If we keep that in mind, it is impossible not to feel admiration for the writer's courage in the face of many and severe misfortunes. But we never keep it in mind for long, for Rolfe's genius itself makes us forget it, leading us into a comic world which is unlike any other that has been created by the imagination. The comedy is largely involuntary; for it is impossible to conceive that the effect which Rolfe intended to produce on his readers is the one he really produces. But the comedy is nevertheless the result of an extremely idiosyncratic and one-sided logic, not of mere literary blundering (Rolfe was a fastidious artist and never blundered), and as such it is inherently interesting and quite unique. There is nothing one can do with such a book but urge people to read it.

V S PRITCHETT   Nothing Like Leather

Listener XIII, 30 January 1935, 211

Nothing Like Leather is a novel quite out of the common because of its union of two qualities which do not come together very often. The long roomy novel describing the complete life-story of a set of characters or of several generations is a recognisable type; but it is often worthless, the treatment being usually so loose and general: everybody knows these large and plain canvases. The short, closely wrought study of some circumscribed situation is an equally familiar form: some of the best work in contemporary fiction has been done in it. The self-confidence of the age does not seem to be great enough to combine these two categories. If a novelist regards life closely—that is, if he regards it at all—he has to restrict his field of vision. If he takes a wide view the separate objects are blurred, often deliberately indeed, for this blurring of outline has become one of the arts of the novelist, the resulting indistinctness providing the best opportunity for the insinuation of his philosophy, which is generally a mystical belief in life. No novelist can relate the fortunes of human beings over a long period without asking himself what the meaning of these happenings is and making some reply. The popular Victorian reply was wedding bells; the popular reply now is more vague and doubtful, particularly since three or four generations began to feature in stories, qualifying the finality of wedding bells; but one can still hear in that reply a distant vibration of bells, though what they are ringing for nobody can quite say. They are at any rate a necessary accompaniment to the large plain novel. There is nothing of this in Mr Pritchett's book; it is both large in conception and close in texture, as novels were before the modern era of doubt, and before they acquired the habit of finishing with a mystical hope in lieu of a happy ending. A history of the permutations of the happy ending since the Victorian Age, showing its gradual refinement into something which is not quite happy and does not quite end, and yet is in some way gratifying, would make instructive reading. But Mr Pritchett's novel would not come into that survey, for it ends very definitely; the hero dying at the right time, to use Nietzsche's phrase.

The chief character in *Nothing Like Leather* is Matthew Burkle, a sly, reserved, acquisitive but not unlikeable man, who beginning as a clerk in a tannery rises in middle age to wealth and influence. Mr Pritchett's treatment of the tannery provides an admirable example of the difference between his novel and the kind of long novel I have been mentioning. In that one would have found long and detailed descriptions of the various processes through which hides are put before they can be turned into leather, with incidental hints of the strictly technical emotions which they excite in Matthew Burkle at their successive stages, and accounts of business raptures when they are sold at last as leather. There is none of this nonsense in Mr Prichett's book; he obviously knows what his tannery is like and gives us a vivid impression of it; but he does not burden us with information and we do not feel after reading the story that it is our duty to run a tannery. He is not really concerned with Burkle's business emotions, which would have satisfied many another novelist, but with his emotions as a human being; and he shows that as Burkle grows older these become a more and more inextricable tangle of business calculation and natural feeling. It is this grasp of the complexity of an ordinary business man's nature which makes his study of Burkle such a satisfying one. It is not so much that natural feeling pulls one way and business instinct another in Burkle; but rather that both are indissolubly confused, since they are equally natural to him; so that his love for the woman who attracts him is identified in his mind with business ambition, and business ambition coloured with his passion for her. This is one of the finest strokes of imagination in the novel, and it shows how complete is Mr Pritchett's conception of his chief character. Burkle marries early in life, and it is not until he has become the manager of the tannery that he falls in love with Henrietta Petworth, its owner. Their ambiguous relation to each other, which twice actually rises to the point of an explicit avowal, but without result, as if nothing had happened, is described with extraordinary skill. Burkle does not desire Henrietta as a mistress; but her beauty, her style, her social position, her house, her tannery make up together such an impressive symbol of his ambitions that when she tells him that she is going to marry another man and dispose of the tannery, the double stroke is too heavy for him, and in his agony of mind he slips into one of the tannery pits and is suffocated. All this part of the story is brilliantly conceived, and the end itself is completely convincing. The one unconvincing stroke in the book is Burkle's beard. He actually grows it to prove a thesis of Mr Pritchett (curiously, the same thesis is found in Mr Bates' novel): thethesis that a man in middle age recapitulates the development of his father, no matter how much he may have disapproved of him as a child. Burkle's father wore a beard and bullied his children; Burkle acquires a beard and bullies his children. The conclusion is arbitrary and does not arise inevitably from Burkle's character as actually portrayed in the story. This is not a major point, and it is not unduly insisted upon; yet it obviously means something to the author. Apart from it there is little fault to be found with the book, except an occasional patch of over-writing. Burkle himself is a palpable creation; Dorothy his wife and Henrietta his employer are equally good in their different styles; there is a succession of scenes described with the most vivid exactitude and sometimes with beauty; and the book grows of itself until it seems to become a part of one's experience. It is certainly a remarkable piece of work and should be read.

DOROTHY CHESTON BENNETT Arnold Bennett: A Portrait Done at Home

Scotsman, 24 January 1935, 622

There have been very few books written about Arnold Bennett since his death a few years ago: fate in that respect has been kind to his memory. But it has been kindest of all in inspiring the writing of this volume, which is not only perfect in its sincerity and its general temper, but also a literary work of unusual distinction, and surely one of the most delicate tributes that have ever been paid to a famous writer by one who knew him intimately. To say that its author is a critic of extraordinary intelligence can give no idea of the exquisite quality of this book; for her excelling gift lies rather in the most delicately poised and penetrating intuitive sympathy. There are no revelations of the ordinary kind in this volume, and little gossip; its justification is that after reading it one feels one understands Bennett more intimately than one does even after reading his letters. Yet it invades no privacy and tells nothing, one feels, that its subject would not have wished to be told. And it is in itself a remarkable feat of imaginative understanding.

On Meeting Famous Persons

The author, then Miss Dorothy Cheston, first met Arnold Bennett in March 1922, in Liverpool, where she was acting in his play *Body and Soul*. Her account of their meeting will give an idea of the active sensitiveness which characterises all that she writes:

> I had already met a good many well-known or famous people, and my experience in doing so had decided me that one must always be prepared on such occasions to take the onus of the introduction upon oneself, to be, if possible, the contributor to the occasion, because the position of famous persons renders them inevitably both sated and over-exposed. It was not their business, but one's own, to find the remark which would decently cover the bare crude moment of introduction to somebody they had never, or barely, heard of.

From that evening Bennett's friendship with Miss Cheston grew steadily until late in 1923 they decided to join forces and live together. The description of their hesitations and scruples before they took this step is perfectly frank and unaffected, and leaves one with a high respect for the sincerity and consideration exercised on both sides. But it is for its analysis of Bennett's character, as a man and as a writer, that the book is perhaps most truly remarkable. The analysis is unusually close and intimate; yet it never impinges for a moment on what the most sensitive taste might consider impermissible. It is indeed a model of what such a book should be.

Scheme of his Imagination

The book is interesting in three ways: as a description of the relations between two sensitive human beings over a number of years, as a portrait of a remarkable man, and as a sidelight on his work: for one cannot read it without understanding better the scheme of Bennett's imagination. The most trifling things that the author mentions conjure up the novels before our eyes. Take, for example, this description of Bennett's flat in George Street, Hanover Square:

> The general aspect gave one a feeling that his taste, either by nature or development, found expression in curves and a certain flowingness not ordinarily considered masculine, but which was not precious or "arty." There was a tendency to baroque—but not Italian baroque, Victorian, rather—whose massiveness tempered the almost feminine manner of this taste. The whole was subdued by the faint shabbiness of, for instance, old Empire stuffs and darned Aubusson, subdued especially by the sense of an ordered profusion of so many things that in a crowded life had their use.

That expressed with admirable precision the dandified solidity of so much of Bennett's work, as well as the feeling of abundance and of the wearing process of time which makes *The Old Wives' Tale* such an impressive novel. Or take this comment on Bennett's preoccupation with the machinery of existence:

> I think that the machinery and contrivances of life were to him the toy-boats, the railway lines and signalling apparatus, which in his boyhood he had never possessed. It seemed that when this mood—which I call his 'gas bracket' mood—prevailed, his countenance was at its most open and gleeful.

The 'gas bracket' mood certainly prevails a great deal in Bennett's novels, sometimes a little disconcertingly; but this interpretation of it, while not perhaps justifying it, makes us understand it more deeply and gives it a new significance. Or take this:

> Of Arnold Bennett's moral beliefs that which he felt perhaps more keenly than any other concerned the power of growth inherent in ordinary human weaknesses. Weaknesses only, at first so gentle and hard to detect! Indeed it is true in all ways that time, and the dramatic movements and changes it accomplished, was "his subject."

It was here, too, that he was most truly a great writer, in his feeling for 'the dramatic movements and changes' accomplished by time, making small things, whether weaknesses or virtues, great, and in turn making great things small; and *The Old Wives' Tale* is his best book because there this feeling is stronger than in any other novel he wrote.

Forestalling Caprice

This intuition of the capacity of weakness to grow made Bennett a moralist, and a moralist of a particular kind. What he seems to have most insisted upon in his life was a deliberate and unusually strict control of his impulses, and a conscious planning of his time.

> Although he fully savoured in his mind the imaginative and even the spontaneous aspects of every action, he proceeded—usually with a success he was a little vain about—to forestall every capricious and spontaneous aspect of it.

The author blames this excessive deliberation partly on an unhappy love affair in his early life, which was followed by a broken engagement. 'Through it he was turned, at a critical period, more towards the deliberate processes of his mind, and more away from the instinctive.' She is also inclined to attribute his comparatively early death to this firm adherence to deliberate living at the expense of impulse; for the plan of work which he drew up in his most vigorous productive years he insisted on sticking to when his bodily powers were declining. 'He believed,' she says.

> with a kind of unsophisticated faith (for faith it was) in the efficacy of wisdom being imparted, and the power of humanity to improve itself. This was the very note of his especial optimism.

It was also the faith of a man who believed that the mind can dominate impulse, and who actually dominated his own impulses to a degree which must excite our admiration. But towards the end his deliberative mind seems to have hardened until, instead of acting as his servant, it helped to drive him to his death. The passage in which this development is traced is deeply moving.

The picture of Bennett which emerges from this comparatively short study of him is more than usually complete and extremely sympathetic. It is a little classic of its kind, full of the most intimate understanding, and for the most part extremely well written, as the quotations will show. The letters from Bennett himself are of the liveliest interest.

I COMPTON-BURNETT A House and Its Head

Listener XIV, 24 July 1935, 174

It is a great pity that Miss Compton-Burnett should be considered a novelist who can be enjoyed only by the eccentric few. It is true that she writes in a style and adopts a method of representation that nobody else could have thought of and nobody, so far as I know, has ever ventured to imitate. But on the other hand her prose has almost every virtue that prose in the beaten English tradition could possess; it is clear and logical and plain; it can express the most subtle distinction with ease and wit; and it is almost fantastically exact; the only virtue that it lacks being colloquiality. This last fact is probably what discomfits a reader when he first takes up one of her books, for they consist very largely of dialogue, and one naturally expects dialogue to be colloquial. Yet this difficulty can be got over quite easily, it seems to me, if one accepts these dialogues for what they are, that is as a literary form, not a spoken one, as dialogue, not as conversation. They follow a different law from the conversations in ordinary realistic novels, and are used to produce a different pleasure. And that pleasure presupposes in the reader a degree of intellectual curiosity as well as a delight in the use of words. If he can bring these to the reading of Miss Compton-Burnett's books, he will find that in addition to this intense pleasure in the form they will give him almost everything that the English novel at its best gives him: character in abundant variety, comedy, tragedy, and a criticism of life of unusual incisiveness and depth.

A House and its Head is less closely constructed than Miss Compton-Burnett's last novel, *More Men than Women*, but it is far richer in character and incident. It contains one very horrible figure, Mr Edgeworth, the head of the house mentioned in the title, as well as a fine deathbed scene and a murder; but in conception it is comic, the comedy being provided by a terrific chorus of busybodies, most of them middle-aged spinsters. About half-way through the book, conversation takes the bit between its teeth and runs away with everything else, so that one does not care much any longer what is happening. That is perhaps a fault, but what a fault, and what conversation! In humorous dialogue at its best there is a quality of timelessness; it soars above action and place, and evokes a picture of a little group sitting perpetually talking, for centuries perhaps, while all the rest of the world is rushing about; the Falstaffian scenes in *Henry IV* produce this timeless effect, and *Tristram Shandy* also, which is a sort of continuous dialogue between the author and the reader. The second half of this book is almost comparable to these. The action goes on, but it has lost the reality that it had at the beginning; it has all turned into conversation. This is a fault in structure, but a fault transfigured into a virtue. A worse defect is that the chief dramatic characters, Mr Edgeworth and his family, lose their outline during this process; the talking chorus gets the upper hand so much that they end by becoming mere members of it.

The story begins with a breakfast-dinner scene introducing Duncan Edgeworth, his wife, his two daughters, and his nephew, the members of his household. After breakfast they go to morning service and we become acquainted with the gentry of the village, the clergyman, the doctor, and the various churchworkers. Mrs Edgeworth dies shortly afterwards, and her widower, after going on a visit to a relative, returns with a young and beautiful wife. She bears a child to his nephew, which he takes to be his own. After a few years the error is discovered, and the young wife runs away, and Mr Edgeworth marries again. Shortly afterwards the child dies in mysterious circumstances, and presently it is found out that it was murdered at the command of his younger daughter Sibyl, partly out of spite and partly out of calculation. The murder is hushed up. The older daughter Nance, the most admirable character in the book, then gets married to the rector, and the story ends. There is enough violent incident in the book to make a melodrama; but it is described parenthetically, and what Miss Compton-Burnett is really concerned with is the impact of the minds of her characters on one another, their endlessly subtle awareness of each other, and the inexhaustible vagaries of the popular imagination as it is shown in the gossip of the better-class people in the village. The peculiarly alert dialogue might have been made to bring out such things; it is a vehicle of expression so exact that a single word may give away the character that utters it (and none of the others is likely to let it pass); almost a fault of the book is that even the fools are clever. The portrayal of the various characters has the same exquisite precision, and when they are decided characters it gives them a quite extraordinary force. Compared with Mr Edgeworth even Gourlay in *The House with the Green Shutters*, repulsive tyrant though he is, seems a harmless human figure. Mr Edgeworth degenerates somewhat as the story goes on, it is true, but up to his third marriage he is a superbly imagined character. The chorus of church-workers is beyond expectation or praise. This is a novel so much above the ordinary level, so proportioned, so serious in conception and witty in execution, so exalted in the intellectual imagination it displays throughout, that one cannot speak of it in ordinary terms. It has faults, but it moves on such a level that even these would seem virtues if they were found in an average good novel.

T L BEDDOES The Works of Beddoes ed H W Donner and *Thomas Lovell Beddoes* by H W Donner

Scotsman, 5 December 1935, 6

After Blake, Donne, and Hopkins, Beddoes is the latest of the great English poets to be resurrected. Tentative attempts have been made during this century to disinter him: Sir Edmund Gosse edited him (not very carefully, it seems) in 1908, and Mr F L Lucas brought out a volume of selections a few years ago. Many people must have got their first acquaintance with his longer works through the late Lytton Strachey's essay in *Books and Characters*, a stimulating but very journalistic performance. Dr Donner has now produced a complete edition of Beddoes's extant works, admirably arranged and annotated, and written a critical biography of the poet, using the material in the Browning Box and all the other material he could get his hands on. It is possible that some more information about Beddoes will yet turn up; much about him, and particularly about the years he spent in Germany and Switzerland, still remains dark and inexplicable; but here at last are all the known data for judging him as a man and a poet.

His Stature as Poet

There can be no doubt that he was a great poet; the difficulty is to determine just how great he was. Dr Donner claims that he deserves

> a place among that great Romantics, side by side with Blake, Wordsworth, Coleridge, Lord Byron, Shelley, and Keats, different from all, but at his best an equal of the greatest.

There is no difficulty in agreeing with this: the only question is whether 'at his best' he did not excel all these poets, with the possible exception of Blake and Wordsworth. Dr Donner maintains that he was essentially a romantic poet whose romanticism was obscured by the Elizabethan extravagance of his diction. But at his most tremendous it is hard to attach any label to him. Is this romantic?

> I begin to hear
> Strange but sweet sounds, and the loud rocky dashing
> Of waves, where time into Eternity
> Falls over ruined worlds.

Or, at a different level, is this romantic?

> As I heard the snaky mermaids sing
> In Phlegethon, that hydrophobic river,
> One May-morning in Hell.

Or take the line that Strachey admired so much:

> Like the red outline of beginning Adam.

Or the marvellous speech by Athulf in 'Death's Jest-Book', too long for quotation, beginning

The spell of my creation is read backwards,

in which he describes his passions swelling and growing 'like brutes conceived' until he seems

A wild old wicked mountain in the sea,

where the consciousness of the murder he has just committed

Shall be created and become a Lion
All alone in the darkness of my spirit,

and murderers

Will come to live upon my rugged sides,
Die, and be buried in me.

There is no use in calling this Elizabethan; Webster at his most terrifying never rose above such a height. And there is no use in calling it romantic either; none of the romantic poets, except Wordsworth now and then, had this overwhelming vision of mortal guilt. Coleridge and Keats, when they attempted similar things in 'Christabel' and 'Lamia', fell far behind this prodigious scope. For the astonishing thing about Beddoes is that when his imagination is at full stretch it is impossible to conceive that any other human imagination could go further. It may be said that he is excessive at such moments; but he is also supreme.

In the mere mastery of language he was also unrivalled among the English romantic poets. Shelley sounds thin beside him, Keats lacking in vigour, Wordsworth threadbare. Where among them can we find language used with such unconditional power as in this?

All is ready now:
I hold the latch-string of a new world's wicket;
One pull—and it rolls in.

Or as in this?

Once more I'll see thee, love, speak to thee, hear thee;
And then my soul shall cut itself a door
Out of this planet.

Beddoes has been accused of a literary use of language; but what distinguishes verse such as this from most romantic verse is the naturalness of its syntax and something vigorously colloquial in the turn of the phrases beneath the magnificence of the rhythmic movement. All the characters in 'Death's Jest-Book' talk like giants, it is true, but they talk colloquially; and the result is blank verse which possesses in an almost unique degree the qualities of ease and splendour.

Beddoes and Browning

The reason why Beddoes has been considered a lesser poet than his contemporaries is easy to understand. It was partly because he could not impose a satisfying form on his rich genius; Keats in his short life achieved measure; Beddoes never quite did so. But a deeper reason is that he was more than a romantic in an age when the romantic convention was supreme. His poetry was most sincerely admired by Landor and Browning, who were not entirely subject to that convention; and on one side, indeed, in his humour and his love of the conceit, he was like Browning. But when he sent 'Death's Jest-Book' to Barry Cornwall, a conventional romantic poet, Cornwall at once condemned it, and told him to write it over again. 'Death's Jest-Book' is not by any standards a coherent drama; but it is at least a colossal anthology of dramatic poetry on the theme of death and immortality; and we can see it now as one of the greatest poems of the nineteenth century. The strong supernatural cast of Beddoes's imagery is still held up against him; but supernatural imagery is surely fitting in a drama dealing with death and immortality, and we know that the problem of immortality was the ruling problem of Beddoes's life, and the cause of his preoccupation with anatomy, for he hoped to find in the body itself a scientific proof of survival after death. Of the major poems produced in the nineteenth century surely only one, 'The Prelude', can be said to excel 'Death's Jest-Book' in intrinsic interest and sustained genius.

His Opinion of the Drama

Dr Donner's biography is by far the most complete that has yet appeared, but it is not a satisfying interpretation of the man Beddoes, simply because we have not yet the data on which to base such an interpretation. Beddoes was certainly one of the strangest as well as the greatest men of his time, and his attempt to set fire to a London theatre with a lighted five pound note was not the oddest incident in his life (he had a great contempt for the drama of his time). But this biography should be read in conjunction with the poems. They themselves are indispensable to anyone who claims in future to know English poetry. And by these two books Dr Donner has rendered a major service to literature.

RUDYARD KIPLING

Listener XV, 5 February 1936, 272

Kipling's great virtues as a writer were a quick eye and a quick ear, a retentive memory, a quite astonishing power of mimicry, an inquisitive intelligence, and, some distance behind all these, a genuine sympathy with the human passions. His worst fault was a narrow philosophy. This did not interfere with the exercise of the virtues just mentioned, except for the last one; but it qualified that in all sort of ways. His philosophy was the philosophy of an administrator; he admired men who could give and carry out orders. The institutions he liked best were the Army, the Mercantile Marine, and that part of the Civil Service which deals with the administration of things, not with the writing of letters, or indeed with writing of any kind. He admired the subordinate ranks in these institutions just as sincerely as the superior ones, enjoying equally the society of engineers and privates, and ship-masters and generals. But they received his approval, and his imaginative understanding, only so long as they knew their places. If they did that he was content to allow them any latitude in other respects; indeed the more completely they showed themselves to be human when they had nothing else to do, the better pleased he was with them. He had almost a liking for Original Sin (off duty); and the vigorous profanity of soldiers in their free hours was a proof to him both of their humanity and of the virtues of discipline. He approved of discipline, and he loved Human Nature. He believed firmly in a social hierarchy in which every class, or rank, had its own function, and he was endlessly interested in the people belonging to these classes, so long as they did not question their condition, or grumble against it, or botch their jobs. These classes in their inter-relation made up his image of society, and the bungler, the climber and the reformer were equally noxious intruders there. For in their various ways they disturbed the man who was doing his job, and to do one's job efficiently was to Kipling the sole guarantee of civilisation and above all of Empire. He would not have agreed that to err was human in a ship's engineer, and technical uncertainty, military or engineering weakness, was far more heinous to him than mere sin, of which he could write with unexpected sympathy.

His understanding of human beings was thus qualified in the most complicated way by his philosophy, which was the philosophy of one who is managing or at least overseeing the practical destinies of an Empire. Actually he did neither of these things; but by the power of mimicry which was one of his virtues and dangers as an imaginative writer, he identified himself so completely with the people who did as to make no difference. His attitude was consequently, like Carlyle's and Nietzsche's, rather that of a man of action than of a man of letters. Like all men of action, he saw human beings as means and not as ends; and since there is no choice for a means but to perform the function it was designed for, he had no place in his scheme for liberty. On the other hand he had an intense realisation of the vital difference between good work and bad, whether it was in administration, or in ship-building, or in seamanship, or in engineering.

Behind all these there was a conception of the world as a contrary and yet just entity which would inevitably respond to the right action and inevitably kick against the wrong one; something which was neither quite mechanical in its reaction nor quite instinctive: a cross between a high-spirited horse and a smoothly running engine, which demanded both intuition and technical skill to be mastered. This conception was a perfectly serious one, and imaginatively effective; but in the terms in which he stated it Kipling showed how much he was under the influence of his age, an age of expansive Imperialism; and of his class, a class which was peculiarly identified with the ends of Empire. For he believed that the young men of the English middle classes, which roughly meant the young men from the public schools, were alone competent to deal with this touchy monster. At the beginning of one of his best stories, 'Drums of the Fore and Aft', he asserted that 'God has arranged that a clean-run youth of the British middle-classes shall, in the matter of backbone, brains and bowels, surpass all other youths', and he prophesied that 'when all men are at the mental level of the officer today', the Army 'will sweep the earth'. He also referred in this characteristic passage to 'the intense selfishness of the lower classes'. These generalisations sound very strange now, when political opinion from the extreme Right to the extreme Left recognises that reform is urgently required, and that even youths belonging to the middle classes may stand in need of improvement. They bring back the full atmosphere of a period when the British middle classes felt they had the world well in hand and would continue to do so as long as they were left undisturbed by busybodies. Kipling, with his acute suggestibility, his capacity to take on the exact colouring of the class he admired, expressed this view authoritatively and without ever questioning it. He accepted it as a permanent and satisfying conception. Yet it was simply the view of his age and his class. It was also a completely static view, and that was why he was so impatient with reformers. He was inclined to look upon society in general as a larger edition of the Army, and so reform always had to him a suggestion of insurbordination.

In all this he was, like Carlyle and Conrad, who were also born outside England, against the main English literary tradition, which is purely human and based on liberty. He did not speak the same language as Marlowe and Milton and Blake and Wordsworth. His gospel, again like Carlyle's and Conrad's, was a gospel of work and hero-worship. Carlyle came from a country which was both poor and Calvinistic; Conrad from a long and indecisive struggle with the sea; and Kipling from the fatalistic and imperfectly settled East. It was natural, therefore, that they should have recognised with more than ordinary clearness the virtues of work, and that the idea of liberty should have roused their scepticism and even their hostility, as unjustified in the nature of things. Kipling had a profound understanding of the vital difference between good work and bad; he had hardly any appreciation whatever of the value of thought, and here he was unlike Carlyle, whose conception of work was considerably wider. But it excluded just as strictly the idea of liberty.

In spite of all these things, there remains in Kipling's stories a warm human sympathy which nothing could suppress. The outlets which it found through the defences he raised round it were sometimes, certainly, so narrow that it turned to sentimentality or facetiousness. His convictions were always at war with his sensibility, but they never succeeded in quite subduing it. He expressed it with almost complete freedom only when he wrote of children or for children, and that was probably because children are not quite in the working world. Many of his stories about children are sentimental; but in a story like 'Baa, Baa, Black Sheep' he shows the most sensitive understanding of the sufferings of an ill-used child; there is hardly a touch of facetiousness; the sympathy is pure through and through. The *Jungle Books* are delightful for the same reason, though even in them one feels that Kipling is only painting another picture of his social hierarchy, and that he likes the various animals mainly because they know their stations. And a great deal of the charm of *Kim* is due to the fact that the main figure is a boy.

But Kipling's understanding of human nature was erratic and partisan; and where he was unquestionably remarkable was in the quickness of his eye and ear, his gift for mimicry, and his story-telling, which was an elaboration of that gift. His dialogue is superb:

> An' there they sat, the damned deevidend-huntin' ship-chandlers, deaf as the adders o' Scripture.

He throws off casually such description as this:

> A Clyde-built iron boat, a flat-bottomed, pigeon-breasted, under-engined, bull-nosed bitch of a five thousand ton freighter, that would neither steer, nor steam, nor stop when ye asked her.

Such strokes as these show his true genius as a writer.

MARGIAD EVANS Creed

Listener XV, 11 March 1935, 512

Creed is Miss Margiad Evans' third novel, and it shows the same qualities as *The Wooden Doctor* and *Turf or Stone*: that is a strained intensity occasionally degenerating into rant, and an imagination of such force and purity that the only word to fit it is genius. Both the rant and the genius are more obvious in the third novel than in its predecessors; they have grown side by side; perhaps it is the author's line of development; at any rate it would be impertinent to draw to her notice the virtue of discipline which often constitutes the chief merit of writers less well endowed. 'I begin to write', she says in a short note, 'relying on the force and fine senses of each moment. That will be my strength. Nobody has ever seen any complete thing instantaneously. Such a vision would mean a pause, which there is not. . . . What I offer you as reading is real, though I outstrip each page and at the end am different.' All the best passages in this novel, one feels, were written on this plan, and so it justifies itself; but Miss Evans also tells a story involving about a dozen separate characters; that story has a plot, and a plot cannot be managed by relying on the force and fine senses of each moment; it requires the exercise of deliberate judgement. Miss Evans has tried in this story, it seems to me, to strike out a form more suitable to her gift than she found in her first two novels. She has certainly poured abundant genius into it; but the force and fine sense of each moment differ very greatly in quality, and what she offers as reading is sometimes real and sometimes unreal, as unreal as this scrap of dialogue:

> 'I see Dollbright on Saturdays in the shop. He is a clerk, not a bogey-man. I suspect his soul is behind his ear, and it's a fountainpen'.
>
> 'I thing it's a passionate and angry soul and God have mercy on its passage—'
>
> 'Now you're serious.'
>
> 'So I am!' exclaimed Ifor Morris, astonished. 'That's the second time he's got me.'
>
> 'I'm not interested in my enemies.'
>
> 'Enemy . . . Enemy!' Ifor Morris cried, becoming excited, 'that's it, that's he. A wild enemy to us and to our century, with the primitive strength to *condemn*. A bigot, but how one can fear him!'

I give this as an instance of the false intensity into which Miss Evans can fall when she misses the real.

Miss Evans' greatest virtue is nevertheless intensity and immediacy of imagination. It is shown most obviously in her visual power. That, again, has several degrees. At its lowest it results in such admirably accurate description as this:

> Below him traffic squirted mud and water at the pavements. Wheels sounded as if they were tearing a skin off the road, and blue reflections travelled swiftly under the bellies of cars.

At a somewhat higher level it communicates a frightening life to inanimate things, as in this description of the window of an old clothes' shop.

> Outside Mrs Trouncer's he stopped a moment. A lamp was burning on a bracket, and the shutter had not yet been fastened over the window. He saw the row of boots all with their tongues drawn forward, and the clothes hangers like bones, poking through the flimsy dresses.

To show it at its highest I should have to quote a long passage describing how the hero of the story was overwhelmed by the presence of darkness. I cannot think of a more magnificent evocation of the terror that may be caused by the oncoming of night.

This visual power of Miss Evans, then, is probably what will strike the reader first yet it is merely a secondary and incidental quality of her genius, for a power of this particular kind, it seems to me, is only given to writers to whom the invisible world is still more real. That is why in Kafka's stories, which are concerned purely with invisible conflicts, all the streets and rooms have such an almost oppressive solidity, and why Baudelaire was so painfully possessed by the substantiality of the world. Miss Evans' visual power is, then, only an attribute of her imagination, which sees human beings in relation not to a temporal secular environment, but to an eternal pattern which is in the last resort religious though not by any orthodox standard. Her main figure is Dollbright, an ironmonger's clerk in late middle age, who believes in a God of wrath, and finds salvation by rebelling against that belief. In her description of Dollbright's struggle Miss Evans is not always coherent, but she reaches a level of reality which has been almost lost to imaginative literature and must remain unknown to writers who approach life as a political question. Her vision of life is not the vision of a mere process; it embraces causes and ends as well, as any complete human vision of life must. This, and the intensity of her imagination, is what makes Miss Evans' work so startlingly different from the rest of contemporary fiction. This book is full of faults; but it is the work of a sincere writer and of a writer of genius.

T S ELIOT Collected Poems 1909-1935

Spectator, 3 April 1936, 622

The first eighty pages in this volume are taken up by the poems which have already appeared in *Poems 1909-1925*; the remaining hundred pages contain Mr Eliot's poetic production for the last ten years, except for *Murder in the Cathedral*, which is not included. This second part begins with *Ash-Wednesday*, embraces two unfinished poems, 'Sweeney Agonistes' and 'Coriolan', ten choruses from *The Rock*, four *Ariel Poems*, thirteen *Minor Poems*, and ends with *Burnt Norton*, which is in some ways different from any of Mr Eliot's other poems, and is one of the most remarkable, I think, that he has yet written.

It will be seen from this that Mr Eliot has been considerably more productive during the last ten years than during the sixteen years before; but it is very difficult to judge whether he has been productive on the same level, firstly because a writer of such individuality as his changes the taste of his readers, and they come to his later work with a different mind, and secondly because his style has altered. The alteration has been towards a greater explicitness of statement; *Ash-Wednesday* is far more explicit than any poetry that Mr Eliot wrote before it, and it represents, I think, a turning point in his development. *The Waste Land* is no doubt his greatest work, but there is in it, compared with his later work, a certain blindness both in the despair it expresses and in turning away from despair at the end. Since 'The Hollow Men', where that despair reached its lowest depths, Mr Eliot has never expressed it again; he has taken it as a theme, certainly, in 'Sweeney Agonistes' and other poems; but though he is still in the of it, he is no longer within it. That is to say that he is not so firmly under the influence of his time and is more deliberately concerned with permanent things. The difference may be seen by setting side by side:

> These fragments I have shored against my ruins

from *The Waste Land*, and

> Redeem the time, redeem the dream
> The token of the word unheard, unspoken

from *Ash-Wednesday*. This difference, the difference between despair and faith, is so great that it is very hard to compare the two kinds of poetry that derive from it. A good deal of the second kind is obscure, like the first, but with a different obscurity: not the obscurity of deep darkness, but rather that of darkness against light. It is consequently less heavily charged and more easy to understand, more finally comprehensible. This must be admitted to be in its favour, unless we are to regard obscurity in itself, deep and total obscurity, as a poetic virtue.

The second half of the volume is nevertheless more unequal than the first. 'Sweeney Agonistes', brilliant as it is, is definitely in a lower class of poetry than the rest, and doubtless is intended to be. The choruses from *The Rock* are first of all choruses, that is compositions intended to be spoken and to be comprehensible as soon as spoken. They contain some beautiful poetry, they are original in form, but they naturally lack the condensation which Mr Eliot's poetry has at its best. On the other hand, almost all the shorter poems have intense concentration and perfect clarity at the same time; *Ash-Wednesday* and the four *Ariel Poems* are works of great beauty; and *Burnt Norton* is surely one of the best poems that Mr Eliot has ever written. Its subject is Time and its main text a quotation from Herakleitos to the effect that the road upwards and downwards is one and the same road. This poem is different from the others inasmuch as it is not at all dramatic, being a pure intellectual enquiry into the nature and forms of Time. It alternates between the most close argument and the most vivid imagery expressing the contradiction of Time, a contradiction implicit in the recurring phrase, 'At the still point of the turning world.' It contains lines of great beauty:

> We move above the moving tree
> In light upon the figured leaf
> And hear upon the sodden floor
> Below, the boarhound and the boar
> Pursue their pattern as before.

That is a far more rarefied poetry than

> In the juvescence of the year
> Came Christ the tiger
> In depraved May, dogwood and chestnut, flowering judas,

but it has something in common with it, a sense of the fabulous; the difference is that the second kind is very much more figured and patterned (to use words that recur frequently in it), which means that it is more thoroughly worked out. Imagery which is thoroughly worked out often becomes mechanical and lifeless; but in this poem both the thought and the imagery are intensely concentrated, and gain immensely from the development. Whether this poem owes anything to Dante I do not know, but one might chance the guess that Mr Eliot's later development as a poet has been away from the Elizabethans, by whom he was so much influenced at the beginning, towards Dante.

Mr Eliot's position as a poet is established, and his work has been more thoroughly discussed than that of any of his contemporaries. His influence on poetry has been decisive. That influence was due chiefly to his genius for poetry, but it was due also to certain qualities which he held in common with some other men in his age. He has had an influence on the form and on the attitude of poetry. By this I do not mean that he has encouraged a kind of poetry in which all sorts of poetical quotations and reminiscences alternate with realistic descriptions of contemporary life. This method was employed very effectively in *The Waste Land* because it was a natural part of the scheme; it has not been employed successfully by any of Mr Eliot's imitators, and as a set poetic method it is obviously ridiculous. Mr Eliot's dramatic approach has influenced the form of poetry away from the purely lyrical, and his exercise of the historical sense has influenced the attitude of poetry. The first influence has been entirely salutary; it has led to a necessary reform of poetic language and a spirit of objectivity which had been buried in the degeneration of Romanticism. The reliance on the historical sense Mr Eliot himself seems to have lost in his later work; it does not go with religious poetry; it cannot survive the vision of 'the still point of the turning world.' But even in *The Waste Land* he used it conditionally, for there too, if less explicitly, he was concerned with permanent things, which are not affected by history. When the historical sense is employed without reference to these permanent things it leads to a shallowness of the imaginative faculty, for it robs the individual existence of meaning and can in itself give no meaning to society, since society is still in becoming, and by the laws of history will always be. Where the historical sense has been used in this way, the responsibility is not Mr Eliot's; but it partly explains why his influence should be so great with poets who do not hold his beliefs.

LAURA RIDING Progress of Stories

Listener XV, 23 March 1936, 604

Progress of Stories is a very remarkable piece of fiction. Miss Riding has enough invention for half-a-dozen novelists, and enough intellectual power for a score. She is witty, she is a delightful story-teller, and her style at its best has the perfect ease which comes from being able to say in the simplest words exactly what one wants to say. At the same time she has set herself an enormously difficult task, a task so difficult that I cannot pretend to have understood it fully, after having followed the different stages in it with intense interest. There are eighteen stories in the book, but it is not a mere collection of stories, but a 'progress', as the title indicates, and though the end which that progress reaches may remain obscure to the reader, as it does, for instance, in Franz Kafka's stories, the journey produces so many strange discoveries by the way that he is bound to find it exciting, if he should have any curiosity about life at all. Miss Riding is not in the least like Kafka, has obviously never been influenced by him, and may not even have read him; but she often gives us the same feeling as Kafka does, that we are making discoveries which we cannot put a precise name to, and which can be expressed only in terms of allegory or of fantasy. In the last resort she does not seem to believe in story-telling at all; it is only a final inadequate means in an inadequate state of things. Here again she is like Kafka, who said in one of his aphorisms: 'There is a goal, but no way; what we call the way is only wavering.' This does not prevent Miss Riding from being an endlessly fascinating story-teller for if there is no story it is obvious that every story becomes possible. But in that case these stories are not so much a progress as an ingenious demonstration that there is no real story. For Miss Riding does not get any farther than 'Nearly True Stories', which are all fairy tales; after that she gives a crown to Hans Andersen and confines herself to 'More Stories'.

A reviewer has no concern with an imaginative writer's ideas, unless where they are obviously inadequate; and Miss Riding's ideas seem to me to belong to the kind which can only be learned by a mystical experience. The world she writes of is therefore far better known to her than it can be to any of her readers. She has to tell of it by means of a set of stories, and so the nearer to it she gets the more fabulous her stories become. To the plain reader this fabulousness may seem at first false or affected, yet it is clear that if a writer has a vision of life which is not easy to communicate, fable and fairy-tale become the truest and most natural way to communicate it without compromising its essential character. This does not mean, of course, that it is the only way to communicate a writer's vision of life, as Miss Riding seems to suggest. Yet in these fairy-tales she has succeeded in saying certain things of the greatest importance which could not have been said in any other way. In a short review it is impossible to go into the nature of these things, though a real consideration of the book would have to do so. All I can do is to indicate the plan of the book. It begins with 'Stories of Lives', dealing with 'unequivocally unimportant material. They are about lives *as such*; and all lives, as such, are unimportant. All lives have happened long ago; or, at any rate, they are not happening *now*, however immediate they may seem to the people who are living them. And whatever is not happening now is unimportant; it is merely curious.' But to understand this properly one would have to read the whole book, and particularly Miss Riding's vindication of fancy as against imagination. The 'Stories of Lives' are purely mechanical, and describe with insolent ease the ordinary routine process of existence. The 'Stories of Ideas' are concerned with serious things, but in a diluted form; a good deal of what happens happened long ago, and is therefore more curious than important; though Miss Banquett in the second of the two stories (one of the best in the book) surely rises above unimportance when she finally becomes in her last incarnation, if it can be called an incarnation, 'the continuous end of a story to which there is no end, since she is not.' (This again is not mere verbal play, but a compression of a number of ideas containing a criticism both of life and story-telling.) After 'Stories of Ideas' come four 'Nearly True Stories', the best of which is perhaps 'A Fairy Tale for Older People', which ends again in the defeat of the story as a means of telling the truth, but as a mere tale is magnificent. After this Hans Andersen is crowned, and we have a few more stories. It is difficult to give an idea of the beauty and abundance of Miss Riding's invention. Sometimes it seems to follow too obviously the line of her thought, and to be a transposition of that instead of a creation in its own right; but this happens very seldom. *Progress of Stories* is so purely original, so completely devoid of the second-rate, that all one can do is to praise it.

RALPH BATES and CHARLES MORGAN
The Olive Field; Sparkenbroke

Listener XV, 29 April 1936, 843

The Olive Field is a very much better novel than Mr Bates' last one, *Lean Men*. Like that it deals with the revolutionary struggle in contemporary Spain, but states the terms of that struggle far more objectively and comprehensively, with greater knowledge and mastery. In temper the novel it resembles most is Tolstoy's *War and Peace*; for it describes a political condition in purely human terms. In a note at the end Mr Bates defines his aim. 'This is a novel of the Spanish Revolution', he says. 'It is, however, the human drama and spiritual conflict of that revolution which has moved me. I have therefore tried to keep political matter out of this book save when it becomes a dramatic reality.' Mr Bates' knowledge of the political forces in contemporary Spain is clearly adequate for his purpose; but his triumph is that he has incarnated these forces in the everyday life of his numerous characters, and expressed them in terms of pure human experience. This required, above all, a resolve to state the whole truth, to take all the factors into account, on every plane of feeling and thought, and in every class. Here Mr Bates has succeeded beyond praise. He is clearly on the side of the working classes in Spain; but in his descriptions of them and their enemies he is no more for one party than for another; he is merely concerned to understand and to tell the truth. His two priests, Father Martinez and Father Soriano, are just as convincing as his workmen, for he gives to them the same ungrudging and objective sympathy; and all his characters, with the possible exception of Don Fadrique, the music-loving aristocrat, are complete figures, with all the faculties of normal human beings. Mr Bates' continuous grasp of the wholeness of his characters and of the complete scheme of forces within which they move raises this novel quite out of the common level. His aim is an ambitious one, and on almost every essential point he seems to have succeeded in it.

The scene of the first three-quarters of the book is Los Olivares, a small town in an olive-growing district in Andalusia; of the last fourth, the mining district of Asturias where the revolution broke out in the autumn of 1934. The olive field of Don Fadrique is the centre of the action in the first part. Mr Bates describes in beautiful and loving detail the relation of the workmen to the trees they tend; and some of the finest passages in the story are about the trees themselves. There is a revolt of the workmen during the olive harvest; soldiers are called out; arrests are made; and a procession is shot down in the streets of the town. The olive fields lie waste; Don Fadrique decamps; and the workmen emigrate in groups to other parts of the country. Mudarra, an Anarchist, and Caro, a Communist, go to the mining district of Asturias, and become leaders in the Revolution of 1934. Mudarra is captured, tortured and killed, Caro escapes across the hills with the girl he has married. The novel covers such a large field and describes so many aspects of life that it is hard to say on which side it is best. The accounts of violent action are very effective in a sober and objective style; but perhaps best of all is the description of the work on the olive field and the life of the little town adjoining it. There is a magnificent account of a hail-storm and its effect on the trees; there are also several exquisite passages on music, a subject which Mr Bates can never leave for long, and a sermon on liturgy by Father Soriano which is something of a *tour de force*. The last part of the book, in spite of the violent action which makes it exciting, is not quite so good as the first three-quarters; Mr Bates does not get the same inspiration from the landscape and the life of the people; and the relations between Caro and his wife Lucia strike one as being falsely conceived and badly worked out. Nevertheless this is a story containing about half a hundred vividly drawn figures shown in innumerable situations, some of them comic and some tragic, and all informed with a quite unusual completeness of imagination. It is a book which no intelligent reader should miss.

Mr Morgan's novel *Sparkenbroke* is also concerned with an ambitious theme, but it seems to me to lack almost all the virtues which make Mr Bates' story so well worth attention. Its theme, to quote the dust-cover, 'is the nature of love and of arts, as qualities of the imagination, and their relationship, as aspects of the same ecstasy, with the idea of death itself.' This is a theme, or a constellation of themes, which has often been treated parenthetically in works of imagination; but in an unallegorical story it cannot be much more than a subject for conversation. There is, indeed, a good deal of conversation about love and death and imagination in Mr Morgan's story; but like all direct thinking put into the mouth of an imaginary character, it gives the impression of being at second-hand, as if the character had been listening to the author, and was merely retailing his opinions for effect. The character who does this is Piers Tenniel, Lord Sparkenbroke, who is a poet, novelist and mystic. He is a man teased by intimations such as those described in Plato's *Phaedrus*, quoted by Mr Morgan: 'Now every human soul must have seen the realities of that other world, else could she not have entered into this body. But to recall those things by means of the things of this world is not easy.' Accordingly Sparkenbroke broods on death, which is the gateway to that other world. To say anything at all on such a subject one must possess the purest utterance, an utterance as pure as those two sentences from Plato. This is a fair example of Sparkenbroke's:

> 'You are a child still,' he said, and she was dumb. 'So the doctor told you of Sparkenbroke, I should have liked to hear it. You had better go back to him. Now. Go and ask the doctor and the priest about death's fulfilment. . . . Or shall I tell you again what the fulfilments are? Poetry is one; and love, perhaps—"the beast with two backs"; and death is one, it may be. But if you're a good doctor with his head screwed on, or a priest with a taste for scholarship, or a girl just out of school, then one is flesh rotting in the grave, and one is my corrupt body feeding on your corrupt body, and poetry—well, what is poetry to you?'

That passage seems to me to be painfully false. A genuine belief in immortality cannot be expressed in such an accent of petulant superiority. The real fault in this passage is that Sparkenbroke is not thinking of actual love and actual death when he mentions them; they do not evoke any image either to him or to the reader. When Mr Bates writes of death we at least see the corpse; he faces the consequences of the events he describes. Mr Morgan looks past it, or it may be that this effect is produced by the fastidiousness of all his characters, a fastidiousness that makes them ignore all in the objects they regard except the noble aspect. Apart from the nature of love and art, the story is concerned with a triangular love affair between Sparkenbroke, his honest friend George Hardy, and a young woman called Mary. All three seem to me to be quite unreal, and they are presented in a smoothly oiled style which is securely padded against the impact of experience.

WALTER DE LA MARE The Wind Blows Over

Listener XVI, 21 October 1936, 786

The Wind Blows Over is a collection of short stories, the first of which goes back to 1904. The whole gives in a concentrated form the persistent strangeness of Mr de la Mare's imagination. Strangeness is a vague and perhaps misleading term, for the strangeness is a response in the reader's mind to a world unknown to him, or only guessed at moments, while it is the world about which Mr de la Mare writes the whole time, even when he seems to be writing about what is called the ordinary world. The strangeness can be felt as clearly in some apparently straightforward descriptive phrase as in the accounts of supernatural experiences, for instance in a few words such as

> One low thundery evening, during their brief solitary journey through the churchyard into the hedged-in narrow lane by the coach-house and stables.

It can be felt also in the casual observations:

> Her young days over, she too had been tethered up like most humans to a peg on the common.

The temptation is to enjoy an imagination of this kind for its mere difference, treating it as one usually treats ghost stories: that is, as make-believe. Yet there is something quite uncompromising in it; no attempt to escape from life (in the current cliché), but a steady resolve to face life and the ultimate implications of life. In these are included the implications of death as well, and 'What Dreams may Come', the first story in this volume, should prove to anyone that Mr de la Mare does not deal with mere fancies in his stories, but with realities which most of us normally do not take into account at all.

'What Dreams may Come' is an account of a journey towards death from which the dreamer just returns and no more. There is a bus smash, and a woman, or something that had once been one, finds herself sitting with 'the remains of a broken envelope, scribbled over with what appeared to be a singularly eccentric handwriting'. She wanders through a dark country and presently comes to high iron gates with what look like coats of arms shielding them. She remembers as she enters the name 'Emmeline'. At the door of the house she is met by a servant. 'Somewhere, *some*-where she had seen this dark lean meditative face before—these clothes even, the dove-grey waistcoats, the funeral morning coat.' He conducts her to a little room, and says: 'My master will be here directly,' and goes away again, taking with him the piece of scribbled paper which she had given him. In the room is a portrait of the 'master', and she is seized with a frenzied fear in looking at it and knows that there is something which she must do at once, 'that on this depended her everlasting peace, and that in but another moment she would be too late'. She goes into the next room, where there is a muffled form lying on a bed. 'How cold these lips must be—*would* be! And did she really *want* to waken the sleeper?' Then she lifts a corner of the sheet. 'Emmeline in all her dreams had never seen a face so youthful or more lovely. It was drawing nearer to her, too, the lips a little parted as if in astonished welcome of her kiss.' At this point Emmeline at last wakens to find a nurse bending over her. The journey is a journey between life and death; the form on the bed, as first dreaded, is her own body, which she might have lost forever if she had waited for another moment. The extraordinary thing about this story is the originality and exactitude of the imagery, the feeling that the shapes in this allegory are more solid than the ordinary shapes of life. The things that Mr de la Mare sees beneath the surface of life are most terrible, and one can feel this terror even in the story about the amusing old mad woman, Miss Miller, one of the most brilliant performances in the book. 'A Revenant' describes a lecture by a professor on Edgar Allan Poe, and the appearance of the poet himself to confound him at the end. It contains, among other things, some very fine literary criticism. The decisive quality in this volume is the quality of Mr de la Mare's imagination, which goes too deep for a reviewer to follow it in a short notice such as this.

WILLIAM GERHARDI Of Mortal Love

Listener XVI, 25 November 1936, 1018

The dust-cover informs us that Mr Gerhardi's latest novel is 'one of those "stories of a simple heart" which is the novelist's supreme ambition and delight, but the achievement of which is invariably put off from year to year'. Mr Gerhardi has for long had an ambition to write a simple love story, the dust-cover continues, and he was urged by the late Katherine Mansfield not to abandon it. Here we have it. But

Mr Gerhardi's imagination does not work simply; it cannot help taking in the odd and disconcerting implications of a situation, no matter how ordinary in appearance; that, indeed, is what makes him such an interesting writer. *Of Mortal Love* is probably the best novel that he has yet given us; it has the most admirable unity and balance; it is written in one key and yet achieves variety; it is, indeed, a deeply human and sometimes beautiful piece of work. It is human, however, on somewhat the same level as *A Sentimental Journey,* where Sterne attempted the simple style; the humanity, that is to say, is less a matter of feeling than of faith. It is never simple and direct, but it does seize the beauty of simplicity and directness as only a complex imagination to which they are inaccessible could. Mr Gerhardi is like Sterne in many ways; and the pure and effortless clarity of the style of this story only serves to emphasise that resemblance. There is nothing here to hide the fascinating equivocality of his imagination.

Mr Gerhardi suggests Sterne, but he also reminds one of Chekhov and the Flaubert of *L'Education Sentimentale*. He tries to see his heroine, Dinah, the main figure in the story, simply as a human being, as Chekhov would have seen her, but also as a typical figure, as Flaubert would have seen her. His imagination is not so warm as Chekhov's nor so cold as Flaubert's; it flies towards the warmth, but the cold pulls it back again; and this conflict is shown in the figure of the hero Walter, who is always blowing hot and cold, and is drawn from Flaubert mainly. Yet this fluctuation of imagination does not produce an uneasy impression, but rather one of the utmost naturalness and ease, as if Mr Gerhardi, having kept his characters rotating with his right hand for some time, lightly tossed them over to his left to see what it could do with them. The ease of this movement is beyond praise, and it is accomplished without any damage to the characters, who remain equally convincing on the right and on the left. The mere choice of these two characters brings out in the most simple and effective way the two aspects of the love story which is the subject of the book; its simplicity and its complexity; for Dinah is sanguine and single-minded, and Walter is sceptical and involved. One almost overlooks the skill which Mr Gerhardi masks under this extreme simplicity, but our very unconsciousness of it makes the total effect all the more moving. To analyse that effect, in which so many apparently disparate elements are fused, would take more space than a review could run to. But though never simple, it does give a feeling of harmony. The actual portrayal of the characters has something of Chekhov's direct human sympathy; for Mr Gerhardi lets his malicious wit play over them and then dismisses it, leaving them unaltered, as if he had made up his mind about them, changed it, and then changed it again. All this happens in the most natural way. I have had to exhaust myself in comparison, because it is very difficult to give an impression of this story, so apparently simple and so really complex. It is very long, yet there is not a dull page and nothing that one could have wished left out. It contains scenes of great beauty; and it has a really impressive balance and symmetry.

C S FORESTER The Happy Return

Listener XVII, 3 February 1937, 240

In *The Happy Return* Mr Forester describes the fortunes of a British frigate which was sent out to Spanish South America during the Peninsular War on a ticklish errand. His story resembles the ordinary historical novel in no way, yet it makes one feel that this is what a genuine historical novel should be like. There is no laborious detail, no concentration on period effects; but throughout Mr Forester never loses sight of the fact that in the first decade of the nineteenth century there were certain limitations to people's ways of thinking and to people's actions which do not exist today. These limitations he observes as his characters have to observe them; and the action of the story is like the working out of a problem with a few antiquated but on the whole workable notions, while stubbornly leaving out of account how it could be worked out today. This vigilant blindness, or happy ignorance, encloses the action in its period far more securely than any amount of historical detail could have done; and unlike the production of historical detail it requires an unsleeping imagination. This story is one of the most brilliant that Mr Forester has yet given us, and his powers as a storyteller have already been proved.

Captain Hornblower of the frigate *Lydia* receives instructions from the Admiralty to sail from England to the Gulf of Fonseca on the Pacific coast of South America and to remain out of sight of land and hostile observation by other ships until he reaches it. He does so, the voyage taking over eleven weeks. He has further instructions to assist a certain Don Julian Alvarado, a large landowner who calls himself El Supremo and leads a rebellion against the Spanish monarchy. El Supremo is a sadistic madman, but Hornblower fulfils his instructions and also captures the only Spanish warship in the Pacific, the *Natividad*. In her and his own frigate he transports El Supremo and his army to La Libertad. While Hornblower is resting news comes of an alliance between England and Spain, so that after capturing the *Natividad* and handing it over he has now to seek it out and fight it a second time. He does so and after two bloody encounters sinks it. Thereupon the Spaniards refuse him permission to call to refit at any of their ports in South America. He seeks out a remote island, puts in there, repairs the ship, and sets out for home. At Panama he had been forced to pick up Lady Barbara Wellesley, Wellington's sister; the dangers they pass through bring them together, they fall in love, but Hornblower draws back at the last moment. He leaves the lady at St Helena. The title of the story may be regarded as semi-ironical.

The really extraordinary thing about this story is the way in which Mr Forester has entered into Hornblower's mind and the problems that confronted him. The feeling of isolation in the Pacific amid innumerable dangers and difficulties, with no hope of communicating with England, is rendered with especial power. There is an expansion of time and space, an exciting realisation of these two things as Hornblower's most palpable enemies. The frigate *Lydia* is the instrument with which he fights them and an enemy of which he knows nothing until it comes in sight. The descriptions of the two bloody battles between the *Lydia* and the *Natividad* are extraordinarily vivid, again because Mr Forester never loses sight of what could actually be done at the time, and that was bad enough. There is hardly a blurred line in this superb narrative, except perhaps in the description of Hornblower's relations with Lady Barbara.

NEIL GUNN Highland River

Listener XVII, 9 June 1937, 1164

Highland River is the work of a distinguished writer, but frequently pulls one up by its semi-perfections. Mr Gunn is concerned with life beneath the surface, and has an intense pleasure in the sensual world. But one cannot help feeling as one reads that he loves his theme so much that he cannot bear the thought of finally capturing it in words and depriving it of its freedom. In a very interesting passage he indirectly raises the question, Do we really want to know what we set out to know?

> Kenn has an urge to be explicit, even to labour what is infinitely elusive, because the farther he goes towards the source of his river the more he feels there is in this very elusiveness the significance which he would like to hold.

That is a very elusive sentence, and this is a very elusive book. The Highland river of the title is the river by whose banks Kenn was brought up, but it is also symbolically the river of Kenn's life, and by implication the river of life itself. Mr Gunn fishes all sorts of strange and significant things out of it, and leaves all sorts of strange and significant things in it. He is a fascinating writer because he is a writer fascinated, and willingly fascinated, as the hunter is fascinated by the quarry. The fact that there are so many hunting scenes in the story, accounts of poaching salmon and trapping rabbits, is probably symbolically important; for by some ancestral hocus-pocus the trapper is generally a lover of freedom, and the huntsman unconsciously identifies himself with the creature he hunts. Kenn, pursuing the upward course of his Highland river, is really pursuing himself; he is both hunter and quarry, and is torn between the equally fatal alternatives of catching himself and letting himself go. There are, in any case, many signs of vacillation in this story. Some of the scenes are magnificently described. Mr Gunn has a subtle perception of the hidden life of natural things and their effect on our minds, and this gives the whole story a poetic richness. The style is very uncertain, and sometimes actually insensitive.

There is a great deal of unconvincing ancestral musing in the book, speculations on the Picts and the Vikings and their survival in the mind of Kenn. Nevertheless this is probably one of the best books that Mr Gunn has yet written; it is packed with hints and intimations which tease or irritate one's mind, at least stir it in some way. There is some false poetry; but there is also genuine poetry, and genuine meditative thought.

EDWARD UPWARD Journey to the Border

Listener XIX, 16 March 1938, 597

The first book in this list is so extraordinary in its quality, has such concentrated seriousness, and does so effectively what it sets out to do, that it makes the other three, in spite of their good qualities, appear less serious than they ought to be. Technically, *Journey to the Border* is brilliant, and the problem it deals with enormously difficult; the precise statement of a fanciful and yet quite common view of the world, or rather the statement of that view in terms of fantasy; the development of its consequences, which brings the hero to the border of madness (hence the title); the crisis; and the final approximation, both reluctant and grateful, to a view of things as they are. Mr Upward describes all this with a continuous concentration, a continuous invention of clairvoyant incident, which satisfy one's mind and imagination at the same time. The gradual emergence out of this fantasy into the actual world—the most difficult part of the theme—is perhaps not so successful as the rest, and contains one or two absurd touches; but it shows such insight into the evasions and false hopes of the mind, such a comprehensive knowledge of the hero's problem, that it justifies itself.

The chief figure in the story is the tutor (an actual tutor) who is discontented with his situation and seeks refuge in an imaginary world of his own. The purpose of the story is to elaborate that world, and convey the hero through it until he reaches its extreme end; then to make him realise its implications, so that for his own good he has to turn to the actual world. The tutor creates an imaginary world which he hopes will satisfy him; but that does not dispose of the actual world, which is always there, continually breaking in upon his imaginary world and distorting it in all sorts of ways, most of them frightening. In describing the tutor's fantasies and the distortions which wrest them out of his control, Mr Upward is really drawing a picture of society and of the individual's relation to it. The most intimate social criticism in the book is therefore in the fantasy itself; for the personal wish and the objective fact fight together there on the most immediate stage they can find: the consciousness of the individual. The action covers only a few hours. The tutor is taken to the races by his employer. He tries to invent devices for refusing to go; what he calls to himself techniques:

> From this morning on he would be as fantastic, as expansively imaginative, as he liked. He would do just what he liked. More than that, he would do it in such a way that no one would realise he was doing it; they would merely think that he was at last settling down to country life. He saw it clearly now—he would pretend to be one of them. He would wear a check cap, borrow the boy's fishing-rod, examine rabbit-holes, shoot at bats from his bedroom window with an air pistol. He would be the maddest, the strangest of them all—with the advantage that whereas for them their behaviour came naturally, for him it would have all the attractions of a voluntary, a limitless extravagance. He would be invulnerable.

He imagines several devices for avoiding the races; to be frankly irresponsible, go to bed, hide in the kitchen garden, and so on: but when the time comes he meekly goes. On the road he tries to change the look of the countryside to his wishes; it obediently consents, but only for a while, only as long as he intensely wills it; and he always remains conscious that it will change back again. He tries to kill thinking and feeling within himself, for then

> he would automatically destroy the world of his serfdom, the only knowable world, which after all was nothing more than an evil decoration created by thinking and feeling.

But all he succeeds in doing is to bring them to a torturing standstill, and he is glad to have them back again. Throughout the extraordinary incidents, partly real and partly fantastic, which happen to him at the races, he is driven nearer and nearer to the frontier of his imaginary world, until at last he sees his own body passing him in the opposite direction, and in a long dialogue with himself clears up the fantasy and is left with the actual world, in which lies his sole hope of satisfaction. Mr Upward resembles Kafka in some ways, particularly in the logical coherence of his fantasy, and in his mixture or rather correlation of fancy with realism. But he is an original writer, and this is probably the most striking work of imagination which has appeared since Miss Djuna Barnes' *Nightwood*, a very different book.

GRAHAM GREENE Brighton Rock

Listener XX, 21 July 1938, 153

Mr Graham Greene sets himself in his stories to tear off the superficies of life and present us with the quivering nerves, showing us how this inoffensive-looking but terrible machine works. *Brighton Rock* is probably his best novel up to now; but it gives the impression that he has acquired such a distaste for flesh and blood that the average sensual man, or rather the average sensual woman, becomes a melodramatic figure. The main character in the book is a boy of eighteen brought up in the slums of Brighton with a horror of sex and drink, and a contempt for human life which is shown in cruelty and a wild desire for power. He murders a member of a rival racing gang, then murders one of his own followers for fear he will tell on him. For the same reason he marries Rose, a young girl who works in a restaurant. But Ida Arnold, a middle-aged, comfortably amorous lady, feels that it is her duty, as an acquaintance of the man who was murdered, to see that justice is done. To Mr Greene, the dust-cover says, she represents:

> the everyday ethical world . . . the world of legal Right and legal Wrong, in which sexual passion is regarded as a bit of natural fun and not a mortal sin, in which the nearest you get to heaven and hell is an Ouija board.

Pinkie, the boy, who is damned, and Rose, the girl, who is saved, have on this assumption 'things in common', and their real enemy is the world of Ida Arnold, which at last manages to destroy them. Mr Greene is a writer who sees one aspect of life with intensity: in this case he sees that the good and the evil are more real than the well-intentioned, who are neither hot nor cold. Ida is a good sport described with blistering axioms; Mr Greene's hatred of her makes her the most original character in the book. Possibly it distorts her a little as well; one can hardly believe that such a good-natured, lazy, come-easy, go-easy woman would take so much trouble to hound down a wretched boy of eighteen. She might feel glad when he is caught, as so many people very like her feel glad when a murderer is hanged; a shocking and hateful emotion due more to laziness and want of imagination than to actual vindictiveness. But Mr Greene does not convince us that Ida, with her philosophy of the pubs, would have gone so far out of her way to see what she called justice done. She is all the same an original character. The boy Pinkie is made dreadful and pitiable by the intensity of Mr Greene's imagination, but he is not a palpable character; he is an evil product of an evil environment, a living criticism of society, and on that plane genuine. The presentation of the theme is brilliant, and has the economy which comes from a grasp of the essential factors of the situation. The dialogue is perhaps a little too clipped, too immediately effective, yet it is sometimes moving. The total effect of the story is powerful without any concession to the obvious means for rousing our feelings or any relaxation of intellectual integrity. It is a sincere comment on our life which deserves serious attention.

R C HUTCHINSON Testament

Listener XX, 29 September 1938, 678

Testament is a novel of enormous interest. It is very long, roughly about three hundred thousand words. It comprises in its action a number of first-rate themes: the War, the Russian Revolution, and behind these the problem of human salvation. It contains a great number of characters, all of them vigorously outlined, scenes of ordinary social comedy, domestic scenes, war scenes, purely horrible scenes. It has an impressive central figure, an extremely acute and intelligent 'good' man somewhat in the Dostoevskesan style, whose actions form a sort of ethical measure for all the events that take place. It has a philosophy based on religious values, and shows a grasp of the permanent elements in human character. It is long, intricate, detailed, but not shapeless: for everything is related to a definite and deeply felt conception of life. There are numerous faults in it, the chief of them being a love for the spiritually melodramatic which Dostoevsky also had. Its description of the Russian revolutionists is probably biased. Its love scenes are sentimental. But it is a novel of unusual scope and it is closely wrought; the work of a deeply human imagination which takes nothing at its face value; and no one who tries to follow what is being said in fiction can afford to miss it.

The story is told by Captain Otraveskov, a Russian painter who serves in the War, lives through part of the Revolution and finally escapes to Paris. In an internment camp in Austria he meets Count Scheffler, a fellow captive, who helps to nurse him. Scheffler is the 'good' man and becomes the central figure in the story. He is outwardly insignificant, inclined to be short-tempered, has a stammer, and is offhand in his behaviour; but he is quite incorruptible, very intelligent, and very kind-hearted. The two men are transferred to a Russian convalescent camp during an exchange of prisoners. There Scheffler is condemned by a court-martial for refusing to return to service with four hundred men who are physically unfit. By the ruses of a clever lawyer the sentence is suspended. Shortly afterwards the Revolution breaks out. Scheffler is transferred to one prison after another, without his friends' knowing where he is. After the Bolshevists come into power he is treated for a while as a popular hero, both because of his action while in the army and because he had been well known before the War as an advocate always willing to defend revolutionaries. But he ruins his prestige with the Bolshevists by defending an innocent man whom they want to condemn. A case is hatched against him; he stands his trial in turn, is offered an amnesty if he will make a public confession of crimes which he never committed, refuses to do so, and endures his sentence. The last scenes describing the trial and the preparation for it are extremely horrible. Scheffler's behaviour is consistent throughout, under the old régime and the new. He is an embodiment of a kind of human goodness which is independent of the goodness demanded by political régimes: and he has something both of Socrates and the ordinary man in him. Mr Hutchinson's main moral purpose was probably to present this kind of human goodness in as powerful an imaginative form as he could find, at a time when there is a growing tendency to ignore it. There can be no doubt of the power with which he has done so.

The story contains much more than this main line of action, though everything has some relation to it. The tale of Otraveskov's search for his wife, who had got lost while he was a prisoner in Austria, is highly exciting, much more so than some of the obviously adventurous incidents, such as Otraveskov's successful attempt to smuggle himself into one of the prisons where his friend was kept which strikes one as unconvincing. There is a whole series of exciting dramatic scenes, described with convincing power: the interrogation which led to Scheffler's condemnation by the court-martial, numerous incidents during the Revolution, the final battle between Scheffler and his judges. There are numerous scenes of social comedy, interviews between Otraveskov and men of influence when he was searching for his wife and trying to get help for Scheffler, accounts of St Petersburg parties. The detail of the story is unusually rich and piquant, again like Dostoevsky's:

> He led me out into the vestibule and up two flights of stone stairs. He walked very slowly; his boots were too big for him, or else the laces were broken.

The detail itself, often ridiculous, sometimes humiliating and pitiful, convinces us even when the situation is melodramatic. The 'Russian' atmosphere is produced with extraordinary skill, though one feels it owes something to the great Russian novelists. The religious part of the story is the weakest; but its feeling for character and incident and its dramatic power are very unusual; and for imaginative excitement it probably surpasses any novel that has appeared for a considerable time.

PATRICK WHITE Happy Valley

Listener XXI, 22 March 1939, 489

Happy Valley deals with the life of a small Australian town, and contains a great number of characters, all of whom are seen from the inside. The great merit of the book is its closeness to the hidden, instinctive life of the characters; its weakness is its too obvious derivation from Lawrence and Mr Joyce. It moves on two levels; one of genuine powerful imagination, and the other of impromptu fancy. At its best the writing is very good indeed, as in this impression of a hot day:

> Then they got on their horses, Roger and Sidney, and rode down towards the flat. It was yellow and burnt up. The hills were burnt brown, and scabrous, quite bare in the heat, in the shimmering of heat that was liquid and apparent, the whole landscape melting and fused into an indeterminate shape beyond the margin of the eyes.

But at other times it can be full of echoes:

> Hilda Halliday was almost forty. Oliver was thirty-four. But they were happy, she said. Sitting on the seat in the Botanical Gardens, in the warm smell of Moreton Bay figs, he said he would write a poem. She was wearing a yellow hat that made her look slightly pale. And of course Rodney was pale, he took after her, not Oliver, and it was not anaemia as everyone said.

To get a meaning into thought-associations—and Mr White deals at length with thought-associations—one has to impose a pattern upon them, and the pattern is always artificial, an aesthetic design, convincing merely as an arrangement. That day in the Botanical Gardens when Dr Halliday said he was going to write a poem is an integral part of his wife's thought-association pattern, and for most of the other characters there is a corresponding motif, which has to recur so that the pattern may exist. The result is a kind of mechanical spontaneity reached by an enormous simplification. This applies, however, only to Mr White's method, which weighs heavily on the book. He is clearly a writer of unusual imagination, with a substantial grasp of things, and a sense of pity which goes far beyond conventional pity. Only one or two of the characters are really individualised; they are felt rather than outlined, but they are felt with intensity. There are touches quite beyond the usual, as when a wretched school-teacher's life seems to be typified as he sits miserably tapping a bad egg with his spoon. This touch is far better than the murder scene which follows, and it is in such crystallisations of misery that Mr White shows he is an original writer.

HUGH KINGSMILL and R P WARREN
The Fall; Night Rider

Listener XXIII, 25 January 1940, 190

These two novels, both of them remarkable, belong to different types of imagination. Mr Warren has been compared by a well-known American critic to Tolstoy; Mr Kingsmill is more like Flaubert. It is not that Mr Kingsmill owes any debt, technically, to Flaubert, but that his imagination works in somewhat the same way. Mr Warren produces an effect of expansion, and Mr Kingsmill of crystallisation. The novelist can render his vision of life either by embodying it in a great number of different situations, or by compressing a great number of possible situations into one, hitting with mathematical accuracy the one chord which will evoke a sequence of associations. The expansive method can be easy-going and yet produce a novel that is worth reading. Mr Warren, starting with a dramatic central situation, keeps on introducing characters not because they are necessary to that situation, but because they happen to be living in the part of the country where the drama is going on. This weakens the dramatic effect, but, on the other hand, the characters themselves are sufficiently interesting to compensate for it. But the writer who sets out to crystallise a situation is setting out, ultimately, to crystallise man's situation; the truth of the whole lies in its balance; an irrelevant character, no matter how interesting, is merely an inexactitude, an error which nothing can repair. The remarkable thing about Mr Kingsmill's novel is that while moving on a level of intense imagination, it keeps this balance. It is the result of a concise organisation of experience and has consequently great formal beauty; not beauty of texture merely, though that is sometimes exquisite.

The book begins with a visit by William Barr, a man of fifty, to his wife Rose, with whom he has not lived for twelve years. She asks him to provide her with grounds for a divorce; he does so in the last chapter. The intervening chapters tell the story of his married life with Rose, a morbidly possessive woman, and his romantic love affair with Ruth Oldacre, which ends unhappily. The book is a study of two types of love, the kind which is really a love of exercising power, and the kind which gives as well as takes. Both are described with extraordinary truth in a succession of scenes in which, as in certain dreams, a whole gamut of experience seems to be formulated. These scenes are not merely true to the characters,but typical; the words used by the lovers, though simple and even banal, have an unusual weight of meaning (again as in Flaubert), as if they had come to the lips of countless lovers in countless generations by an irrevocable choice, their repetition always bringing the same astonishment. The enchantment in the description of the meetings between William and Ruth is achieved by apparently ordinary means, and is not a particular enchantment, but the enchantment of romantic love itself. On the other side, some of the conversations between William and Rose call up years of misery, and their maddening repetitions produce an effect resembling the effect of poetry. There are some wonderful dreams near the end, when William is lying in hospital suffering from concussion. In these he finds a formulation of the harmony which lies behind the discords of life. Whether a concussion was necessary to secure this is the only debatable point in the story. But it contains so much meaning beneath the transparent grace and concision of the writing, that it is impossible to do justice to it in a short review. It is a work of mature art.

Night Rider is a first novel and a very long one, and has been hailed as the best novel that has appeared in America for several years. Its theme is a Kentucky Tobacco War which broke out early in this century, a war of the growers against the ring of buyers. The chief figure is Perse Munn, a young lawyer who gets involved in the war against his will, and after committing arson and murder, ends by being rounded up and shot by State troopers. Mr Warren is a writer of strong and vivid imagination, with an intense vision of the physical world, and a less intense divination of the evil in the human heart. His descriptions of natural scenes, of passing moods and memories have sometimes a moving poetic truth; but though he is aware of the intricacy of human character, his view of mankind is at bottom naive. The night riders who scrape tobacco fields, terrify non-joining tobacco growers and set fire to warehouses are, when their tricks of speech are subtracted, merely he-men of colossal dimensions. Mr Warren, like Tolstoy, looks straight at every character that comes his way; he knows every wrinkle in their faces: but one feels that, unlike Tolstoy, he wears spectacles, and that they do not quite fit him. His anxiety to render everything exactly makes him furnish every noun with one or two or three adjectives, or with a simile (sometimes beautifully chosen), and we often feel that we cannot see the things themselves for their qualities. He has the disadvantage of dealing with a set of men who are voluble and at the same time inarticulate, so that when they do manage to say something definite it produces an effect of false impressiveness:

> 'Not often, any place, a man's too sure why he's doing something', Mr Munn said. Then: 'Not often, but sometimes, by God'.

It is hard to know what to make of such glaring incongruities. They would not matter very much if they were mere lapses; but one feels they are bound up with Mr Warren's view of human life. The more violent scenes are all tinged with this false impressiveness, and Perse Munn's gradual demoralisation by his acquired taste for violence is unconvincing because it is inarticulate, or articulate only in this rhetorical way. Behind the story is an oratorical conception of fate. On the other hand, it evokes vividly a feeling of the texture of living; we see Perse Munn standing at his bedroom window on a spring morning, riding home in the dusk and hearing the sound of a stream near by, watching his wife gardening and trying to catch the expression on her face before she is aware of him, the expression which is hers alone and which he can never know. There are countless impressions of this kind which come from a deep spring of life and are akin to reverie. The heroic action is overdone, the he-men too big and too stupid in spite of their impressive silences. Mr Warren is certainly a writer of poetic imagination; the difficulty is to take the whole story and the assumptions behind it seriously.

L H MYERS The Pool of Vishnu

Listener XXIV, 1 August 1940, 175

In *The Pool of Vishnu* Mr Myers rounds off the pattern of life which he evolved in *The Root and the Flower*. The last volume leaves a deep impression on the mind and adds greatly to the impressiveness of the complete work. The reason for this is that the book is not merely an addition to what went before, but its completion; we see at last the extent and the shape of the structure; and the structure is an embodiment of human life as seen by a writer of integrity, practical intelligence, and religious wisdom. There is probably no other modern work of imagination which shows such a consistent effort to see life completely. This is not the same thing as to see it in detail, though detail is the subject-matter of every pattern; it is rather to be aware of the factors that make up human life and to give to each its due importance; for a complete picture of life depends finally on a just evaluation of the things which constitute life, not on observation however miscellaneous. The passion for completeness of vision is rare even among novelists, whose ambition it to describe life, and it requires as its condition a state of high tranquillity, for to see everything in its relation the observer must be calm. It is possible that some readers of this book may be aware only of the tranquillity, in which the cities and castles and crowds of medieval India are mirrored as in clear water, so that even the scenes of violence and horror have a sort of serenity. But the serenity comes from the mood in which these things are seen, and from the passionate resolve to give them their relevant place in a whole which, merely by including them, changes their obvious significance.

Probably Mr Myers could not have carried out his task of imaginative evaluation on such a scale except by taking as his theme a society remote from ours. The remoteness really gives a more exquisite point to his criticism of our life. We see the medieval characters in his story confronted by all the moral and social and religious problems of man, and certainly as well equipped to answer them as we are. The society he describes has a more cultivated upper class than ours and a more downtrodden lower class; but that is all. There are customs and ceremonials which are strange to us, but no more intrinsically strange in themselves than ours. There are honest reformers and honest conservatives, and dishonest men of all views, as there are now. This society is somehow held together by means of, or in spite of, this congeries of human types, a ramshackle society not unlike our own, threatened simultaneously by stagnation and by change. The right way is as clear and unmistakeable in this society as it has always been, but there are only a few with the courage and perseverance to keep to it. This is human society as Mr Myers sees it existing in medieval India and no doubt today. His social criticism is accordingly both exact and objective in an unusual degree.

But the social criticism, excellent as it is, is only a part of the story, and the least important part. For Mr Myers' ultimate aim is to evaluate experience, and particularly experience where it is most intense and significant—in man's moral and religious relations. He has the distinction, rare in a novelist, of being more interested in good than in evil, and the ability to make goodness interesting. The main figure in the story is Prince Jali, whom we meet first as a sensitive boy bewildered by the diversity of life and the changeableness of his own nature. He is involved in false relations, and assumes false personalities, but in the end learns virtue and wisdom. The stages in this process are of entrancing interest; we feel as we read that, like Jali, we are learning more and more about the nature of goodness and of life. The various scenes are clear and in the main effortlessly natural—the result of a rare moral and aesthetic discrimination. The fineness of the writing can be shown only by quotation:

> Edged with crimson, her sari was caught in at the waist, and revealed the little gold sandals on her feet. Jali's gaze returned to her eyes, the sky-blue of which was so dreamy that one could look into it without meeting her. In these moments she was to him less a person than a thing—a tranquil and lovely thing that it was natural to stare at. No doubt the person in her was accustomed to retire, leaving you this liberty, and only when you had your fill would she gradually re-inhabit herself.

In this passage there is a sophistication carried forward to simplicity which informs the style throughout the book. The effect is one of clarity containing innumerable shades of meaning. The structure of the story gives the same impression of clear and ordered complication. Those who know *The Root and the Flower* will be sure to read this book; those who have not should read both.

VIRGINIA WOOLF *Between the Acts*

Listener XXVI, 24 July 1941, 139

The appearance of Virginia Woolf's last novel makes one realise with renewed force, almost objectively, what a loss her death is to English literature. *Between the Acts*, though comparatively short, is both one of her most ambitious and most perfect novels. It reminds one indirectly of several of its predecessors, *Mrs Dalloway, Orlando,* and *The Waves*, in particular, for in it she weaves into one pattern the themes with which she dealt separately in them.

The means by which she achieves this result are quite simple; she describes a summer day, and stages in it a pageant of English history, thus packing ages of change, separation and vicissitude into a few hours. In all her novels she is preoccupied by the fact of separation, and therefore by memory, which gives us our keenest apprehension of separation—the separation from ourselves; confronting us across a gulf with what we were and what we are. Beyond this recognition she had a sense, sometimes faint, sometimes vivid, of a union of some kind behind the separation, a union among the living, and between the present and the past, the living and the dead. This recognition, a mystical moment, appeared only when the present became quite motionless, no longer a floating bridge between the past and the future, but pure present from end to end, a simultaneous intensification and expansion of the instant of living. She was concerned with it not merely as a mystery but as a fact of experience; the novels which mark her progress as an artist, *Jacob's Room, Mrs Dalloway, To the Lighthouse, The Waves*, deal more and more essentially with the finest, the most elusive and profound kind of experience, trying to catch it in the flying moment, its perpetual vanishing place. The flying moment is infinitely rich, infinitely worth preserving, but is gone at once. Separation is self-evident; the union of all things, past and present, can be seized only by a rare act of the imagination. The sense of separation in *The Waves* is almost unbearable. In this last novel it is expressed even more strongly, but along with it an evocation of the moment of realisation, when all things know that, in spite of themselves and Time, they are bound together.

In its treatment of these two aspects of life *Between the Acts* surpasses all Virginia Woolf's other novels, and is perhaps the most complete expression of her world of imagination. Memory has inevitably a large place in it; memory which, as in her other novels, opens like a gulf beneath the ordinary surface of life, displaying a strange and disconcerting landscape. The memory is not confined to the actual lives of the people who remember; but goes far back. Old Mrs Swithin, early in the summer morning, recollects older things:

> She had been waked by the birds. How they sang! attacking the dawn like so many choir boys attacking an iced cake. Forced to listen, she had stretched for her favourite reading—an Outline of History—and had spent the hours between three and five thinking of rhododendron forests in Piccadilly; when the entire continent, not then, she understood, divided by a channel, was all one; populated, she understood, by elephant-bodied, seal-necked, heaving, surging, slowly writhing, and, she supposed, barking monsters; the iguanodon, the mammoth, and the mastodon; from whom, presumably, she thought, jerking the window open, we descend.

The rhododendron forests in Piccadilly recur throughout the book, along with images of the dead perpetuating their memory through time:

> the old families who had all intermarried, and lay in their deaths intertwisted, like the ivy roots, beneath the churchyard wall.

Parallel to the dead, forming a strand in the complete pattern, are the herds of domestic animals and their keepers, who might easily have lived among the past generations, and belong to them as much as to the living. Bond, the cowman

> contemplated the young people hanging roses from one rafter to another. He thought very little of anybody, simples or gentry. Leaning, silent, sardonic, against the door he was like a withered willow, bent over a stream, all its leaves shed, and in his eyes the whimsical flow of the waters.

This exquisite image suggests the timeless life of the farm servant, and prepares us for the chorus of peasants who serve as a static background to the various scenes in the pageant. Finally there is the audience, made up of the neighbouring gentry, who live as much in the present as anyone can live, that is, never quite there.

The changing past, the unchanging or more slowly changing life of the herds and the peasants, and the present itself—the sum total of past change and the involuntary cause of change to come: these make up the strands of the pattern. The audience, the contemporary characters, are at odds with one another, despondently or complacently lost, except for old Mrs Swithin with her faith in a reality beyond the reality of the moment. The pageant unrolls before them, a Chaucerian scene, an Elizabethan scene, a Restoration scene, a Victorian scene. Finally comes the Present Day, representing

> Civilisation (the wall) in ruins; rebuilt (witness man with hod) by human efforts; witness also woman handing bricks.

The audience applaud this flattering idea of themselves; but then the players appear holding up all sorts of mirrors 'hand glasses, tin cans, scraps of scullery glass, harness room glass, and heavily embossed silver mirrors'. The members of the audience are caught and split to pieces in this chaos of mirrors; they do not know where to look; they want to run away. A voice out of a bush addresses a long denunciation to them, ending:

> *Look at ourselves, ladies and gentleman! Then at the wall; and ask how's this wall, the great wall, which we call, perhaps miscall, civilisation, to be built by* (here the mirrors flicked and flashed) *orts, scraps and fragments like ourselves.*

But after this castigation the voice asks them to attend; a record of music is played on the gramophone, and the orts, scraps and fragments are for a moment resolved into a unity. It is as if the pageant had flared up into a different reality; as if experience had suffered a violent displacement, nightmarelike at first, and then pleasurable beyond expression. The scene is an extraordinary piece of imagination, though whether quite successful is doubtful. The nightmare part is very fine, and in its bare directness unlike anything else by its author; the resolution of the nightmare is not so effective as it should be, is slightly unconvincing, more because of the way in which it is said than because of what it says. Perhaps if Mrs Woolf had lived to make the final revision of the book this might have been avoided; perhaps all that was needed was a slight alteration in the wording which only she could have made. But as it stands this scene embodies more intensely than any other scene in her novels the essential quality of her imagination.

Apart from *The Years*, a reversion to her early style, her prose has shown an increasing economy ever since she wrote *Mrs Dalloway*. She has never written better prose than the prose in this last book, with its flashing, almost imperious curtness, its exact colouring, and its rapid, unhesitating movement. One is tempted to go on quoting from it impression after impression perfectly rendered. The characters stand out with unusual solidity and clearness in the exquisitely radiant atmosphere which fills this as almost all her books: a light unlike any other light. What we remember chiefly in her other novels is that strange light; but from this one we shall remember with equal distinctness the characters and the working out of the situation, the symbolic form in which a woman of genius saw the human state.

PATRICK WHITE *The Living and the Dead*

Listener XXVI, 31 July 1941, 175

The Living and the Dead is not a book that can be dealt with in the everyday vocabulary of the reviewer. To read it is an experience resembling one's first experience of the work of Joyce and Lawrence; it is of the same order; it has the same unexpectedness; and one feels that it may turn out to be even more significant. Mr White has a passionate spirit of exploration, in his dealing with experience, which is given only to writers to whom imagination is a calling. He examines, or rather enters into, the world of experience, ordinary and extraordinary, with an insistence which itself is a gift; for the essential mark of the writer who illuminates life for us is that he does not stop where other writers stop, content to reach an approximate stage, but pursues his search for meaning.

In one respect Mr White has a great advantage over Joyce and Lawrence: that his imagination is dramatic. He creates independent characters and keeps intact the balance between them. Lawrence's characters melt into one another in attraction and repulsion, and Joyce's express the isolated response, so intensely personal that it gives the impression of being impersonal, as the response of any human being would be if he lived alone in the world. Mr White's imaginative region is quite different. He follows closely the feelings and thoughts of his characters, but has at the same time a firm grasp of the changing situation, a grasp of relation. In other words he has an unusually fine sense of order, although the story is an account of the evolution of disorder. As a living construction it has a beauty in itself; the close investigation of thought and feeling is never pursued for its own sake; in all the parts there is a sense of the whole. For this combination of qualities Mr White required an exceptionally flexible style. It has some displeasing idiosyncrasies; it is sometimes restless; but at its best it has the closeness and the imaginative venturousness of poetry, and sometimes an astonishing flow of invention. Compared with what he does in this book with the raw material of experience, most novels seem to do nothing at all.

Criticism has to separate elements of a work which in the work itself are so closely woven together, so much a part of each other, that it is clear they cannot exist in separation. The quality which gives the most immediate sense of the unity of a work of imagination is style; when the writer's means closely fit his ends, the style seems to take everything upon itself, and give shape and substance to all that it describes: scenes, characters and objects seem to be created simply by the terms in which they are expressed. Mr White's style has this fine congruity, not always, but nevertheless to an astonishing degree; its general effect is to animate everything, to make everything vividly present, without losing that sense of the relation between the present and the past, the moving sequence, which makes it possible for us to read experience. The book tells the story of the Standish family from the end of last century until the present day; but it does not give the impression of a number of stages, separated by decades, or illustrated by public events: we have the feeling, instead, that we are watching Time's hand moving, not merely catching sight of it when it has reached this point or that. The plan of the story—though not its method—is retrospective. We are shown Elyot Standish at the beginning, as he returns from Victoria after seeing his sister Eden off to Spain to offer her services to the Republicans; and the rest of the story is an explanation of him and how he found himself there. The story of his mother's romantic marriage, disillusionment and gradual degeneration is the main episode in the book, and by far the most successful. Elyot himself, who is the test character in the story, the living man among the dead, is like most test characters not quite convincing. Some of the later situations, the love affair between Eden and the workman Joe Barnett, for instance, are conceivable, as well as necessary to the plan of the book, but inadequately worked out. But the force with which Mr White has embodied in the story of a single family a sense of disorder gradually and invisibly spreading to its end and the end of an epoch, is a proof of the depth of his imagination. This is a novel which no reader can miss.

HUGH WALPOLE The Killer and the Slain

Listener XXVIII, 1 October 1941, 443

A Great number of the late Sir Hugh Walpole's novels show signs of his obsession with evil. The evil that struck his imagination was not ordinary evil; it did certainly involve such things as selfishness, envy, greed, lust, treachery, even murder, but it went beyond them and became an active principle hostile to goodness, instead of a mere deviation from goodness. A man may be selfish, envious, greedy, treacherous, even murderous, and yet have a sincere longing for virtue. But the evil that Walpole was concerned with was deliberate, specialised evil, and its principle was enmity, its spirit the spirit which denies all that ordinary men in their hearts long for.

His best novel, *Mr Perrin and Mr Traill*, is a close study of a destructive enmity between two men. In his more fantastic stories such as *The Prelude to Adventure* and *Portrait of a Man with Red Hair*, he describes characters in whom enmity has become full-blown and is directed with positive enjoyment at all that is good or happy. The combination of evil with enjoyment is what makes these characters so original and so unlike ordinary characters. Even Goethe's Mephistopheles, though he is the spirit of denial, does not enjoy evil in this wholehearted way, his enjoyment is poisoned by disillusion; he does not have the abominable joviality of Walpole's shabby provincial fiends. These people are jovial because they believe in evil, because they have a faith, a thing which Mephistopheles, as he knows all about evil, lacks altogether. They are half-baked devils who hope that if they stew in wickedness long enough they may grow perfect. And so they fling themselves into it with a perverted religious fervour.

Hugh Walpole's main originality as a writer lay in this imaginative grasp of evil aspiring towards evil; but the grasp was incomplete; he fished up from the abysses he dredged in all sorts of fantastic nightmares more likely to frighten himself and his readers than to illumine the real character of evil. This happens particularly in his full-length portraits of bad men, where one cannot tell whether the finishing touches are put on to bring out the truth or to produce a thrill. There is truth in these portraits; but it is obscured by fancies born of fear and by the curious human desire to experience the thrill of fear.

The Killer and the Slain is a study of possession. The good man, driven to desperation by the persecution of his genial enemy, kills him and is afterwards slowly invaded by him. He becomes so completely the man he murdered that when he meets a sort of replica of his former self he is filled with murderous hatred. At the end, when he is on the point of killing this man who reminds him of his good days, he has a moment of clarity and kills himself instead. This scene is moving, but the meaning of the story is obscure. That Tunstall, the bad man, should possess Talbot, the good man, may signify that evil lives on after the death of the evil-doer, or that to rid oneself of evil by violence is to invite evil to do its worst; indeed, it may mean a dozen things. But it is hard to tell which of these Walpole intended it to mean. One feels that, as he wrote, the story took possession of him as Tunstall took possession of Talbot, and that the story killed the meaning, as Talbot killed himself. The book shows signs of weariness and exhaustion, particularly in its repetition, a fault rarely found in its author; the melancholy reason for this may be sought in his last long illness. Flashes illumine the moderate horror at rare intervals; the end is impressive; but as a whole the book is sad reading.

JAMES T FARRELL and JOYCE CARY
Ellen Rogers; To be a Pilgrim

Listener XXVIII, 17 December 1942, 795

When you begin reading *Ellen Rogers* you feel it is going to be like a hundred other sordid novels showing people living on the physiological plane, where love is sexual satisfaction, discontent frustrated appetite, and disillusion and sadness mere appendages of natural egoism. The title of the book prepares one for something of the kind, making one think of *Esther Waters* and *Sister Carrie* and a whole class of fiction which finds its symbol in some deliberately commonplace name. But in the middle of hard-boiled, insectlike sexual intrigues, Ellen Rogers falls in love, disastrously, and the atmosphere changes in the most astonishing way. On the surface—and the surface matters—the story is still sordid; but gulfs open beneath it. Ellen is carried into circles of delight and torture where her egoism and vanity and calculation fall from her, so that her life, which might have been frittered away in a waste of meaningless satisfactions and dissatisfactions, ends as a tragedy. Ed Lanson, the cause of her disasters, is a figure so equivocal yet so vivid that it is almost impossible to decide, after an intimate acquaintance with him for several hundred pages, whether he is worthless or not. He, not Ellen, is the chief triumph of the story.

A leaflet attached to the book gives the information that Mr Farrell is working on a projected series of twenty-five novels. He regards himself as a realist, and the obvious writer to compare him with is Theodore Dreiser. But in spite of his realistic method, he is essentially an imaginative writer, and his picture of life has an exhilaration which Dreiser's lacks. It is the dangerous exhilaration which comes from a sense of imminent tragedy; it has a touch of violence; Mr Farrell's imagination is a savage imagination, genuine and unbroken, but not quite humanised or civilised. Whether he is a truly tragic writer it would be hard to say; his province in the present book lies where tragedy is always impending, and where the actors with a sort of perilous excitement invite it by venturing a little further towards it, until they find themselves caught. The suicide of Ellen Rogers, when it comes, is almost a foregone conclusion; the excitement lies behind her, for it consisted in going a little too far, in inviting the tragedy with more and more daring, not in the tragedy itself.

The figure of Ed Lanson shows that Mr. Farrell is a writer of original imagination. Lanson is both a highly individual and a highly typical character. He is a half-baked proletarian superman, whose greedy philosophy of life is nourished on what Nietzsche scornfully called 'modern ideas', of which he was himself one of the chief purveyors. Lanson is the type of the natural rebel and the amateur revolutionist, who believes that life should be free and spontaneous, and measures its freedom by the whim of the moment; immensely attractive when the whim is to his liking; immensely disconcerting and disagreeable when it is not; and increasingly artificial as he discovers that life will not live up to his expectations and continue to be free and spontaneous. He eventually turns himself into a convincing imitation of the free and spontaneous man, and it becomes impossible to distinguish where affectation ends and nature begins in him. The power of Mr Farrell's imagination is shown particularly in his description of Lanson's changing moods; he is not merely copied from nature, he is created; and it is not his truth to life that impresses us, but his truth as he comes from Mr Farrell's hand. Certain of the scenes are like nothing that could be written by a merely observant writer, but are pure imagination: the fantastic philosophical argument between Lanson and a college boy, or the scene where Lanson threatens to commit suicide unless Ellen believes a lie he told her, and almost does so out of simple, defiant vanity.

Mr Farrell achieves these original and subtle effects in spite of his style, which is without grace or taste or even ordinary simplicity and naturalness. It is a half-baked style used to describe a half-baked superman, and so it is not entirely incongruous. The effect of the book is achieved by sheer imagination which in spite of the style makes itself felt somehow or other, and by the dialogue, which is superb.

To be a Pilgrim is another remarkable novel, but in a quite different style. Mr Farrell's story is closely knit and concentrated; as we read it nothing matters to us but Ellen Rogers and Ed Lanson. Mr Cary's book is a sort of assembly of experience in the mind of the old man who tells the story; it is the harvest-home after the gathering in of the sheaves, and also—a possible weakness—a rough and ready gospel. Whether Mr Cary subscribes to the views of old Uncle Tom on life it is hard to say; at any rate they are very plausible in an old man who remembers the Victorian Age, and Mr Cary states them with sympathy and eloquence. The story, which consists in a running diary written by Uncle Tom, deals partly with the present and his niece Ann and his nephew Robert, modern young people whose ideas are repellent or ridiculous to him, and partly with his long-since-dead sister Lucy, his brothers Edward and William, and other old friends. This natural juxtaposition of the present and the past provides a vivid contrast of two ways of life, and an implied criticism of the present-day. The criticism is not satisfying, since the past, in spite of all its blunders, is seen as essentially good, and the present as falling short of it. The problem would be easier if one could tell how far Mr Cary agrees with Uncle Tom; but perhaps the form of the novel forbade him to do that. We must take Uncle Tom's philosophy as a point of view and leave it at that.

The great beauty of the story consists in its evocation of memory, and its sense of the almost inexhaustible wealth of life that can be enshrined in the mind of one old man. Uncle Tom's diary is packed and bursting with life. The memories of childhood are particularly fine; the character of Lucy, a wild. Brontëan child and woman, is magnificently realised. Mr Cary has as powerful an imagination as Mr Farrell, but he has also a humanism nourished on tradition which gives all his scenes a warmth, a richness of association, partly sad, partly happy, which adds immeasurably to their effect. This book is by far the best that Mr Cary has yet given us; it is an original attempt to embody a complete vision of life, and it contains several scenes as vivid and beautiful as anything else in modern fiction. If it were not for an occasional too positive and emphatic statement, one might even be tempted to accept Uncle Tom's philosophy.

MARY LAVIN   Tales from Bective Bridge

Listener XXX, 29 July 1943, 134

When one turns from these two good stories to Miss Lavin's *Tales from Bective Bridge* one enters a completely different atmosphere. What distinguishes Miss Lavin's work is the quality of beauty, an unsatisfactory and probably misleading term, but the only one I can think of. It is due chiefly, perhaps, to an exquisite fidelity and aptness of imagination, which determines both her vision of life and the form she gives to it. The most immediately striking example of this is 'The Green Wave and the Black Wave', a story of death at sea, told in the traditional Celtic epic style, a style which enables her, as none other could, to evoke the primitive sense of the elemental forces of nature which still exists among fishermen and fishermen's wives in remote places. The fable of the perfectly beautiful woman is another instance of Miss Lavin's exquisite use of form to express exactly what she wishes to express. These two stories are exceptional in style; the others deal with ordinary situations (with the qualification that to Miss Lavin no situation is ordinary) in the manner of the modern short story, that is with a skilful use of implication. Probably the best of these is 'Miss Holland'; it tells how one vulgar remark opened the eyes of a well-meaning refined middle-aged woman to the nature of experience. If it had been handled even a little less surely, it would have appeared artificial and unreal; but as it is, it is a little masterpiece, and packs into a few pages an incorruptible and somewhat Stoic judgment of life.

One of the most striking things about these stories is their variety. 'At Sallygap' contains the tragedy of a man's life, 'Brother Boniface' its fulfilment. 'Love is for Lovers' is a sardonic social comedy, turning, as in 'Miss Holland', on the effect produced by a few words casually dropped. The first story and the last in the book are the least completely satisfying, perhaps because the themes they deal with are apart from ordinary experience; but the final judgment Miss Lavin passes on that experience is as sure as it is in the other stories. Her certainty of judgment is, indeed, one of the things which make this such an impressive book. Miss Lavin obviously knows the formula of the short story as it is currently practised; but she has no formula; she adapts her form to her purpose, and boldly takes the road she thinks right. She is a remarkable writer, with a fortunate union of imagination and intelligence, a style to serve all the purposes which she needs it for, and an original vision of life. This is her first book, but she is already mature.

KATHARINE BUTLER HATHAWAY
The Little Lock-Smith

Listener XXXI, 6 April 1944, 390

It is very difficult to place *The Little Lock-Smith* by the ordinary classifications. It is neither autobiography nor fiction in the usual sense. It contains no information, no dates, no encounters with famous people, no references to public events until the very end, where, in a postscript, the War seems to have overtaken the narrator. It mentions few physical circumstances of the heroine's life, but these are extraordinarily vivid, for they have a second significance as objects in her spiritual autobiography. The story is an account of a transformation of physical deformity into internal beauty, a detailed record of one of those transmutations which possessed the imagination of Rilke in his later poetry. What makes it remarkable is a passionate imaginative conviction of the reality of the inward life which goes on almost, one would say, in disregard of the outward forms of existence. It is this internal life that Mrs Hathaway describes.

The narrator is an undersized hunchback. As a girl she had lain on her back for several years clamped down on a frame, with a halter round her neck to keep her head straight. The revolt of her spirit against her body began then; perhaps it should be called an escape rather than a revolt: she succeeded in making of her immobility and discomfort a sort of special privileged state, so that while all who saw her were filled with pity or repugnant curiosity, she enjoyed a unique happiness, unique since it was the direct outcome of her illness. This happiness was interrupted only by terrors at the thought of infinity, which came upon her at night.

She received her first shock at the age of fifteen, when she was allowed to get up and for the first time saw her stunted, misshapen form in a mirror. This shock recurred for several years afterwards. During her illness she had created an internal image of herself as a beautiful woman; she felt as she thought a beautiful woman would feel; now she could establish no connection between the caricature in the mirror and herself as she had known herself and still knew herself. For a long time she suffered a violent oscillation between these two images—herself as she was in her own mind, and herself as she appeared to others. The second image recurred only as if by accident, an accident outside her; but the recurrence was so painful that at last she forced herself for the sake of her own peace to appear to conform to it, and to become the quaint, amusing, prematurely sage dwarf that people expected her to be. Here the story becomes like a fable of human developmental in general, and describes a universal predicament known, more or less vaguely, to everyone. What gives the story its significance is that, though it deals with a violent exception in human experience, it expresses over and over again in symbolical form the half-guessed experience of almost anyone. It is in her description of this kind of experience, which is vague and half-conscious with most people, but passionately clear and self-evident to her, that Mrs Hathaway shows the originality of her talent. The hunchback imprisoned in her body has something of the same absolute sense of liberty as Emily Brontë had in the damp and dismal vicarage in Haworth. It is a quality found more often in women's books than in men's, especially in its absoluteness.

The story tells how the heroine succeeded in overcoming her temptation to conform to a false image of herself and chose instead to express her inner image. The problem here is again a universal one. There are one or two dubious touches in the account of Katherine's salvation. The epilogue with its references to the War strikes a violently jarring note; and before that, in the story of the house, the style is sometimes ovestrained to achieve an effect which might have convinced us more if there had not been such a display of effort. But the book is the work of a very remarkable writer, and the record of a singularly undeviating effort of the mind. The writing itself is wonderfully natural, free and resourceful, capable of expressing the most obscure states of mind with clarity and ease.

FORREST REID Young Tom

Listener XXXII, 6 July 1944, 22

In *Young Tom* Mr Reid introduces us again to the boy he has described so exquisitely in *The Retreat* and *Uncle Stephen*. This book, like the other two, has a radiant lucidity, a crystalline serenity which seems to maintain intact the very essence of childhood. Mr Reid is an original writer, but his originality is easily overlooked because there is in it not a single touch of violence, or even of emphasis. The incidents he describes seem to have no importance in themselves; they have no general bearing, provide no criticism of society, touch on no urgent problem. The kind of life he deals with is in a sense outside society and time, for Tom has hardly realised yet that time flies, and accepts his small world as it is, not knowing that it is part of a larger human whole with laws which would distress him if he were aware of them. He is in a state of innocence; the book is a description of that state, and ends with a first intimation of evil, when Max Sabine shoots a squirrel.

To preserve this sense of innocence and present it untarnished is one of the most difficult feats imaginable for a writer. Sentimentality is an almost universal fatality for those who write about childhood; exaggeration, sophistication, idealisation, the faults which maturity brings and childhood itself lacks, all easily come in. One fancies that Mr Reid has been saved from these defects by a philosophical conception of childhood somewhat similar to that of Vaughan, Traherne and Wordsworth, though he does not explicitly show it. Only those who hold some such conception of childhood can write about it without sentimentality or the sham brutality of *Stalkey and Co*; and this is probably the best justification for it. At any rate, in spite of certain features which would have brought any other writer to grief—Tom's friendship with his three dogs, his conversations with them, his visions, and a ghost which visits him—the story carries our belief throughout, delights us, and never outrages either our minds or our feelings.

Yet notwithstanding the perfection with which every scene is set down, a book such as this would not be of any real importance if there were not an assumption behind it, and if that assumption were not finally mystical. The story moves us because it shows experience breaking into innocence, a universal event which after we have grown up we generally forget. If we do think of it, we tend to set it outside time, as a fabulous occurrence. Mr Reid describes it lightly, almost parenthetically; but Tom's realisation of evil when Max shoots the squirrel, the burst of rage which makes him steal the gun and fling it into the river, his growth in worldly wisdom when, after stubbornly refusing, he agrees to apologise for his action, are like those events in early history which seem to prefigure the stages of human development. In spite of the scrupulously unemphatic tone of the story, each incident stands out, and we are conscious of great issues behind all the happenings. Mr Reid's handling of the fantastic and the supernatural is extremely skilful, almost too skilful sometimes; the sight of a ghost, one feels, should cause some slight perturbation. The account of Tom's dream of the Chinese demons, on the other hand, is magnificent. Tom goes for a walk one summer morning, and finds a door in a hedge that he had never noticed before, and is led into an oriental garden. Things get worse and worse and he is about to be captured and killed, when he wakens in his bed. He sleeps for a few hours and then wakens into the same morning, but without the door in the hedge. The surprise Mr Reid springs here, a surprise evoking his whole vision of the double meaning of life, is very fine, and leads the imagination into strange speculations. His three books about the childhood of Tom will probably remain as one of the most original and most perfect works of imagination of his time.

SOMERSET MAUGHAM The Razor's Edge

Listener XXXII, 27 July 1944, 106

Mr Somerset Maugham has glanced now and then at the religious type in his later novels. In his latest, he draws a three-quarter-length portrait of a religious man—a religious genius, one would be tempted to call him if he were not compressed into such modest dimensions; at any rate, the exceptional type of man who sets himself to follow the path of perfection. The portrait is not entirely convincing, whether through Mr Maugham's fault or the inherent difficulty of the subject it is hard to say. No one, probably, has ever succeeded in drawing a convincing imaginative portrait of a saint, and Mr Maugham's Larry Darrell has the attributes of a saint, including the most essential one, liberation from the tyranny of the self. Dostoevsky twice tried to draw a similar figure, in Myshkin and Alyosha Karamazov; he managed to make them astonishing, like all his other characters, but one has the suspicion that they are not quite real. Such figures are bound to fascinate the imagination of novelists who have either a religious view of life or an omnivorous interest in it; yet Myshkin and Alyosha and Larry Darrell are exceptions to the ordinary human rule; they live the life which we omit to live, which we have a distant feeling sometimes that we should like to live if we could regard it as remotely possible, but of which we know less than nothing.

To the ordinary reader, the ordinary human being, Myshkin is convincing mainly as a vague wish-fulfilment, since he exists for him in the world of aspiration, not in that of experience. When an actual religious genius like Traherne or Blake speaks we believe him, for he speaks out of experience, and he does not have to bother about verisimilitude; he can flout it, and very often does so. But the novelist describing a religious genius does have to bother about verisimilitude; he has to strain to be more convincing than he is about his other characters (who speak for themselves since they speak to us). We can see Dostoevsky doing this and we can see Mr Maugham doing it; and as we become aware of this effort to convince we throw in our weight too; for every reader wants to believe; that is his constant character, on which all storytellers depend. Yet if the story is about a mystic or a saint, something goes wrong. The reader is divided between his admiration for the skill of the author and his vague disappointment with the effect. He may believe Blake and remain unconvinced by any imaginative portrait of him.

There are degrees of unconviction, nevertheless. Mr Maugham makes the young American Larry Darrell as convincing, one feels, as he could have been. Certain things about him, his appearance, his way of talking, his direct evasion of the ordinary claims of social life, his refusal to let his friends know his address, are all convincing. His diction, on the other hand, fails him when he has to say anything involving his deeper feelings. Poor Sophie Macdonald is murdered in a brothel in Toulon. Larry had wanted to marry her, but on the eve of their marriage she had run away from him to resume her life of drinking and drug-taking. This is what he says about her after her burial:

> She had a lovely soul, fervid, aspiring and generous. Her ideals were greathearted. There was even at the end a tragic nobility in the way she sought destruction.

What he says may all be true, but one cannot believe that a man who had pursued truth and goodness for so many years would have used just these terms. They make Larry look amateurish.

The great triumph of the book is Elliott Templeton, the man of fashion, the worldling who pursues the social life with American efficiency. He and the people among whom he moves are intended to provide the artistic contrast to Larry's search for the true life. They are superbly presented, with a perfect mixture of sympathy and irony. The description of Elliott's death in all its stages is surely one of the best that Mr Maugham has ever written. A novel such as this does several things at the same time. The picture of America in the opulent 'twenties and of Paris in the early 'thirties evokes an impression of a whole world moving towards the present war, and unwilling to be retarded in its movement. Larry, if his friends or we could have believed in him, might have been the brake. But there is enough in this novel, apart from Larry, to make it one of the best that Mr Maugham has written.

ROSAMOND LEHMANN *The Ballad and the Source*

Listener XXXII, 26 October 1944, 470

Reading *The Ballad and the Source*, one realises with a shock of surprise how defective the average good novel is. Most such novels do something well, have one interesting quality, exhibit one characteristic turn, like a commonplace man redeemed by a sense of humour, or a plain woman saved by pretty hair. A slight tinge of character, a well-managed idiosyncrasy, even speaking out of the corner of the mouth, laconically, in the style of Mr Hemingway's imitators, is sufficient to constitute distinction. But between such qualities and the qualities which go to make up a novel like *The Ballad and the Source* there is an enormous difference, the difference between a rough sketch and a picture filled in and completed. What strikes one at first about Miss Lehmann's story, as something novel, is its thoroughness. Thoroughness can be the most boring quality imaginable or the most delightful. To delight us it must be continuously enlivened by invention or discovery, which is the same thing; it must tell us more about the subject than we ever expected to learn, bring out the implications suggested by the rough sketch, and not merely describe ordinary properties which we could have conjectured for ourselves. This thorough and deliberate going into a subject gives shape and proportion to a story, makes us feel that it is important and has a meaning—otherwise why examine it so carefully?—and gives the reader various kinds of pleasure, the pleasure of watching a design unfolding, of sharing an enquiry into experience, of acquiring new knowledge of life.

The second notable thing about this book is its story-telling, in which it revives with brilliant success an older tradition than the one we have grown used to. It is essentially a full-scale study of one woman, Mrs Jardine. We see her first as a charming woman in late middle age, sensitive, sympathetic, slightly unconventional, her charm magically heightened by the adoration of a girl of twelve, through whose eyes she is seen. This first impression remains with us all through the book, but after it has been fixed, all the rest of Mrs Jardine turns into a series of stories, and becomes the 'ballad' of the title. These stories are told by older people to the young girl whose first impression of Mrs Jardine sets the mood; her adoration suffers shock after shock as it becomes clearer that Mrs Jardine is a stubborn egotist who destroys the happiness of everyone who comes close to her, yet it remains strong enough to give these stories a legendary quality, the aura of romance which a child's imagination gathers round anyone who has done strange or excessive things in the past and is much talked about. The skill with which Miss Lehmann presents Mrs Jardine as she is and Mrs Jardine as the girl sees her is beyond praise in its apparent simplicity. Mrs Jardine is of course seen through several eyes as one story follows another; through those of the maid Tilly, through her own (the most revealing of all), and through those of two or three other people. But their stories only corroborate one another and show what an awful woman Mrs Jardine was; what puts her life beyond the reach of facile judgment and raises it to the level of the ballad is the imagination of the young girl who listens to everything and in listening transforms it.

The Ballad and the Source is full of poetic imagination and of acute observation; it holds a very fine balance, at least until near the end; Mrs Jardine herself is a wonderful portrait, realistic and legendary at the same time, one of those figures who tease the imagination after we have learned all we can about them. She could only have been described in a series of stories, because she is one of those women who are much talked about. Perhaps we tend to forget how much people are talked about in general, and how much of our time we spend in talking about them; and that may be one of the reasons why the stories about Mrs Jardine, as they accumulate, put a slight strain on our credulity. We are not used to this way of writing a novel or presenting a character, though it is the way characters are presented to us in ordinary life.

All the part of the book which deals with Mrs Jardine as she was when the young girl met her in the first chapter has the enchantment of memory and childish imagination. Later, when we see her through our own eyes as an ageing woman living her life according to her nature, she inevitably loses something of her mystery and becomes more ordinary; probably Miss Lehmann intended this to happen. The end of the book, where Ianthe, the daughter, returns to revenge herself on Mrs Jardine, is by far the least imaginatively convincing. Up to this point the excitement of the story is accompanied by the excitement of discovery; but here the story runs away with itself and becomes something much less significant; the incidents move us merely as they would in an ordinary exciting story. Ianthe's madness was probably necessary in Miss Lehmann's scheme to point finally the destructiveness of Mrs Jardine's character. But in spite of many fine touches it is not quite convincingly described. This is almost the only weakness in a remarkable novel.

L P HARTLEY The Shrimp and the Anemone

Listener XXXII, 16 November 1944, 554

Among stories of childhood *The Shrimp and the Anemone* is not in the least like any which have come to be accepted as the best of their kind: those of Mr de la Mare or of Mr Forrest Reid, for instance. In spite of this, Mr Hartley's book has a good chance of somewhat the same kind of distinction. He differs from Mr de la Mare and Mr Reid in showing childhood as a miniature replica of adulthood, with the same essential problems, the same struggles, the same certainties and uncertainties concerning moral issues. But being new, discovered only for the first or second time, these problems and uncertainties are seen more freshly, have more of their original surprise in them than they will have again; they are apprehended with the undivided attention, as one might study a strange animal, or consider an idea in a Socratic dialogue; the overpowering weight of the adult cliché has not yet crushed their novelty out of them.

Mr Hartley takes as his hero an exceptionally enquiring and open-minded boy of nine, Eustace, places him in a situation strewn with pitfalls, and gives him a losing battle to fight: puts him, in other words, in what to the author appears to be the human situation. Eustace's reflective powers strike one at first as too sustained and too efficient for a young boy, but as one goes on reading one begins to doubt this impression, and then to remember all sorts of things one had forgotten about childhood, and finally to accept Eustace as a convincing enough child. In any case he taps a source of childish memory rarely drawn upon. The first impressions of childhood, being new and vivid, and the wild fancies of childhood, being unique, are easy to remember and return spontaneously to our minds; but our first reasonings about this or that practical problem fade into a general chain of reasonings which runs through our whole life, part of a process which we automatically accept, because we could not conceivably exist without it. What distinguishes these first reasonings from our later ones is that they are less bound by custom, and therefore more true in intention, though the premises from which they start are quite inadequate by adult standards. We remember most easily what is peculiar to childhood; Mr Hartley makes us remember what is common to childhood and maturity.

His story is really a story of the irreparable wrongness of the human situation. The book opens with a symbolical incident. Eustace finds an anemone devouring a shrimp in a rock-pool. The problem presented by this occurrence bewilders him. Should he rescue the shrimp? But if he does that he will rob the anemone of its dinner and perhaps make it die of hunger. He appeals to his elder sister Hilda, a girl of decision. Without hesitating she scrambles down, detaches the shrimp, and in doing so disembowels the anemone; and both die.

In the story one imagines that Eustace is cast for the part of the shrimp, and Hilda for that of the anemone. That is to say, they are over-poweringly attracted towards each other, and fatal to each other; yet both are right from their own point of view. Accordingly there is no solution for their problem: if Eustace eventually detaches himself (there is no indication in the story that this will happen) he will suffer for it; and if he doesn't, he will suffer in another way. This is the somewhat grim moral of the story, overlaid but never quite concealed by the amusing comedy and the charm of the presentation. Mr Hartley has chosen a child's story, with cruel felicity, to point a pessimistic reading of life.

This story presents a situation so perfectly in all its complicated simplicity, that the mere workmanship produces a feeling of pleasure. But once that is exhausted, one is struck by the fine sense of proportion which can suggest with almost equal power the point of view of the shrimp and the anemone, though the one is the devourer and the other is in perpetual danger of being devoured. In human terms, the problem is not quite so simple as this; we are made to feel that Eustace can never be quite devoured, and that Hilda will always remain obscurely disappointed; she is really the most pathetic character in the book. And she is only one of the many mouths waiting to engulf the small boy Eustace—the most dangerous, because she wakens in him the desire to be engulfed. The nicety with which Mr Hartley sets Eustace in his exact position among all those claims and dangers, and defines a whole series of perils of which the boy is unconscious, is very striking. This is what gives the story its unusual depth of suggestion, for though the subject-matter is childhood, the real subject is the human predicament.

CHARLES WILLIAMS All Hallows' Eve

Listener XXXII, 1 March 1945, 246

The dust-cover of his latest story introduces Mr Williams as a writer of 'supernatural thrillers', and then praises his 'profound mystical insight' and 'understanding of human relations'. A writer of profound mystical insight who writes thrillers about mystical things strikes one with a sense of incongruity; we receive thrills through our nerves, and mystical illumination through another organ of perception. Yet Mr Williams has clearly a subtle apprehension of spiritual entities unknown to or vaguely guessed at by most of us; he can distinguish and discriminate where we conjecture or see nothing at all; and to follow the development of his story gives one the sort of pleasure which a mathematician might get from a difficult and entrancing problem; for he deals with the unknown and constructs out of it an imaginative world which is clear and coherent.

In the course of this he produces a succession of first-rate thrills, all of them with a reasonable foundation, and all accounted for by the terms of the strange world into which he takes us. At the same time these thrills leave us with the knowledge that we have gone too far, that for some obscure reason we have courted the contact of something inimical and slightly destructive, and have yielded to a fascination. Mr Williams' thrills are far rarer than most; they touch the imagination as well as the nerves; yet one has a feeling that they do not essentially come from his mystical insight, but rather from something much more specialised, his implied or actual belief in the black arts. To get the full impact one would have to believe in the powers of necromancy; to those who do not believe in these powers they will remain merely well-contrived thrills, consequently not to be taken seriously. Yet the story is a serious story dealing with problems far beyond the scope of the realistic novelist. The result is a feeling that Mr Williams has not chosen the right form to embody his remarkable vision of life and time and eternity. The style, which is close and exact but insistently rhetorical, confirms this impression; Mr Williams seems to be forcing the style to do what should have been done by the plot.

Yet if one discounts the necromancy and the more calculated thrills, there remains such a wealth of rare insight and imagination in this story that an appreciative reader is bound to return to it again to extract new meanings. Mr Williams, to paraphrase the note on the dustcover, traces the story of people who are on their way to Heaven or Hell, without having reached either. Two of them, young girls, are newly dead and at the beginning of the journey through eternity which the author furnishes with such interesting milestones. The others are still alive, and one of them, Simon the Clerk, a magician, has been alive for a few hundred years. Simon is overmastered by the desire for that absolute power which is said to corrupt absolutely; and he is not content with power over the living, but wants to extend it over the dead as well, and rule in the kingdom of shades. Such an idea for a story sounds as wildly improbable as it could be; but the conflict itself is endlessly fascinating, both as an intellectual construction and an imaginative invention. The strict logic of the various happenings, the mathematical certainty with which the conflict is worked out for good or evil, produces a formidable impression, and almost makes one believe that magic is an art which deserves respect. Some of the thrills have an intense imaginative quality; as when in the picture of Simon and his disciples, the disciples take on the shape of beetles after one of his adepts has looked at them. Touches such as this show what an original and profound writer Mr Williams can be.

ALDOUS HUXLEY, HENRY GREEN and ANNA KAVAN
Time Must Have a Stop; Loving; I am Lazarus

Listener XXXV, 5 April 1945, 386

After reading Mr Huxley's latest novel one is left wondering whether his mixture of misanthropy and mysticism is an incongruous or a harmonious one. The first half of the story has such a close resemblance to his early work that it reads like a period piece dating from the 'twenties. The faint nausea at the physical appearance and habits of human beings, the disgust at their enjoyments, the sardonic relish of their illusions, are all here as they were in *Antic Hay* and *Those Barren Leaves*. Some of the characters whom Mr Huxley displays with every sign of disgusted enjoyment are good by ordinary standards and some bad by any standards, but he has an equally low opinion of both; they are all ridiculous. Kind Mrs Ockham is like a pug, 'a pink, hairless pug with a bad complexion'. Handsome but unkind Mrs Thwale is always giving a 'delicate little grunt of laughter'. When Eustace, the fat, elderly man of the world, lights his last cigar, 'Damply, lovingly the unweaned lips closed on the object of their desire. He sucked at the flame of the little silver lamp, and a moment later the teat was yielding its aromatic milk, his mouth was full of smoke.' A profound distaste for all the habits and odours of the physical world except those which are aesthetically pleasant reappears again and again. These evocations are brilliant, and they are accompanied by that feeling of pleasure which a writer feels in exercising a gift of whose genuineness he is certain. And a writer who is able to do something supremely well probably has no choice but to go on doing it.

But the book has a second aim besides indicating the absurdity of life as the intelligent middle classes live it. Sebastian, the main figure in the story, resolves to work out his salvation, and salvation, according to Mr Huxley, can be attained only through liberation from ordinary desire and through love. To believe this is doubtless to believe that the life which most people live is ridiculous and disgusting. It is the very thing from which we must flee if we seek the kind of salvation in which Mr Huxley believes. The faint doubt one becomes aware of after reading this book is whether Mr Huxley, having fled from it, has really got away from it. Disgust attaches us just as closely to things as love does, and is as intimate and inescapable. Pity, an emotion which Mr Huxley distrusts, is far less narrowly personal, though for him it may have the disadvantage that it leads to action, and he seems to distrust all action which is not in some sense—a high sense, doubtless—self-regarding. He is a sort of spiritual isolationist; he believes that a few, if they try very hard, will be able to save their souls; he regards all movements for general improvement as mere illusions. If he were to found a new religion he would not look for his disciples among fishermen, or their modern equivalent, but among that quintessential part of the intellectual elite who have reached the point where they have begun to doubt or to despise their election. His distaste for ordinary human life makes his disbelief in the possibility of human improvement in general easily comprehensible. It helps also to explain his extreme detachment from the world and what the world in its blind way is striving for. One has the feeling sometimes that Time itself is to him a form of evil. All serious attempts to attain excellence create in ordinary people a certain feeling of estrangement, even a slight dismay. If Mr Huxley's detachment strikes one as being excessive, even perverse, it is at least a demonstration of his sincerity. But how in his detachment he can still dislike his characters as heartily as he did twenty years ago is another question.

Mr Henry Green's latest novel, which is mostly about English domestic servants in a big house in Ireland, is, in comparison with Mr Huxley's, simple and charitable. Mr Green has a gift for yielding to his subject so spontaneously that his very style capitulates to it. There are moments in the present book where the writing almost suggests that of *The Young Visiters*; such extreme susceptibility to the suggestions of the subject is almost a fault. He has virtually a separate style for each character; if he had had a foreign maid among his collection, he must have fallen into pidgin English whenever she appeared. Charley Raunce, the butler, is dealt with as man to man.

> 'Oh, I don't know,' he replied, cautious and as if he was shy.

The women have a general style of their own to comfort them:

> 'Oh dear,' the nanny said come over limp. 'Arthur, I see yes, Arthur.'

The comedy is simple, broad and on the whole sweet-tempered, but it goes on without much variation; the characters speak like maids and children and men-servants without intermission, whatever happens. The problem which bothers some of them, whether they should go on living safely in Ireland when their friends are being bombed by Germans in England, is solved by circumstances rather than by impulse or reason. In its mere power of mimicry the book is quite extraordinary, and often very amusing; but one has the feeling that it has no basis; Mr Green yields so completely to his theme that he is left with no opportunity to think about it.

Miss Kavan's latest volume of short stories shows a concentration on the subject which puts her into a different world from Mr Huxley or Mr Green. It is a restricted world, a world mostly of isolation and mental anguish, and the unrelieved misery of those who cannot get out of their isolation or understand their anguish. Her main strength lies in the seriousness with which she takes into account things as they are, a seriousness which never degenerates into bitterness or disgust even in contemplating the hopeless and the incurable. The first few stories deal with life in asylums and mental homes. The later, and by far the more remarkable ones, take us into an exterior world which resembles that of Franz Kafka, and are explorations of the meaning of experience. 'The Brothers' is a story of guilt and its continuance as a thing in itself long after the guilty act has ceased to have any effect. 'The Gannets' is purely visionary, a description of something which could not possibly have happened, and yet raises an echo in the mind which tells us that something corresponding to it has happened and does happen.

Like some of the stories which follow it, it can't be compressed into a rational formula; we do not know the world in which these things are happening, and yet we feel their truth, and feel that they are telling us something which could be told in no other way. One of the stories, 'All Kinds of Grief shall arrive', resembles Kafka so strikingly that one wonders whether here Miss Kavan has been consciously influenced by him. But in all the others she is very definitely herself. There is no classification to cover this kind of imaginative writing; it cannot be called symbolic, and still less allegorical. It is definitely a new kind of writing, and seems to have begun with Kafka. To harness it to allegory would be to distort it and take away its meaning by substituting a more obvious meaning for it. To readers who have no gift for catching hidden significances it can have little meaning at all; to those who have, it probably holds more meaning and is more worth consideration than any other kind of contemporary writing which comes under the heading of fiction. It starts generally from some total conception of the human situation, rather than from an actual incident or scene; it requires an equal application of the intellect and the imagination, and above all a gift for continuous invention. Miss Kavan has these gifts in their undiluted state, along with the style of a born writer. This is a very remarkable book.

EVELYN WAUGH ***Brideshead Revisited***

Listener XXXIII, 28 June 1945, 722

Mr Waugh's new novel is a remarkable one; remarkable as coming from the author of *Decline and Fall*, and remarkable in itself. He insists that it is a serious book, and it is so obviously serious that the assurance is unnecessary. But Mr Waugh has always been serious when it came to the point, even in his comic books where there is invariably an end to the fun, and generally a painful one. He has always shown a curious kind of humanity, too, in these somewhat cruel books, the humanity of a writer who has resolved to try inhumanity for a start to see how far it will take him, so that he might find its limits. This seriousness and humanity—still with an unrelenting core—have become explicit in his latest book. He still persecutes his characters as he has always done, but he is sorry for them while he persecutes them. He still shows his preoccupation with odd characters and characters obviously heading for misfortune, but the misfortune is not comic, the oddness is not caricature. Everything is complex.

In *Brideshead Revisited* Mr Waugh deals with odd Catholics, as he once dealt with odd schoolmasters. They are Catholics who have strayed in all sorts of queer or usual directions, and find their way back somnambulistically, by unorthodox paths, or by none at all, simply following what seems their natural inclination: to Mr Waugh all these strange apparently fortuitous divagations fit ultimately into the vast, all-embracing, mysteriously moving orthodoxy and rightness of the Catholic Church. The Church is the point of return for all those circuitous journeys; the story traces a graph of them and brings them to their pre-ordained place. Ostensibly the characters live in a certain social setting, but in reality each of them is following out a secret journey of his or her own without being aware of it, or becoming aware of it only when its destination comes in sight. To suggest all this from the outside—and Mr Waugh works from the outside by choice—to convey the shape of this invisible pattern which is the real pattern of the story, must have been extraordinarily difficult, and how far the attempt has been successful it would be hard to say. The clearer the religious pattern becomes, the more the characters passively conform to it, and the less convincing they are as characters. This was probably unavoidable; at any rate the second half of the book strikes one as being much below the level of the first.

Oddness is merely an emphatic degree of individuality, and Mr Waugh gets the utmost drop of oddness out of his characters by seeing them, almost without comment, from the outside. His narrator is a non-Catholic moving among Catholics, fascinated and disconcerted by their ways which are strange to him, and never—in the story—quite understanding them. He alternates between sympathy and complete lack of sympathy, and is perpetually correcting the one attitude by means of the other. The Catholic family of Lord Marchmain is like a group which is perpetually revolving, so that we see various aspects of them in rapid succession; the result is not a blur, but a series of perfectly clear pictures, each at surprising variance with the others, each adding something new, yet each a piece out of which the final image is built. This surprise, this objective complexity, keeps the story continuously fresh and in a sense entertaining. Taken separately the episodes are serious, but their arrangement produces an effect of wit. The conduct of the story is brilliant, especially in the first half; the writing is clear, flashing and pointed. One beautifully finished episode follows another; point after point is subtly made; there is no dullness, no sense of insistence; we feel that the author is dealing with real experience at first hand; the atmosphere of youth, of early manhood, and of middle age are freshly evoked; countless difficult situations are handled with admirable firmness; each episode is convincing in itself; the story is packed with life; but when one comes to the end one wonders whether the total effect is really convincing, and whether all that has been crammed into the story adds up to the meaning which the author wishes us to read into it. Whether this is so or not, it is a remarkable novel which falls away in the second half, it is true, but contains scenes of great beauty, and is filled with imagination.

The story records the memories of Charles Ryder, a Captain in the present war, when the course of duty brings him back to an English country house which he had known as a young man. The members of the family who once lived in it, Sebastian Flyte, his sister Julia, his brother Brideshead, his mother Lady Marchmain, are all called up in his mind. His friendship with Sebastian is perfectly described; the weakest part of the story is the account of his love affair with Julia, which is curiously rhetorical in the romantic style. Sebastian becomes a dipsomaniac, but in spite of this manages to fulfil his fate as a Catholic, ending as a servant in a Catholic monastery in North Africa. Julia, after promising to get a divorce and marry Charles, finds at last that she cannot go against the law of her church, though she has been for a long time a renegade member of it. Old Lord Marchmain, who has long since left the Church and lived with his mistress in Venice, returns to it again when he is on the point of death. The story is written, one feels, to explain why these things must have happened, and few would agree that it succeeds. But it contains so many other virtues that this does not matter finally.

C S LEWIS That Hideous Strength

Listener XXXIV, 6 September 1945, 274

Mr C S Lewis's new book continues a modern tradition of religious fiction which seems to have been initiated by Chesterton, and whose most distinguished representative was the late Charles Williams. It popularises a religious message by casting it into the form of a thriller; it is both highly intellectual and highly melodramatic; insistent in its orthodoxy, careless in the freedom of its invention. In Charles Williams and Mr Lewis it depends for its melodrama on excursions into the supernatural; there they find—especially among the evil spirits—shapes and powers more terrifying than ordinary humanity, even in concentration camps. They take their stand on good, and from that vantage-point allow themselves to be safely fascinated by the vast supernatural machinery of evil, and to extract from it an edifying thrill. One feels that Charles Williams, with his learned acquaintance with demonology and witchcraft, could have written a book as extraordinary as James Hogg's *Confessions of a Justified Sinner*. But Hogg lived among a people who still actually believed in possession by demons, and Williams did not. The result was that Hogg produced a masterpiece, and Williams a succession of remarkable thrillers, brilliant in their curious powers of imagination, but incapable of evoking genuine belief. We accept Hogg's supernatural occurrences because he and the people he knew accepted them as part of the popular conception of evil. But Charles Williams's magicians and Mr Lewis's visitants from Venus and Mars have no part in our current conception of good and evil; so that their intrusion does not seem to bring us to closer grips with our moral problems, but to divert us from them. Both writers do evoke with intensity an atmosphere of evil; but it is like a conjuring trick, a matter of technique. Compared with the sense of evil which Georges Bernanos can produce by describing the life of a fairly ordinary French village community, it seems artificial and unconvincing. After reading this curious kind of fiction, so correct morally and theologically, so lax artistically, one's first feeling is that human history is guided or misguided, and souls saved or damned, by a process less purely melodramatic.

Mr Lewis calls his story 'a modern fairy-tale for grown-ups', and as a fairy-tale it has considerable merits. If we did not have to believe in it, any more than we have to believe in Snow White, it would be a delightful book. But it is obviously intended to be much more than a fairy-tale; it deals with a contemporary danger to the whole world (though what that is it would be difficult to describe in a few words), a danger which Mr Lewis dispels by summoning a number of good spirits and Merlin from his grave to be their servant. The more realistic parts of the story are by far the best; the staff of Bragdon College are described with an exact satirical touch that is delightful, and the villainous clique who run N.I.C.E. (an establishment which is trying to get all mankind into its power so as to dehumanise it and turn it into an efficient machine) are perfectly convincing until they get too thoroughly mixed up with the supernatural forces. The story itself is as exciting as any thriller, and brilliantly contrived till near the end, when Mr Lewis surfeits us with wonders, and with one scene of really excessive horror. The moral keeps intruding every now and then; but one would have taken it more seriously if one could have taken the story seriously. Writers of religious thrillers cannot have it both ways; they cannot make our flesh creep with fictitious horrors and at the same time put us in a proper frame of mind to appreciate a theological moral. As soon as melodrama becomes theological, theology becomes melodramatic.

W H AUDEN Collected Shorter Poems

Observer, 30 April 1950, 7

This volume is the first to give some idea of the scope and variety of Mr Auden's poetry. The variety is remarkable, sometimes disconcerting. The scope is wide. Mr Auden writes in every mood, uses any form and any vocabulary that comes to his hand, and invents where he can find none. The book accordingly contains a mass of poetry written on a surprising diversity of subjects and in moods which range from the jocularity of the music-hall to high seriousness. There is nothing to give it unity but the author's cast of thought and imagination. Yet that is always perfectly recognisable.

The poems seem to be rather tumbled out in any order than arranged, and the reader has every now and then to change his mood in agreement with them. No doubt this adds to the liveliness of the book and emphasises the sense of variety, yet it is somewhat distracting. The student desiring to find a graph of Mr Auden's development as a poet will not find it here. But that can be studied elsewhere by those who wish to do it.

The word 'clinical' has often been applied to Mr Auden's poetry. Yet the chief impression one has after reading this collection is of a tormented humanity. Certainly in his earlier work Mr Auden seemed to be resolved to understand human beings by diagnosing and classifying them. Yet that seems to have been a short phase, and he soon passed to the more universal imaginative operation of understanding them for their own sakes. Diagnosis and classification are short-cuts; they reach a specific truth of their own which convinces a part of our mind, but only by leaving out the things which would convince us fully. The diagnosis and classification have gone. But Mr Auden has still such a quickly moving imagination that he is still predisposed towards the short-cut, jumping the slow stages by which we reach an understanding of life. This, perhaps, is the reason why he sometimes seems so allusive. The disadvantage of the short-cut in his early poems was that it jumped to conclusions, its advantage in his later ones, that it reaches the truth a few yards before us, and surprises us with it.

The variety of this poetry was only made possible by an extraordinary mastery of form, a more than usually complete capacity for the vigorous and felicitous use of language. It is impossible to illustrate it in a short review, and when one has mentioned such perfect conversation pieces as 'Musée des Beaux Arts', meditations on contemporary troubles like '1st September, 1939', the fine metaphysical poem on Pascal, the grotesque fantasy of 'Through a Looking Glass', the purely lyrical poems, the popular ballads, one has hardly touched the diverse interest and richness of the book.

Mr Auden has been blamed for lack of seriousness; yet he is surely the most serious poet of his generation:

In the nightmare of the dark
All the dogs of Europe bark,
And the living nations wait,
Each sequestered in its hate;

Intellectual disgrace
Stares from every human face,
And the seas of pity lie
Locked and frozen in each eye.

That is serious enough, and not less serious because its author can write in a different mood:

My second thoughts condemn
And wonder how I dare
To look you in the eye.
What right have I to swear
Even at one a.m.
To love you till I die?

The imagination moves and lives with equal right in these two worlds. The rare thing today is to find a poet who is at home in both.

The reader may feel somewhat hustled and disconcerted by the diversity of these poems. Perhaps they might have been more considerately arranged. But they are the work of an extraordinary poet.

DAVID GASCOYNE A Vagrant and Other Poems

Observer, 24 December 1950, 7

Mr Gascoyne belongs to no school. He has no style except his own, which is so pure that it seems to leave no room for idiosyncrasy. The poets of Mr Gascoyne's generation aim directly at idiosyncrasy, either their own or that of the age, 'the contemporary idiom', as if it were an essential virtue of poetry. When they chose, instead of a personal idiom, the idiom of their age, they came to write in an easily interchangeable vocabulary, and sometimes gave the impression of appearing in chorus, with one voice, sometimes their own, sometimes that of Mr Auden, predominating over the others, and the ground base of Mr Eliot rolling with an admonitory note in the background.

One of the pleasures of reading Mr Gascoyne is that of listening to a voice speaking with its own inflection and not at all in character. For idiosyncratic poets are forced to speak in character, both those who create the character, like Mr Auden, and those who assume it. So that to find things said simply in the way in which they can best be said is in the present state of poetry a great relief. No poet of his generation abuses English so little or uses it with more precision and felicity than Mr Gascoyne.

This is due in part, perhaps, to his sense of the permanent in human experience, for that makes utterance simple and unaffected. In this volume he deals chiefly with contemporary life, but his imagination, while deeply concerned with that life, passed straight through it to the permanent. That, indeed, it may be plain, is the only way in which the contemporary can be illuminated and given a meaning beyond itself. In 'A Vagrant', an imaginative statement of our dilemma today, and in 'Innocence and Experience', an impression of a typical contemporary encounter, the implications are brought out with an exactitude which only a permanent vision of life could have given. There is irony in both poems, but it is not the irony of an ironical temperament, but that which is sometimes fitting in the most serious treatment of the most serious theme. The mood in both poems, and in most of the others, varies from stanza to stanza, giving them a fine variety and unexpectedness, but the point from which the situation is viewed never changes. That is the ultimate virtue which holds all the other qualities of these poems together. It produces that rare thing, a balance.

Mr Gascoyne is a Christian poet and unorthodox. Perhaps the best short description of his creed is to be found in a prose poem, 'The Second Coming', which ends with the words, 'all propaganda that is not true Christian revolutionary propaganda is sickness and falsehood.' In a sequence of short poems, 'Fragments Towards a Religio Poetae', he tries to define his beliefs about God and man, but not very strikingly. These beliefs can be more clearly felt in the poems where he implies without trying to define them, poems dealing concretely with experience as in the title poem, 'Innocence and Experience', 'Reported Missing', 'Birth of a Prince' and the strangely beautiful poem 'The Sacred Hearth':

> Mysterious and unrecapturable moment, when I stood
> There staring back at the dark white nocturnal house,
> And saw gleam through the lattices a light more pure than gold
> Made sanguine with crushed roses from the firelight that all night
> Stayed flickering about the sacred hearth.

In such poems Mr Gascoyne never goes wrong, though dealing with the most difficult matters. His sureness here is perhaps what distinguishes him most as a poet. It is a rare quality, and poetry cannot afford to do without it.

WALTER DE LA MARE Winged Chariot

Observer, 24 June 1951, 7

A charming woodcut by Miss Joan Hassall on the title page of this beautifully designed book shows a number of objects: the sun, the moon, the stars, the two hands of a clock, an hour-glass, three birds flying, some flower-buds, a pyramid and an urn. These properties will be found in Mr de la Mare's stories and poetry fairly often; no other writer brings so many wild remote things as well as mechanical domestic things so deeply into human life, and makes them so much a part of it that we become aware, for instance, of the quaintness and pathos of clocks, these housemaids of time. In this poem he takes the things which time itself offers in its endless attempt to explain itself as the subject of a prolonged musing monologue. Most of them are circular, or revolve, returning to their mark in a month or a year, and seem to say that time goes round. The pyramid and the urn stand outside, as shapes left behind by time in its passing.

The woodcut is a little pictorial anthology of the main themes in the poem, and these Mr de la Mare has elaborated with a felicity and ingenuity and occasional quaintness which are his alone among living poets. We can wrestle with time or stand and contemplate time, and all of us are bound sometime, perhaps, to do one or other or both; but to enter into these moods, and through them try to enter into the moods of time itself, is a different matter; and that seems to be what Mr de la Mare has tried to do. Reading the poem we feel that we are seeing time begetting and measuring itself in all sorts of curious modes simultaneously: by the tick-tock of the clock, and sand trickling through the neck of the hourglass, the changing notes of the cuckoo, the life-span of the elephant, the revolutions of the seasons and the heavenly bodies, the accumulation of memories in the mind, the growth and decay of the generations. Nothing, we feel, can be thought of that is so constantly ingenious and busy as time (the poem gives a great sense of time's busyness). Yet time is a thing that perpetually runs out like the sand in the hour-glass—the tragic symbol of time, the opposite of the immovably optimistic clock.

In this endless movement which would leave a sort of nothingness behind it if it were not for memory, what is it that remains with us? Mr de la Mare would say it was the moments of true apprehension of suffering and compassion, of delight and love. That is the traditional answer, to be found in almost all human writing from the start, and in a sense all writing is about time. It is in the single strokes of imagination or fancy, of humour or wisdom, that the value of the poem lies. It tempts one to quote, but a short review can give only a slight idea of its felicities. Of the cuckoo:

> How stealthy a craft to jilt her eggs and young
> And put them out to nurse their whole lives long . . .
> Two idle summers and a sundering sea,
> And all small honest birds for enemy.

Of the time before clocks:

> By candle Alfred set his hour to pray:
> And, once, Man merely Sunned his life away.

Of waste places where the wind never comes:

> Those deserts where no zephyr stirs.
> And coins gleam on, which age-gone travellers
> Dropped from their camel-caravans.

These curious and delightful imaginations illumine a serious and tragic yet affirmative vision of time

> Which robs the unfolding flower of its bud

and man of the life he does not want to leave. The humour and wisdom and rare genius are Mr de la Mare's.

GRAHAM GREENE The End of the Affair

Observer, 25 September 1951, 7

Economy of statement is demanded by this age of literature, and probably no writer has carried it further in the novel than Mr Greene. Other times felt they could be leisurely, and though this made them say many thing they need not have said, it allowed them also to say many things we cannot say now; we do not have the time. We are economical with time, for though the possible future of mankind stretches far further in front of us than it did for Dickens and Thackeray, our own future seems short; so that if we have anything to say, we have to be brief. Proust and Joyce and Thomas Mann are the last writers in the great garrulous tradition, who gather so much gratuitous humanity into their stories. They still did not feel that time was running short.

In the first half of this novel Mr Greene's skill and economy reach a point which one feels he will never pass. The story is told in the first person by a novelist who knows so much about his craft that he despises it. He is a discontented, envious, jealous, suspicious, aggressive, unhappy man. He falls in love with the wife of one of his friends; in his jealous mind his love becomes simply an 'affair', with the appropriate development. He describes the affair apparently with the utmost frankness and sincerity; but as he sees it out of his envy and jealousy, everything he says about it is false. When he says sincerely that he loves, he is lying; and he does not speak the truth even when he says he hates. To have brought all this out in a straightforward narrative told by a man doing his best to be truthful, is an extraordinary feat. For Mr Greene has created a character, made him tell his true story, and yet indicated at every point that it is false. The real story, when we read it in the diary of his mistress, whose love was love, is quite simple, but already almost known.

Mr Greene is concerned in this book with the relation between love and hate. To the narrator, Maurice Bendrix, it is a crucial problem, but as everything in him is falsified by envy and jealousy, one feels that the problem is falsified too. Bendrix is really frustrated because he has a thirst for power which can never be satisfied: it brings the unhappiness which he calls hatred; it reduces his love for Sarah to the dimensions of an affair; and it is the indirect cause of her death. He tells us all this without ever becoming aware of it. After her death he still nurses his love or hate for her; but what he calls love and hate are really the frustration of his power over her. When she turns to the Catholic God, he is jealous of Him as of a rival power. Thinking of the time when he was happy in his love for Sarah, he reflects: 'I hadn't during that period any hatred of God, for hadn't I in the end proved stronger?'

The story raises questions which the reader has to answer. Economy, one feels, has been pushed to the point where Mr Greene cannot make his own statement. But the inference seems to be, as far as one can seize it, that hatred of God may be the road to love of God. Yet Sarah had no hatred. If, as the last sentence in the book seems to imply, Bendrix is on the desperate point of conversion, one cannot help thinking that he will be a jealous and difficult worshipper.

The dingy or ignoble minor characters are beautifully portrayed. Bendrix himself is a wonderful study, perhaps the most remarkable figure in Mr Greene's world.

ANGUS WILSON Hemlock and After

Observer, 13 July 1952, 7

This novel is a description of life breaking up, and of a part of society as Mr Wilson sees it. Three of the characters have reached their purgatory, being honest and intelligent, but the rest are going downwards, thoughtlessly or willingly, without resistance, to their various respectable or disreputable hells. With apparent deliberation Mr Wilson has collected this strange miscellaneous crowd to illustrate the disintegration of life: social climbers, spivs, criminals, political fanatics, fellow-travellers, homosexuals, disillusioned liberals, middle-class commuters to rural towns (who to Mr Wilson seem to be necessarily damned), people stuck in jobs as in busy little hells, perverts in their limbo. All, except the despairing liberals, descend a moving staircase to the deeper and greater hell that awaits them: the breakdown of civilisation which they foreshadow. Mr Wilson is a moralist and has written a very disagreeable book, as moralists who hate evil and are simultaneously fascinated by it are apt to do. He is to be taken seriously.

The main and most likeable character in the story is a conscientious liberal somewhat in the style of André Gide: a man who holds it right to try all things, but omits to hold fast to that which is good simply because the trying itself has become his good. After years of married life Bernard Sands yields to his homosexual inclinations; his wife suffers a mental breakdown; his children disapprove; and his reputation (he is a grand old man of letters) is breathed upon. He is sincere, high-minded, and a man of good will, and he has just succeeded in getting Government backing for the opening of an old English country house as a home for young writers. Simultaneously he finds himself troubled for the first time by a sense of evil. An absolute liberal—and Bernard pushes his creed as far as it will go—may be incapable of acknowledging evil, since all things to him are things to be tried. The sense of evil bit by bit undermines the creed on which Bernard has built his life, though he still goes on living in accordance with it. All this comes out in his dubious speech at the ceremonial opening of the writers' house, and everything else, as if in sympathy, goes disastrously wrong. All the separate kinds of evil in the story come together in an orgy of spite, perversion, indecency, and general disorder. This scene seems to be designed to gather up all the threads of the story, but something has gone wrong with it, too; the disorder has got into the description. The result is a very curious mixture of farce and melodrama.

Mr Wilson has written some of the best short stories of his time. This, his first novel, is not the novel of a short-story writer; it is well planned and it has a theme. The theme is defined in the blurb as 'the contradiction between the need for authority and the distaste for power . . . exemplified in the conflicts and uncertainties which beset Bernard Sands and bring about his death.' The book indeed states a real problem, though not so clearly as these words suggest. The criticism of liberalism of the Sands (and Gide) kind is admirable. Yet the numerous social misfits in the story do not really illustrate the thesis, but rather obscure it. If our life is falling to pieces, these are certainly some of the pieces; but the cause of the fall still eludes us. It may be that Mr Wilson is following Zola's example and giving us one section only of the breakdown. His picture is certainly one-sided, and his selection of characters specialised.

But the characters themselves are crammed with uncomfortable life, and violently real. It would be hard to find a character more substantially evil than the detestable Mrs Curry, who welcomes blackmail, perversion, prostitution and anything else that comes, makes money out of them all, and drenches the whole in baby blue sentimentality. The book has brilliance, wit, savagery and, sometimes, imaginative sympathy. It has a serious purpose. But it is hard to discover where its moral centre lies. A recognition of the weaknesses of liberalism is not enough.

EVELYN WAUGH and ERNEST HEMINGWAY Men at Arms; The Old Man and the Sea

Observer, 7 September 1952, 7

These books, both by experienced novelists, are somewhat unlike what we have come to expect. We are surprised by a slight lack of professional assurance and accomplishment. The authors seem to be reaching after something more significant, and imperfection has slipped in. How the novelist is to deal with imperfection now that the novel has become recognised as a technical feat, is hard to say. It was not a question which worried novelists in earlier times. But now the novelist must offer a triumph and avoid any sign of a struggle with his subject. And since the novelist offers it, the reader has come to require it, for a triumph is a reassuring thing.

Yet we apply other standards to the great novelists of the past, we accept Scott's insipid heroes and heroines (and how many of them there are) for the sake of the scores of living characters, knowing that these could never have breathed in the conditioned atmosphere of a neat contemporary novel. Melville's Moby Dick and Captain Ahab tear wide gaps in his imaginative structure. We accept the faults for the sake of the greatness. It is true that the greatness, both in Scott and Melville, is something that breaks in; there are enough chinks to admit it. But the contemporary novel has become so neat and tight that only a double miracle would allow the miracle to happen.

Neither of these novels may be great; but there is one character in *Men at Arms* of a quite different size from any other that Mr Waugh has produced, and a really heroic piece of narrative in *The Old Man and the Sea* told with a simplicity which shows that Mr Hemingway has forgotten that he is a tough writer. He does, at the start, expose his sentimentality more openly than he has done before; but that is a thing which we have to accept for the sake of the superb writing which follows, just as we accept the tears of Dickens. The first few pages are almost strangely sentimental, with relapses into the 'ands' of children's storybooks;

> Everything about him was old except his eyes and they were the same colour as the sea and were cheerful and undefeated.

But this gush of sentimentality is a mere discharge of inhibitions, a sort of ceremonial purification; and as soon as the long battle with the great fish begins the toughness and the sentimentality are gone, and Mr Hemingway is in the world of free poetic imagination where he is really at home. If the reader can survive the first few pages which introduce him to the old man, the boy, and the fish, he will be rewarded. For Mr Hemingway is essentially an imaginative writer, and his imagination has never displayed itself more powerfully than in this simple and tragic story.

Mr Waugh's story is uneven compared with his earlier ones, but the unevenness is due mainly to the fact that it contains something better than he has ever given us before; the character of Apthorpe, a comic invention full of poetry. For most of the book Mr Waugh exercises the admirable talent which he has shown so often; a talent not so much for original creation as for hitting off with the fewest strokes a number of general types, so that we immediately recognise them. There is a scene between a husband and a wife who has left him and been unfaithful to him with several men. It is brilliantly done, and we recognise that this is exactly what 'that kind of woman' would say and do. But Apthorpe is in a different world; he is not this or that kind of man, and not so much observed as created; and he remains throughout a mystery, a comic mystery teasing the mind with possibilities.

The main figure, Guy Crouchback, whom Mr Waugh treats with a different kind of seriousness, is uninteresting in comparison, as main figures in novels, old and new, tend to be. Perhaps he and Apthorpe were necessary to each other, and Apthorpe could not have come into existence without Crouchback, requiring a touch of the same seriousness. The picture of army life is brilliant, with a touch of genial brutality. But Apthorpe is wonderful.

I COMPTON-BURNETT Mother and Son and The Novels of I Compton-Burnett by Robert Liddell

Observer, 6 February 1955, 9

I have read Miss Compton-Burnett's novels as they came out, for a quarter of a century, and always with increasing admiration, although they are variations on a single theme. No other novelist is so constantly like herself as this great writer: I borrow the epithet thankfully and with a sense of its justice from Mr Liddell. Yet what stares one in the face is the quite extraordinary form which she has chosen, or which chose itself, for the presentation of her view of life. It ignores the established conventions of the novel; there is nothing else like it; nothing in it that can be imitated and so influence the future of prose fiction. Nevertheless it completely justifies itself. That is the puzzle.

Mr Liddell knows the novels intimately, and his excellent introduction to them will be helpful both to Miss Compton-Burnett's admirers and to those who stand on the brink. He is particularly good where he points out the diversity beneath the apparent sameness of the characters. (The sameness is mainly caused, I think, by the fact that Miss Compton-Burnett always deals with the same subject.) But he does not say much about the form of the novels, and the form seems to me of prime importance; I feel that without it this writer could not have evoked the atmosphere or produced the intensity of effect which is her mark.

I would like to throw out a few ideas on this problem, for the first response of any reader, on taking up one of her books, is, Why on earth should she write in this particular way? Why is there such a striking absence of description? Why do we have no image of these people about whom we know so much? If we could clear up this mystery I feel we would have a juster idea of the originality and economy of the means which Miss Compton-Burnett employs for her purpose. That, as everybody knows, is to lay bare the frustrations and distortions caused by domestic tyranny.

Mr Liddell begins aptly by quoting a harrowing passage from Amiel's 'Journal', enumerating the various horrors bred by constricted family life: the suspicions, rancours, hates, venomous words, slips of the tongue; the catalogue is endless. This is Miss Compton-Burnett's province, and no other writer has explored it so thoroughly. Now as to her form. She is so exclusively taken up by the domestic passions that if she had described her characters and how they are dressed, their houses and how they are furnished, she would have been distracted from her real subject.

Her characters live in country houses which, for all we are told about them, might easily be the same house. It is lost in the country, but we have no impression of the country. The family seems to live all, or almost all, the time in this house; but we do not know what the rooms are like or how they are furnished, pleasantly or drably. We feel sometimes that the house does not look out on anything, and if we try to form an image of it we see a brute square building, a private prison, and inside three main divisions, one for the elders and betters, one for the children, and one for the servants. The members of this family never get away from the house, even when they visit their friends. It is the place to which they have always to return, so that even their brief moments of escape have the colour of imprisonment. This is what creates in Miss Compton-Burnett's novels such a strong sense of confinement, and also sets her free to study the passions of her inmates, almost as things in themselves, undistracted by any other consideration. The means suit her particular ends; they shape the form of her novels, and no other form would have served.

Her descriptions of the characters have the same purpose. We are given a mere catalogue of features, which belong to the characters but do not express them. Miss Compton-Burnett is not interested in flesh and blood; her characters do not embrace, because they have no bodies, and when they cry we are reminded of weeping fountains. She deals with what lies beneath, the terrifying or vain or pathetic passions. 'Passions spin the plot.' And we see the passions more clearly because we are not distracted by the physical appearance of the people who feel them. We do not ask whether the prisoners in a gaol are handsome; our feelings towards them are of a different kind. Gaols are not filled with good-looking and plain prisoners, but with smouldering passions.

Passions, so closely confined, sometimes lead to crime, and that is the role of murder in Miss Compton-Burnett's novels: it is part of the account. In her latest novel, adultery committed, hidden, and then revealed plays a decisive part, but the deadlier passions are not roused. A magnificent tyrant, Miranda Hume, dies conveniently soon; there is a chorus of children, pathetic and amusing, and a quite delightful woman character, a sweet-tempered egoist and aesthetic pretender, who influences the action but wisely stands apart from it.

Miss Compton-Burnett deals more magnanimously with her family despots than she used to do, seeing the good in their evil. A faint ray of charity falls across the story, and there is a faint hope for the children. Yet her world is a terrible one; we may be thankful that there are other and happier families. But her survey of her chosen field is a profoundly moral task.

J R R TOLKIEN The Return of the Ring

Observer, 27 November 1955, 11

This volume brings to an end Mr Tolkien's extraordinary trilogy, *The Lord Of The Rings*. The ring is carried through many perils into the heart of Mordor, the country of evil, and destroyed there, and the power of Sauron, the demon, along with it. The hobbits return to the Shire, where a malicious wizard has been working general mischief, setting up dark satanic mills and terrifying and starving the people. He is ejected. Lórien, the land of the elves, returns to its ageless felicity; the human heroes take up their peaceable rule.

What does one remember chiefly after reading the story? The journeys, the adventures, the magical feats of sorcerers good and bad, but most of all, perhaps, the country which Mr Toklien has invented, and the exactitude with which he has charted it. There is nothing else I can remember that is like that country; it is as strange as the names of its different provinces and landmarks: Mordor, Moria, Erebur, Mirkwood, Minas Tirith, Isengard, Rohan, Lórien. Mr Tolkien has provided maps showing the hills, rivers, woods, castles and walled towns where the different races live: men, hobbits, elves, dwarfs, orcs, and ents, the last a race of trees walking and speaking.

The action has all the fascination of a game between good and evil, and I fancy that it will be played yet in many a playroom; one the size of a city square would be best. We can see Mr Tolkien picking up the pieces which are his heroes in a hard game against himself, and thinking some other astonishing move. His skill is unfailing, for he knows how the game will end.

The feeling that the story is a long and intricate game, and derives its fascination from that, is my chief feeling after reading it. For the astonishing thing is that all the characters, except a few old men who are apt to be wizards, are boys masquerading as adult heroes. The hobbits, or halflings, are ordinary boys; the fully human heroes have reached the fifth form; but hardly one of them knows anything about women, except by hearsay. Even the elves and the dwarfs and the ents are boys, irretrievably, and will never come to puberty. The orcs, who are on the opposite side, are very bad boys indeed, and the Gollum, the most real character in the story, is a most detestable boy. The good boys, having fought a deadly battle, emerge at the end of it well, triumphant and happy, as boys would naturally expect to do. There are only one or two minor casualties.

Mrs Naomi Mitchison is quoted on the dust-cover as saying that one takes the story seriously; 'as seriously as Malory'. This is just what one does not do. The heroes of the Round Table did not end happily. They were as brave as the heroes of the Ring, but they knew temptation, were sometimes unfaithful to their vows, or torn between the opposing claims of love and duty. Boys moving in a boy's world, with a boy's idea of heroism, romance, women, good and evil, are not fully human, and cannot become Lancelots and Tristrams.

The story, then, is not at all like Malory, but it does have a resemblance to Rider Haggard. It is far beyond him in invention; indeed it is far beyond any other story in that class—if that is its class—that I have come across; and that is what makes it remarkable. One must admire a power of invention so inexhaustible as this, and at the same time so controlled. The ring as the symbol of unlimited power, and so of absolute evil, one need not take seriously; but as a magic ring it is very effective, and the focus of the action. And the various races which take part in the war are fascinating creations, though the individuals, no matter what race they may belong to, are stock characters. The style is that of a boy's adventure story, and it suits the action. But of its kind—and it is a respectable kind—this book can only be called brilliant.

KATHLEEN RAINE *Collected Poems*

Observer, 11 March 1956, 7

This volume includes all the poems that Miss Raine wishes to keep. They are concentrated on a single ultimate vision of things. She has discarded, as she explains in her introduction, all poems which do not contribute to that effect. In the list of what she excludes are 'almost all that include any trace of ecclesiastical symbolism', 'love poems of a personal nature', and 'poems descriptive of place and time as such', these mostly from the war years.

'The ever-recurring forms of nature,' she goes on, 'mirror eternal reality; the never-recurring productions of history reflect only fallen man, and are therefore not suitable to become a symbolic vocabulary for the kind of poetry I have attempted to write.'

These few phrases tell us more about Miss Raine's poetry than any critic could, and help to explain why it is like nothing else that is being written today, why it is so much itself, and has so few marks of its time. The imagination and the form are completely their own.

Fallen man has been the great theme of poetry ever since Homer 'and his unchristened heart'. The fallen world is the world where, however uneasily, we are at home with our neighbours, in human time. Miss Raine's is a vaster world; her span of time is all time, from the year one, when man was not, to its end yet to come: it is the time of 'the ever-recurring forms of nature' that 'mirror eternal reality', and among them man, but in a different position in a pattern where all has its place. To Miss Raine the elements, air, water, and fire, are real and seen in their pure working. 'Stone and Flower' was the title of her first book of poems, and 'The Year One' the title of her last. For her natural things have an inviolate life of their own, yet at the same time are moments in the ever-recurring cycle. Time in its perpetual recurrence leaves within our reach the beginning of things:

> Reaching down arm-deep into bright water
> I gathered on white sand under waves
> Shells, drifted up on beaches where I alone
> Inhabit a finite world of years and days.
> I reached my arm down a myriad years
> To gather treasure from the yester-millenial sea-floor,
> Held in my fingers forms shaped on the day of creation. . . .
> They sleep on the ocean floor like humming-tops
> Whose music is the mother-of-pearl octave of the rainbow,
> Harmonious shells that whisper for ever in our ears,
> 'The world that you inhabit has not yet been created.'

Among these ever-recurring forms man alone inhabits 'the finite world of years and days'; beyond him yet in a sense close to him lies the vast cycle of time where all is perpetually transformed and remade. That transmutation, the reality of every momentary form it creates or discards and leaves behind; human life implicated with all that is and has been, stone and flower and plant and the elements of which they are made—this is Miss Raine's theme. Among modern poets it is hers and hers alone; it is not an easy one, and she has had to find many ways of expressing it, perhaps best of all in the wonderful riddling 'spells' in 'The Year One', which resemble those old Celtic spells that mean more than they say and seem to penetrate into the ever-changing meaning of things.

Her poetry is outside all the modern categories; it is pure as from a well-spring, and has a fresh natural beauty undecorated and undefaced by influence. We are fortunate that we should have it, and this book should be read again and again.

GEORGE BARKER Collected Poems and *The True Confessions of George Barker*

New Statesman, 31 August 1957, 252

The central theme of Mr Barker's poetry was stated early; what he has written since merely serves to make it clearer. The development was not continuous; one section of this book is filled with repetitions, as if the imagery had come to a standstill. It is a curious imagery; it is as if an internal vision were trying to break outwards and become visible; the images do not make us see; sometimes we can only guess what they stand for. They are bright and opaque at the same time. This is true of a remarkable poem, 'Calamiterror', which appeared in 1937, and the distance Mr Barker has left it behind can be measured by turning to 'Goodman Jacksin and the Angel' in *A Vision of Gods and Beasts* which came out in 1954. The two poems deal with the same theme. This is from 'Calamiterror'.

> Between the ribs of the violent man
> Beats the red centre of the world of death.
> The ribs like branches hanging meat like leaves
> Makes the green tree red. Coiled in the ribs
> The embryos of life and death lie, one by one
> Ravaging a surgeon's groove of agony,
> Break from the belly, stand on the bloody thigh,
> Cockcrowing like man and babe and bird.

And this is from 'Goodman Jacksin and the Angel':

And out of the horn rumpled sheet
Where nightlong in their forking lock
The hissing kissers slew and mock
That image from which they were cast—
Out of that fouled and rocking nest
In which those justly outcast meet
And mount like stray dogs in the street,—
Out, out the innocent image steps.

The romantic imagery is gone, and the conflict between spirit and flesh, innocence and the horror out of which it comes—for that is horror as Mr Barker sees it—is laid bare. The theme is stripped clean, and the poetry achieves energy and bitterness.

What are we to think of the theme? That Mr Barker is a modern Manichee to whom the world is evil and the spirit a prisoner struggling to get free? There is certainly less 'calamiterror' in the later poem, simply because the issue has become clear. There is still terror when Mr Barker contemplates the way in which we came into the world and the way in which we shall leave it, and the loss of innocence long before that can happen. He has an extreme horror of the flesh, and at the same time the horror attracts him. It is a feeling which others have known, but it has rarely been described with such a combination of truth and despair. It admits of no reconciliation with life, one might think, yet there are moments of reconciliation in the poems, occasional recognitions of a blood-boltered glory. 'Calamiterror' evokes a sort of visceral and obstetric mythology, a Plutonian drama where the heart and the intestines and the generative organs are the actors, and life and death are the chorus. 'Goodman Jacksin and the Angel', on the other hand, is a vision of life; we can recognise it as such; and it has enough power to prevent us from questioning its validity. It reaches far, at any rate, beyond the life that the ordinary Goodman Jacksin knows. The fact that the poem is a dialogue gives it an objectivity which the earlier poems lacked, and helps to persuade us that the world it discusses is the actual world. No vision is complete, and this one does cast light on human experience from some infernal beam.

The True Confession of George Barker was omitted from the collected poems at the publishers' request. It seems a pity. The theme is the same as that of the two poems I have mentioned, and it is stated in a succession of moods, which gives it variety. Technically it is brilliant in fits and starts, fantastic and witty and shocking and flippant in turn; it is one of Mr Barker's best poems. One is as sorry for its omission as for the inclusion of a great number of other poems (no poet can be so good and so extravagantly bad as Mr Barker). Some of these poems show his poetry at its worst: the empty word-weaving the ineffectual images:

Then at my face the shower of rain
Stardusts me with a handful of its brilliants,
Flecking my lashes like worlds.

Such things help to conceal the real virtues of this poetry.

Yet its interest does not lie in its technical skill, but in something more fundamental to poetry, its imaginative power. In that Mr Barker seems to me superior to any other poet of his generation.

II

AMERICAN

WILLIAM FAULKNER and SOMERSET MAUGHAM
These Thirteen; Ah King

Listener X, 4 October 1933, 519

The first two volumes are collections of short stories, most of them well over the magazine length. One or two are compressed novels. Mr Faulkner's 'A Rose for Emily' tells the story of a woman's life in sixteen pages, and tells it dramatically; and two of Mr Somerset Maugham's stories, 'The Book Bag' and 'The Back of Beyond', could easily have been expanded into full-length novels. All three gain immensely in one way by this brevity, for they give us an unencumbered bird's-eye view of human lives which is beyond the power of the long novel, with its inevitable qualifications and its accumulation of detail. We have the pleasure—a very intense one—of seeing all the stages in the development of the action almost simultaneously, or at least of holding them without effort in our minds. Stories of this kind are not a variant of the novel, part of whose point consists in the complication; nor are they short stories in the sense defined by universal practice. One feels after reading them that it is a pity they are not generally accepted as constituting a class by themselves and more deliberately cultivated than they are now.

Mr Faulkner has written more astonishing and inimitable things than these thirteen stories, but probably nothing that shows more clearly the greatness and variety of his powers. There are always passages in his novels where we see him wrestling without disguise with his theme, hitting it in the wind and battering it on the head, and though the spectacle is exciting it is confusing too, and the final effect is one of extraordinarily vital but oppressive prolixity. These stories are written with extreme economy, not the economy which consists in accepting words as counters and using the fewest possible number of them, but the higher poetic economy of making them do things beyond their usual capacity. Mr Faulkner sometimes allows himself a spate of adjectives which Mr Somerset Maugham with his devotion to short and simple statement would never pass, as for example: 'They waited, patient, grave, decorous, implacable; clansmen and guest and kin.' But on the other hand he can express by a sort of poetic shorthand things that are completely beyond the reach of language as the ordinary prose writer uses it. He forces words into a sort of organic identity with the things to which they pertain and does not accept them as mere designations of objects; and this is not mere verbal play, but comes from a vision of the world which is unusually exact and absolutely his own, and so has to be communicated in his own fashion.

The stories in *These Thirteen* fall into three groups. There are four about the War, six dealing with life in the Southern States and three with life in post-War Europe. The third group is the least satisfactory, though it contains one fine *tour de force*, 'Mistral'. Of the War stories 'Victory' is the only weak one, and it is weak quite apart from its vigorously drawn but incredible stock Scotsman and its grotesque Scots dialect: 'A says tae me, a says: "Fritz has a new gun that will carry to Par-ris", a says, and A says tae him: "'Tis nawthing: A hae one that will hit our Cor-rps Headquar-rters." ' But the three others, 'Ad Astra', 'All the Dead Pilots' and 'Crevasse' are superb. The man who tells the story in 'Ad Astra' says:

> After twelve years I think of us as bugs in the surface of the water, isolant and aimless and unflagging. Not on the surface; in it, within that line of demarcation not air and not water, sometimes submerged, sometimes not. You have watched an unbreaking groundswell in a cove, the water shallow, the cove quiet, a little sinister with saturate familiarity, while beyond the darkling horizon the dying storm has raged on. That was the water, we the flotsam. Even after twelve years it is no clearer than that. It had no beginning and no ending.

That is the feeling that permeates these War stories; a feeling packed with pity and horror, and stretching to a horizon that has 'no beginning and no ending'.

This stretching out to vast horizons is the distinguishing quality of all the stories in the book. Though technically brilliant and precise they have none of the 'neatness' which is generally considered essential in a good short story. Many of them do not end in the formal sense at all, but merely stage the setting for some inevitable event which has still to come. In 'That Evening Sun' Nancy, the negro woman who lives in fear of being killed by the husband she has betrayed, inveigles the children of the white people she works for to go with her to her hut when her day's work is done, promising them great amusement. The children go, and see her safely down the dark road and past the ditch where she imagines her husband is lying in wait. When she gets to her hut she desperately tries to interest them in one thing after another; the door is barred; her husband is somewhere outside in the darkness. At last, late in the night, the children's father comes to take them away. Nancy begs him to let them stay; he refuses, but tries to persuade her to go to one of her relatives for safety. But by now she is numb with fear and does not even shut the door when they leave her. 'We went up out of the ditch. We could still see Nancy's house and the open door, but we couldn't see Nancy now, sitting before the fire with the door open.' It is like a vision of infinite danger, and Mr Faulkner's imagination opens again and again like this on vast things. This story, with its terror and its children's grave irrelevant chatter, is not only technically brilliant but inspired from start to finish. The dialogue is as good as Mr Hemingway's, which is to say that it is very good; the imagination of greater sensitiveness and range; the potential power more impressive than that of any other writer of Mr Faulkner's generation. This book should not be missed by anyone who wishes to know contemporary literature.

Mr Somerset Maugham is one of the most skilful novelists writing today. He is both extremely honest and extremely efficient, and he describes life as he sees it and not as he would like to see it. What he does see he sees very clearly and in perfect proportion; but coming to him from Mr Faulkner one cannot help feeling that he sees with only one eye and that the clarity of his view of human life has been reached by leaving out an astonishing number of things. The best stories in *Ah King* are those dealing with practical moral problems, such as 'The Door of Opportunity' in which a clever young government servant in Malay loses his post and his wife's affection by a simple act of physical cowardice which he refuses to acknowledge to himself. It is an extremely skilful and moving piece of work, and the theme is stated with scrupulous justice. The tragi-comic story of Neil MacAdam, a puritanical young Scotsman who leaves his chief's wife to die in the jungle rather than betray his chief with her, is almost as good, and a triumph of ironical statement. It gives us the pleasure of seeing a situation isolated and dealt with in a skilful, almost surgical, way, and though that is less intense than the pleasure Mr Faulkner's stories give us, it is sufficiently rare and quite genuine. The rest of the stories in the book are not up to this level, however, and have actually something of a magazine flavour. A government servant suddenly tells a past love affair without warning to a stranger; it is a peculiarly painful one, and it is spoilt by the chatty after-dinner atmosphere which is its improbable setting. Even Mr Somerset Maugham's style has not quite escaped. 'There was refinement in his face and a spirituality that was oddly moving.' 'A shiver of dismay pierced those hearty, jovial, careless men, and each for a moment remembered that he too was mortal.' The two stories I have mentioned, however, are masterly, and Mr Somerset Maugham's admirers will find the book worth reading for them alone.

CONRAD AIKEN Great Circle

Listener, 18 October 1933, 604

Great Circle is a remarkable novel and a notable addition to a definite class which includes most of the best of contemporary fiction. In other words it is technically inventive and skilful, penetrates far more exhaustively into experience than the traditional novel as it is written today, but at the same time fails to achieve an imaginative resolution of the action, and substitutes for that a moral one. Novels of this kind are generally concerned with the development of a single character; *Sons and Lovers* and *A Portrait of the Artist as a Young Man* are probably the best examples (for the class is a highly respectable one); and all, it seems, that a novel of development can achieve in the way of a resolution is to leave the hero at the end of experiencing a more than usually vivid illumination or coming to a more than usually firm resolution. Paul in *Sons and Lovers* marches towards the city lights with clenched fists, resolved, it is hard to say on what. Stephen in *A Portrait of the Artist as a Young Man* ends by proclaiming his artistic creed and his decision to be an artist. He might have done so at several other points in the last third of the book, and Paul might have clenched his fists as many times without our attaching any special significance to it; but this last resolution, this last clench, seeing that it comes at the very end, must be, we are asked to assume, of a completely different kind. This is the act of faith that the novel of development demands from us. The novelist asks us to forget that life will go on again afterwards, that there are millions of people who have clenched their fists and made resolutions which did not hold, and thousands who have decided to be artists and proclaimed their artistic creeds (which are generally somewhat modified in a few years). In short, after describing with incorruptible honesty a given stretch of experience, the novelist flings himself blindly at a hope or a vague wish-fulfilment, at something which is quite different in nature from life as he has just been recording it. So the novel of development ends almost invariably, after a strict fidelity to truth, on the plane of moral hope. The problem of how to find a satisfactory end to it at all is, indeed, an extremely difficult one; for though this sentimental resolution is obviously none, what conclusion can be set to the story of an individual development except death, which is the only absolute terminus of development? Franz Kafka with his infallible justice in sizing up a situation saw the difficulty clearly and dealt with it in the shortest way. *The Castle*, which is the story of the hero's quest for salvation, for something representing a final illumination, he did not finish at all; but the end he had sketched out for it was almost equally edifying. The hero is told on his deathbed that henceforth he may live assured of his victory, though he has no inherent right to it and it has been granted him simply in consideration of certain auxiliary considerations. Such a solution of the problem makes all others look romantic. And when the hero of *Great Circle* soliloquises inwardly in the last paragraph: 'Life was good—life was going to be good. Unexplored, unfathomable, marvellous and terrible. Filthy, and incalculable. Cruel, and inexhaustible. Like this unceasing swarm of bright rain-drips, like the waves beating on the beach at the Gurnett, innumerable as the atoms in the brain', one seems to be listening to the last cries of countless novelists shouting to keep their hearts up in the darkness that descends so inevitably when one is finishing a novel that is not really finished.

Great Circle belongs to this class, but it is a very remarkable specimen of its kind. Andrew Cather receives a letter hinting that his wife is unfaithful to him. He hurries home when she is not expecting him and finds her with her lover, who is one of his oldest friends. There is a violent scene and Andrew leaves the house and his wife in a rage. That is the statement of the theme. The second section consists of memories of Andrew's boyhood at the seaside, memories tinged with suspicion of his mother, who was living apart from her husband at the time and secretly carrying on a love affair with another man: the couple are finally drowned in a storm and Andrew discovers their bodies. This section, one fancies, is intended as a variation on the original theme and also to suggest the stage of regression: Andrew's mind, unable to endure present misery, flies to his childhood for help. The third section, an astonishing *tour de force*, contains nothing but a long dialogue between Andrew and a friend who is a psychoanalyst. Here all that would technically be called the unconscious content of the situation is poured out in a stream of confessions, apparently fortuitous and sometimes even disingenuous, yet moving towards a solution which always seems to be becoming clearer. After this emotional orgy Andrew (who has been drinking all the time) falls into an uneasy nightmare which gradually fades into calm and happy dreams of his childhood, and from these he at last wakens in his right mind, with all the passion and confusion cleared away. He decides to have a talk with his wife, and before he returns to live with her finally decides to drive down to the seaside resort where he had passed his boyhood. It is during this drive that the illumination comes to him, the chief heads of which are quoted above.

It would be hard to overpraise the sincerity, the psychological skill and technical brilliance of this novel. The dialogue section in particular is an amazing feat of sustained invention and various eloquence. But in spite of all its virtues the book only proves again that from no investigation of the contents of the subconscious, however profound or exhaustive, can a catharsis be extracted. After the furious outpouring of the psychoanalytic section, the dreams and the quiet awakening do become plausible, and for the author to have achieved that was a feat of remarkable finesse. But what he intends to stand for the real catharsis—'Life was good', etc.—is not deducible from the analysis at all, nor is anything more than the alleviation of a very painful but temporary state. Mr Aiken does cast light into the abysses of human passion, however, and deals until very near the end with real and immediate things, touching one on the raw repeatedly. Such a thing happens very seldom in a novel, and so *Great Cirle* is worth very serious perusal. It is, besides, both painfully and pleasurably exciting to read.

JOHN O'HARA, WILLIAM FAULKNER and WALTER BRIERLEY
Appointment in Samarra; Pylon; Means Test Men

Listener XIII, 24 April 1935, 720

If a history of depression in fiction is ever written the contemporary American novel will occupy a high place in it. Depression in American literature is unlike anything we knew after the war; it is both far more simple and far more thorough. One would consequently need to have an independent acquaintance with the United States to judge the first two novels in this list, for it is impossible to believe that they give a true representation of American life. This kind of novel is not a mere result of the present economic depression, for Mr Hemingway set the standard for it some considerable time ago. He described life disintegrating in a vacuum under the onset of sex, alcohol and lawlessness. There was a background to this process, but it was curiously cardboardlike, so that it could be easily changed to suit any scene in the modern world, and with a few touches represent Paris, or Italy, or the United States. In front of it Mr Hemingway arranged a group of Americans and set them to play out their simple static drama. Mr Hemingway is a writer of immense talent; Mr O'Hara, who is a disciple of his, is at least an extremely competent writer; Mr Faulkner has greater gifts than either, and the background to his picture of life, if sometimes grotesque, is far more solid. But the world they all three describe cannot be taken seriously. They have really created a fascinating legend of sex and alcohol. A sociologist might put down this legend to Prohibition; it could be put down with much more plausibility to the overwhelming conviction of the emptiness of American life which so many American writers seem to have. In this emptiness sex and alcohol become unequivocally real; things which can always be relied on. Nevertheless there must be other realities in American life, and the absence of all mention of them in a book such as Mr O'Hara's makes one feel that the effect is unjustifiably partial and inadequate.

Appointment in Samarra shows very clearly what a curious pattern life assumes when these two entities are given a free and exclusive run. Mr O'Hara describes the reactions for a few days of a small industrial town. The chief figure in the story is Julian English, a leading member of the rich and fashionable set in Gibbsville. He is an amiable and likeable young man, and this is how he spends his Christmas week. He begins it by flinging a highball in the face of a man he does not like. As he is in debt to this man, he calls upon him next day to apologise, but is turned away. He goes next evening to a party, having given a promise to his wife that he would not get drunk. They have a tiff at the party, he does get drunk, and afterwards takes his wife to a speak-easy where he dances with the mistress of the local gunman and afterwards spends some time with her in his car. At the club next day a cousin of his wife picks a quarrel with him, and Julian knocks him down, along with two other members of the club. Thereupon he goes for a drive to compose his nerves, and meeting his wife on his way back has a quarrel with her and is told that she never wants to see him again. He goes home, gets drunk once more, and tries half-heartedly to seduce a woman reporter who strolls in. Then, having put on a few gramophone records, he fortifies himself with a last bottle of whisky and commits suicide. The automatic operation of sex and alcohol on a quite ordinary young man could not be better described. The other characters are, like Julian, average sensual men and women responding as automatically but more fortunately to the same stimuli. They are described for the most part without respect and without censure, as if they were curious animals. In performing this feat Mr O'Hara shows the utmost honesty and impartiality, but as these virtues are exercised for an inadequate purpose, they sometimes let him down. For instance, take Al Grecco's musings on his master Ed Charney, the local racketeer: Helene is Ed's mistress and Annie is his wife.

> Al knew Helene really cared for Ed. And she was good for him. You could tell when Ed and Helene were getting along. Ed was easier to get along with then. Tonight, or this after', when Ed showed up at the Apollo, he probably would be in a bad humour. That was the way Annie affected him. Whereas if he had spent the day with Helene he would have been in a good humour. But Al knew that Ed wouldn't think of spending Christmas with Helene. Ed was a family man, first and last, and that was one day in the year he would spend with the kid, at home.

That is a fairly thoroughgoing statement of Mr O'Hara's attitude to life in general, and it issues in sentimentality or unconscious humour, it is hard to say which. In the more dramatic scenes it comes out undisguisedly as sentimentality. Julian makes an abortive attempt to shoot himself:

> He remembered a bottle of whisky he had in the desk, and he had a long-lasting drink of one whisky glass of it. 'Oh, I couldn't', he said, and he put his arms on the desk and his head on his arms, and he wept. 'You poor guy', he said, 'I feel so sorry for you.'

The long-lasting drink of whisky has much the same sentimental significance to Julian as the locket (generally containing a strand of his mother's hair) used to have to the traditional waster. This is what becomes of the hard-boiled convention of fiction in its decadence. But

Mr O'Hara's sentimentality emerges only when he has to acknowledge that his characters are human beings; and his technique, which is very efficient, generally absolves him from that necessity. The book has been a best-seller in America.

Pylon deals with the same two subjects, with danger and speed thrown in. The main characters are three men, a woman and a young boy, who earn a precarious living by winning prizes at flying contests with a worn and tattered aeroplane. A reporter, fascinated by this group and by the woman in particular, joins up with them. The woman is shared between two of the men, and the whole group live a restless and uneasy and confused life which Mr Faulkner seems to have tried to reproduce by the restlessness and confusion of his style. The result is one of the worst books he has written, filled with banal journalistic circumlocutions, in which an aeroplane becomes 'a machine expensive, complex, delicate and intrinsically useless, created for some obscure psychic need of the species if not the race, from the virgin resources of a continent, to be the individual muscles, bones and flesh of a new and legless kind.' Mr Faulkner's temptation to be portentous comes out very strongly in such passages, and also in the spasmodic energy with which he tries to inflate his characters, making them move in a series of convulsive jerks. In the course of these Shumann the pilot loses his life, and his death is a fine piece of sensationalism. The nameless reporter is clearly intended to play a significant part in the story, but he is one of the least credible characters that Mr Faulkner has ever created. What the author conveys by this dislocated story it is difficult to say, and the wordiness of the style tempts one to believe that he does not know very clearly himself.

Means-Test Man is written with far less than Mr O'Hara's literary skill, but it is a first novel of considerable promise as well as a social document of great importance. Mr Brierley, who is himself an unemployed miner, describes honestly and with sensitiveness of feeling a week in the life of an unemployed miner, his wife and his son of seven. He shows how the humiliation of being useless and hopeless eats into the hearts of these people (and of several millions of people like them). Because he does not wallow in dejection like Mr O'Hara and Mr Faulkner, but sets down the poor, petty details of an unemployed family's life with reluctance, as one who feels his sense of decency violated by doing so, his book makes infinitely sadder reading than theirs. The life he describes consists simply of making 25*s*. 3*d*. a week feed, clothe and house three people during a long featureless interregnum; and so the great moments of the story deal with buying odds and ends of food in the shops after the working population have had their pick, and the making of these odds and ends go as far as they can go. The main incident is a visit from the Means Test Investigator, and the account of its effect on the household makes almost unbearable reading. Mr Brierley is not a propagandist; he merely describes. His book will not get so much attention as the other two. Nevertheless it makes their particular brand of dejection look idle; it is the work of a sensitive writer; and it should be read by everybody, if only for the problem of which it treats.

DJUNA BARNES Night Wood

Listener XVI, 28 October 1936, 832

Night Wood is a book which cannot be treated adequately in a review column such as this. It seems to me to be an undeniable work of genius, and the genius is not intermittent, but, with very few lapses, constant throughout, and at the same time of unusual intensity. The book does not belong to any easily definable class; it is not a novel, except in form; and it shows no contemporary influence except, occasionally, that of Mr Joyce. What it reminds one most of is those disquisitions on human life which were more common in the seventeenth century than they are now, and which were always enlivened by imaginative illustrations: in this book the disquisition completely disappears into those imaginative illustrations which form a symbolical picture of the human state as Miss Barnes sees it. If the reader searches for ordinary verisimilitude in this picture he will not find it; the figures in it are not imaginary characters but creatures of Miss Barnes' imagination; they are not drawn from life but created out of her vision of life. They must be judged accordingly. The main theme which they illustrate is given best by a sentence spoken by one of them: 'No man needs curing of his individual sickness, his universal malady is what he should look to.'

Miss Barnes' subject, then, is the universal malady. Her most remarkable quality is a combination of exactitude and strangeness of imagination directed on the various forms of human misery and bringing with it as almost a natural corollary a magnificent eloquence. Take this, as an exact rendering of the extreme of misery:

> Or walks the floor, holding her hands; or lies upon the floor, face down, with that terrible longing of the body that would, in misery, be flat with the floor; lost lower than burial, utterly blotted out and erased so that no stain of her could ache upon the wood, or snatched back to nothing without aim—going backward through the target, taking with her the spot where she made one.

Or this description of a prostitutes' parade on London Bridge:

> They used to walk along slowly, all ruffles and rags, with big terror hats on them, a pin stuck over the eye and slap up through the crown, half

> their shadows on the ground and the other half crawling along the wall beside them; ladies of the *haute* sewer taking their last stroll, sauntering on their last Rotten Row, going slowly along in the dark, holding up their battered flounces, or standing still, silent and as indifferent as the dead, as if they were thinking of better days, or waiting for something that they had been promised when they were little girls; their poor damned dresses hiked up and falling away over the rump, all gathers and braid, like a Crusader's mount, with all the trappings gone sideways with misery.

I should like to quote a dozen passages to illustrate the variety and strangeness and the extraordinary verbal beauty of this book. The story itself is simple and comprehensible enough, and is concerned chiefly with the relations between two women. The eccentric Irish doctor who is the chorus to the story becomes definitely false, considered on any plane of imagination, and not wholly through his astonishing eloquence. Some of the minor characters, on the other hand, are drawn with brilliant wit and force: particularly Jenny Petherbridge, the feeble and ferocious American widow: 'No one could intrude upon her, because there was no place for intrusion. . . . When she fell in love it was with a perfect fury of accumulated dishonesty; she became instantly a dealer in second-hand and therefore incalculable emotions.' Baron Volkbein is also a wittily drawn figure, halfway between a fancy and a portrait, like a dancer caught on tip-toe. But I can only suggest, I cannot give any adequate idea of the quality of this extraordinary book, or of its brilliance and diversity of imagination.

ERNEST HEMINGWAY, MAXIM GORKI and RENÉ BÉHAINE
The Fifth Column and the First Forty-Nine Stories; A Book of Short Stories; The Conquest of Life

Listener XXII, 6 July 1939, 45

The more one reads Mr Hemingway in bulk the more aware one becomes of the central experience with which his imagination is concerned. That experience is a straight left to the point, a bullet in the intestines, a heavy toss in the ring: a facer from Life, or the knowledge that it is coming. All his characters suffer from that aching bruise in the jaw, which is both immediate experience and dulled experience; so that while they know it with mathematical exactitude in their nerves they cannot express it in words, or at most in what Yeats called 'dull, numb words': it is difficult to talk clearly with a sore jaw. Besides, they have very little to tell, because they do not know how that blow arrived: it was a painful surprise. But they do know that Life will hit them again, and exactly on the same spot, and with more and more ease and frequency as they grow older; and this is their and Mr Hemingway's philosophy. *The Fifth Column and the First Forty-Nine Stories* contains a great deal of his work, most of it old, some of it new, and the aching jaw aches fairly consistently throughout it. What emerges is a world where tough healthy men take what is coming to them, getting more and more battered as they advance towards the last facer, when they will be counted out. There is a philosophy of life in this vision of tough men being used toughly, a sort of rough and tumble Calvinism, reminding one partly of Merimée and partly of the music-hall. The best part of Mr Hemingway's art is in the tradition of the music-hall, which is popular and cynical (or was at one time), and as much concerned with low tragedy as with low comedy. There is the same reduction of things to genuine, not merely sentimental, popular terms, as in 'The Killers':

> 'What are you going to kill Ole Andreson for? What did he ever do to you?'
>
> 'He never had a chance to do anything to us. He never even seen us.'
>
> 'And he's only going to see us once', Al said from the kitchen.
>
> 'What are you going to kill him for, then?' George asked.
>
> 'We're killing him for a friend. Just to oblige a friend, bright boy.'
>
> 'Shut up,' said Al from the kitchen. 'You talk too goddam much.'
>
> 'Well, I got to keep bright boy amused. Don't I, bright boy?'
>
> 'You talk too damn much', Al said. 'The nigger and my bright boy are amused by themselves. I got them tied up like a couple of girl friends in the convent.'
>
> 'I suppose you were in a convent.'
>
> 'You never know.'

It is a kind of horrible patter, carried off with ruthless brilliance: murder presented in popular terms which are quite beyond the reach of any merely popular writer. It is up-to-date folk literature, the modern equivalent of the ballad and the broadsheet: a genuine form of art.

Along with the short stories the book contains 'The Fifth Column', a play about the Spanish War. Though Mr Hemingway is an expert writer of dialogue, the play is disappointing, partly perhaps because it vaguely outlines a philosophy of life which is not the philosophy of the tough guy taking it, and partly because it is transparently sophisticated, with the same sophistication which makes a story like 'A clean, well-lighted Place' so painful to read. It is an ordinary, well-meaning, thoughtful play, containing a number of exciting and horrible situations, none of them quite simple enough, or else too simple, and the pathos so unobtrusive that it is as difficult to ignore it as a persistently silent member of a party. Some of the stories are magnificently told, 'Fifty Grand', 'The Undefeated', 'The Light of the World', each of them a feat of reduction and compression: life stripped down to action and sensation, and narrative stripped down to statement. No one has done this better than Mr Hemingway.

A Book of Short Stories, by Maxim Gorki, edited by Avrahm Yarmolinsky and Baroness Moura Budberg reads like the work of an amateur after Mr Hemingway. The description is often weakly poetic:

> The tottering roof added still more to its pitiable aspect. It seemed as if the whole building bowed towards the ground, meekly awaiting the last stroke of that fate which would transform it into a shapeless mass of rotting remains.

The reflections are trite and dated:

> In our present state of culture the hunger of the soul can be satisfied more readily than that of the body.

Nevertheless, in spite of the looseness of the presentation and the lack of any constructive principle, these stories are more genuinely interesting than Mr Hemingway's, simply because they describe a greater variety of experience and describe it more objectively. They are coloured with pity as pity was understood at the beginning of this century: a mixture of humanitarianism and idealism which it is impossible to recreate now. But they have another kind of pity which is at the root of tragic imagination. When it gets involved with Gorki's descriptions of nature it is strained and false, as at the end of 'Creatures that once were Men':

> In the gray, stern clouds, which entirely concealed the sky, there was something tense and merciless, as if they had gathered together in order to pour out flat streams of rain, firmly set on washing all the filth from this unfortunate, suffering and sorrowful earth.

Gorki's approach to nature was aesthetic. But when his imaginative pity is turned on human beings it merely makes him see them more completely and objectively. 'Creatures that once were Men' (a title that might stand for almost any of these stories), describes a dozen or so down-and-outs living in a filthy doss-house. Gorki does not conceal their degradation, yet he penetrates, almost prosaically, to something good in them; he sees in them what they once were. In another writer the sudden discovery of genuine good in weak or vicious characters might seem a mere trick, due to a love of paradox; but in Gorki it comes from a desire to see and understand as fully as possible. In this particular story the portraiture is really striking, and the tragedy of the end, the tragedy of yet one more disappointment, almost justifies the passage about the clouds. Gorki's pity is never solemn; it is lively and filled with humour; sometimes it produces an effect of wit. He is not a great writer; he is not the equal of Chekhov; he probably did nothing much more than describe things that happened to him in his hard and varied life. But he described them with imagination and with a single-minded truthfulness all the more effective because it dispensed with effects. In his foreword Mr Aldous Huxley says that Gorki relied 'at least as much upon verbal texture as upon composition'. The verbal texture is lost in a translation, but it would be hard, nevertheless, to read this book without being impressed.

M René Béhaine's *The Survivors,* the first volume of a long work entitled *History of a Society*, appeared some time ago. *The Conquest of Life*, excellently translated by Edward Crankshaw, is a later volume of the same work. It describes the fluctuations of a love affair between Michel Varambaud and Catherine de Laignes, along with a phase of the Dreyfus trial. It is the work of a scrupulous artist, a man of original mind and sensitive imagination, who may easily be what the late Ford Madox Ford called him: 'the most remarkable living novelist'. Compared both with Mr Hemingway and Gorki, what strikes one in M Béhaine's story is the greater fineness of perception, the greater comprehensiveness of grasp, and a perpetual act of discrimination which seems to begin where they leave off. The analysis of the relations between Michel and Catherine is extremely fine, yet not protracted, and never destroys the balance of the story as a whole. The magnificent thirteenth chapter, in which Michel reads to his friend Lavarenne extracts from the novel which he is writing about his own love affair, the love affair described in the book itself, is a triumphant proof of M Béhaine's mastery of his art and his subject. The main impression which the book gives, apart from its beauty, the beauty of perfectly proportioned parts, is an impression of integrity: one feels that every stroke, every comment is pondered and given its true weight. Yet the final effect is one of lightness and ease. It is to be hoped that the rest of this extraordinary work will be translated.

KAY BOYLE The Crazy Hunter

Listener XXIII, 21 March 1940, 597

Miss Boyle's latest book contains three short novels, and the first two contain probably the best work she has yet given us. They show human life against a background of animal life, the permanent organic background without which there could be no human life at all, though our habituation to urban existence hides the fact more and more completely from us. The background of the first story is a stable and of the second a swannery, and the strange thing is that by their mere unthinking existence they seem to give meaning to all the actions of the human characters. In the third story, on the other hand, whose background is the modern world as people who live in big cities know it, nothing seems to have much meaning, not even the arrest of a bedevilled player in a jazz band for a murder he never committed. The background suits the incident perfectly, and the incident the background, expressing the perfect dissociation of a society which eats beef without knowing anything about oxen or slaughterhouses, and bets on races without having seen a horse. The action is inhuman because there is nothing implied in it but human beings and human institutions, and the institutions, busily grinding on according to their own laws, pay no regard to the human beings. The jazz player might state his predicament something like this: I did not commit the murder; I see that I shall hang for it. And against that provisional cosmopolitan background, there does not seem to be any contradiction, in the statement. The result is a hard-boiled story which reiterates, as Mr Hemingway has done so often, that anything can happen and that it is a waste of time to be surprised. The real mark of the hard-boiled writer is his refusal to be surprised.

Miss Boyle can turn out this kind of story as well as anyone, the kind of story which implies that while life in general does not matter, some small thing here and there, such as a man's being hanged for a murder he never committed, does matter a little. But it is astonishing to see how her powers expand as soon as she describes life against a permanent background, even if it is only a background of horses or swans. Suddenly everything has a meaning, even an embarrassment of meanings, life is seen in relation. The title story is far the best of the three. A young girl in an English country house takes a fancy to a hunter her father has bought. The hunter is regarded from the start as an outsider, for he has no pedigree. There rises an obscure conflict of will over the horse between the girl and her mother, who is a conventional, efficient woman. One day the horse suddenly goes blind. The question now arises whether he should be destroyed—to the mother it is not a question at all, but a foregone conclusion. The daughter secretly takes out the horse every night, teaches him to carry her on his back in the darkness, and at last gets him to the point where he can take jumps. The problem whether the horse is to be destroyed is left unsolved at the end; the mother makes one attempt while the daughter is away, but is frustrated. It is a profound moral discrimination which makes this story so remarkable; the problem is not a simple one to be solved by common sense, but involves the exercise of the full moral sensibility, and throws light on human conduct. Miss Boyle's main fault is still an excessive emphasis, which produces a cataract of violent adjectives:

> 'Hush, now stop, now listen to me,' she said, and at the sound of her voice the horse's head veered awkwardly, but meek, despairing, towards her, the ears quivering antennae-vulnerable, the raised face defeated, directionless, blind, mute.

But there is in the evocation of the relation between the girl and the horse an insight into hidden modes of being as deep as Lawrence's and more completely expressed. The second story, 'The Bridegroom's Body', is a beautiful piece of work, but not quite so convincing. The third story is perfect in its way, but on a much lower level.

ERNEST HEMINGWAY For Whom the Bell Tolls

Listener XXV, 27 March 1941, 460

Some years ago Mr Wyndham Lewis invented a phrase to describe Mr Hemingway's characters, calling them dumb oxen. The phrase was an excellent one; Mr Hemingway's oxen were admirably, convincingly dumb; their inarticulate lowing became them, and Mr Hemingway's integrity as an artist seemed to be involved with the inarticulateness: his strength has always been that he leaves unsaid whatever can be left unsaid. In his latest novel the oxen have begun to talk, surprisingly, like Balaam's ass, and, more surprisingly, in the tones of Miss Gertrude Stein, in which they affirm their belief in liberty, equality and fraternity. Though they still live, like all Mr Hemingway's characters, on the plane of sensation and instinct, their loquacity for some reason raises a feeling of doubt.

From the beginning Mr Hemingway's subject has been the natural man, the natural man frustrated, bedevilled, distorted; no one else has described more movingly the forsakenness of these tragedies on the purely natural level. An animal sadness still hangs round the characters in the present story as they take their winding but unerring road to the gates of the slaughterhouse; but behind the slaughterhouse a symbolic dawn has appeared, and the final kill has assumed the dignity of an ideological ceremony. This symbolical dawn was probably indispensable for several reasons; a writer must find some meaning for life, and cannot leave it in a state of inarticulateness for good; he must come out in the end with his own beliefs. And in this book Mr Hemingway had also to find some explanation for heroism, for he is dealing with heroic action and has essayed for the first time the heroic style. The action is magnificently described, but the style raises a succession of scruples; the afflatus is uneasy and self-conscious, and collapses into gusty imitations of the style of Miss Gertrude Stein with an effect of deliberately attempted lyricism which is painful.

The story covers only a few days and describes an episode in the Spanish Civil War, culminating in the blowing up of a bridge and a fatal accident to the chief character, an American called Robert Jordan. The Spanish peasants who help him in his dangerous errand are superbly described: Pablo, a former Republican leader who has lost his faith and his courage; Pilar, his wife, a magnificently vulgar and vital portrait: the good old man Anselmo, a sort of humble Colonel Newcome; El Sordo, the obstinate, taciturn old farmer—all are astonishingly alive and astonishingly themselves; Mr Hemingway has never done anything better. The weak figures in the story are the American Robert Jordan and Maria, the girl with whom he falls in love. The love scenes are minutely described, but they are all on the level of naturalism, and very little can be said about love on the level of naturalism, where love is merely a sensation:

> Every time Robert Jordan looked at her he could feel a thickness in his throat.

This is one way of expressing emotion, but Romeo and Antony would not have thought of saying that they felt a thickness in their throats; they had so much more to say. The thickness in the throat is a cousin of the lump in the throat; and if the lover remains at this point, he has to fill the ensuing silence with some kind of sentimentality. The great fault of Mr Hemingway's description of love, thoroughgoing as it is in its sensuality, is sentimentality and prettiness. By far the best things in the story are Pilar's account of a massacre of Fascists in a small Spanish town, and various descriptions of Fascist atrocities. In spite of its many faults, this is one of the most striking stories he has ever written.

WILLIAM FAULKNER and LUDWIG BEMELMANS
Go Down, Moses; Hotel Splendide

Listener XXIX, 14 January 1943, 59

Mr Faulkner belongs to the jungle, and Mr Bemelmans to the shaven lawn, school of American fiction. In Mr Bemelman's world we can saunter about at our ease; the objects are familiar and pleasing, and the light lies curled neatly on the grass like a domesticated animal nourished from a great central electrical system. But in his uncomfortable pathfinding expeditions Mr Faulkner is always hacking his way well in front of us: sometimes round a corner, prickly bushes start up before us, branches clash about our ears, the light, when it does appear, bursts out in lurid splashes like blood, making the jungle darkness deeper as it vanishes; we stumble on, hoping to reach some clearing where the shape of the world will show itself to us at last, but the hope is indefinitely postponed. Mr Faulkner has much more genius than Mr Bemelmans, if genius is a quality that we associate with Dostoevsky and do not associate with Jane Austen. But the genius is inextricably entangled with itself, a sort of jungle within a jungle wanting to remain a jungle, fighting against clarity. We have an impression of a ghostly struggle; but we cannot tell quite what is happening, for we are only within hailing distance of the author in the dark. Possibly without our knowing it he has hacked a clear path for himself through the jungle; but if he has, then he has put back all the trees behind him again in the moment which we should have needed to catch up with him. There is a dim feeling that a conjuring trick has been played. For we have to overcome a second time the obstacles which Mr Faulkner has already overcome, but without the hefty axe which he uses to send the branches flying: he keeps that for himself.

Our choice between him and Mr Bemelmans depends on whether we prefer a frustrated Dostoevsky, with all the implicit greatness, to a successful Jane Austen with all the confessed limitation. Mr Faulkner's art consists largely in dramatising the difficulties of the artist. He does not give us a picture of life, but a series of snapshots of the artist struggling heroically to shape a picture of life. The subject-matter, we are perpetually reminded, is inexpressibly difficult, and as the subject-matter is life, the artist's frenzies and convulsions create an impression that life must be a very portentous business. But it is portentous at a remove, for we rarely catch a glimpse of it; the shadow cast by the labouring artist is too deep and too restless, distorting or obscuring everything. To admire a shadow, particularly such a muscular shadow as Mr Faulkner's, is possible for a while; but the admiration ceases as soon as one has a desire to see, a simple but imperious desire, and what we are left with is a homesickness for clarity and light. After all light is the element of art.

In *Go Down, Moses* one can distinguish degrees of obscurity, gradations of darkness. But what makes it hardest to read is the prolixity, the feeling that words here are used mainly as obstacles, piled up like rocks, so that only a trickle of rational meaning is allowed to seep through their craggy masses. The method of narration is so indirect that, in the first story particularly, it is almost baffling, though the story itself is quite simple. This fantastic indirectness is intended, one fancies, to convey a sense of immediacy, to place the story before us without the story-teller, to get rid of everything except things as they actually are. This has been the aim of many writers ever since *Ulysses*, which achieved immediacy in such an astonishing way. But in *Ulysses* Joyce was not telling a story, and Mr Faulkner is, and a story cannot be told by letting things speak, for things have no connected language. If we do manage to make them utter themselves, they are infinitely more clumsy and garrulous than we as natural story-tellers are. And besides, the story is our story; situations, events, accidents, things, are all secondary; the story rises in the human mind and returns to it; it is merely our way of telling ourselves about ourselves. In a great deal of modern fiction there is an inveterate animism or materialism, an assumption that massive and powerful objects, machinery of all kinds, brute events, inarticulate urges, are more real than the human mind. This is probably a reflection of the fact that things in our age take up a vaster area of our attention than they have ever done in former ages. But if we give free speech to these things, and let them babble in their myriad tongues, we plunge ourselves into chaos.

There are no darknesses in the work of Mr Bemelmans; there are scarcely even shadows. He achieves a quite unusual clarity, an effect of gently diffused light. His characters are outlined with more than natural definition; they resemble toys, whose contours are more simple and often more pleasing than the lolloping human form. They are pleasing even when they represent petty despots and villains; and one has a suspicion now and then that Mr Bemelmans in his picture of humanity is a gentle deluder. His Hotel Splendide, which is the scene of all those short stories, is a sort of Noah's Ark of human types carved into such agreeable shapes that even the strictest and the most innocent reader will find no offence in them, though many of them represent highly undesirable qualities. Yet Mr Bemelmans does not try to conceal their wickedness, and the pleasure we get from them is due to the modelling, which is lucid and mildly distorted, and to the general mood, but particularly to a sort of enjoyment of humanity itself, quite without bitterness. Most of the stories are very amusing, but one or two show a wonderfully just and sensitive insight into human life, in particular 'The New Suit', which is fit to be set beside some of the stories of Chekhov. Mr Bemelmans is one of those writers who seem to know their limitations exactly, who show no desire to transcend them, and yet surprise us by transcending them now and then. These stories are so perfectly executed, so amusing and so humanly interesting, that their qualities speak for themselves.

ROBERT FROST *Collected Poems* and *A Witness Tree*

Listener XXX, 26 August 1943, 246

Mr Frost is one of those poets who so evidently succeed in doing what they wish to do that they tempt everyone to point out their limitations. The limitation is so clearly there, as it is not in poets who undertake more than they can manage. But when one examines Mr Frost's limitation one finds that it rises from proportion, and that his proportion in turn is rooted in character. If he were to say more than he says, as people sometimes wish he would, it would destroy the balance of his view of life. As for the character itself, it has the soundness and natural distortion of growing things which have already grown sufficiently to possess a distinctive shape.

The natural distortion is what charms and convinces us in Mr Frost's poetry; we are not listening to a voice, we are considering a human being who has gathered experience from all sorts of places and, as his latest volume of poetry shows, is still gathering it. His accumulation of experience is cautious, stubborn, extraordinarily discriminating without following any perceptible rule, and therefore full of natural surprises. The poetry has no streamlines, no elegances in the urban sense; instead it has a sober harmony of thought, feeling and language attained unexpectedly and unobtrusively by allowing their proper place to the roughnesses and obstinancies of human life. Mr Frost takes account of the things which the streamline cuts through or cuts out in its obsessed pursuit of speed, which it miscalls economy; he is the inspired recorder of these things, and they are so many and so filled with meaning that, beyond the limitation (if maturity is a limitation), we are conscious of the variety and abundance.

To trace Mr Frost's development would be difficult, for except for a few poems in his first book, *A Boy's Will*, all his work is mature. We feel no temptation to use his later work as a criterion of his earlier: both are complete in themselves. His development is shown rather in an increased discrimination; he says things in *A Witness Tree* which he could not have said in *New Hampshire*, that superb collection: things of a miraculous quietness and subtlety. But his attitude has not changed, or it has changed simply by the accretion of fresh experience which has merely confirmed it and clarified further what was already clear. It is a considered attitude; it states a point of view, then half-questions it, then cautiously considers it until a definite implication emerges; and the quintessence of his poetry is in this implication, which is hard to define, but which is constant in all his work, an attribute of character. It could be described only by describing Mr Frost.

As his attitude to life is cautious and considered, it probably finds its ideal expression in the studies of rustic situation, the short stories in verse, which are scattered throughout his books, and particularly in the period which produced 'North of Boston', 'Mountain Interval' and 'New Hampshire'. These poems remind one partly of Wordsworth and partly of Browning, another poet whose gift for describing character seemed to depend on the fact that he invariably wrote in character. There is, of course, a great difference in temperature between the two poets; Browning is tropically luxuriant, and Mr Frost economical and austere. He does not have Browning's devouring interest in the working of the mind and the passions, nor his interest in *why's*; he simply observes the mind and the passions in a given set of circumstances, but into the observation he puts a lifetime of experience, or rather more than a lifetime, for part of the experience is inherited and part borrowed from his neighbours in the give and take of communal life. This gives an extraordinary solidity to his judgements, which are almost always implicit, unuttered, as if they applied to a community of Robert Frosts who do not need to waste words by uttering them. The absence of comment itself has the force of a comment. Mr Frost is like a man who has struggled with a tough adversary (experience), has made headway against it here, suffered rebuffs from it there, and at last has philosophically come to an amicable agreement with it and left it at that. He describes this struggle, never carried to irreconcilable lengths, in a poem in his latest volume:

> I would have written of me on my stone.
> I had a lover's quarrel with the world.

Or, which is to the same point:

> And there is always more than should be said.

The *Collected Poems* run to over four hundred pages. Among these there is not one which is cheap or tawdry or dull or anything but highly interesting. The best of the poems in *A Witness Tree* have a finer quality, a more exquisite clarity, than anything that Mr Frost has written before. The book contains one remarkable poem of horror 'The Subverted Flower' and a metaphysical poem, 'The Most Of It', which ends with a fine legendary image, too long to quote, and 'The Lesson for Today', a sort of dialogue between Mr Frost and the world into which he has lately fallen. This last poem in particular should be read by all who wish to understand this poet's attitude to his work.

WALLACE STEVENS Collected Poems

Observer, 6 November 1955, 10

Wallace Stevens died a few months ago in his seventy-sixth year. Forty years ago, when he first began to be known, he was regarded as odd and tangential: before he died he had established himself as one of the chief living American poets, and his work had become an influence among the younger generation. After reading his collected poems, which fill over 500 pages, I still find his poetry difficult; the accent itself sometimes is hard to catch, and the pervasive personal idiosyncrasy is like an obstruction; one feels the poet is actually reluctant to communicate with his audience, and has set up a barrier which has to be overcome.

No poetry could be more cold and aloof from the ordinary life of ordinary people which seems indeed to exasperate Stevens beyond expression. Combine the aloofness with a vivid sensuous delight in natural beauty, and one may have an idea of the curious quality of his work. All his senses are equally employed, sight, hearing, smell, touch, taste, a very unusual thing in poetry. The opposition between his delight in things and his intellectual revulsion from the drab reality of modern life is apparent even in his early poetry, and the conflict between them is there sometimes very movingly stated. But as time goes on his poetry becomes more and more a justification of his intellectual stance; he follows the speculations of his own mind, turning away from life to an imaginary world of beautiful objects, of peaches and pears—not to the legendary rose which satisfies only three of the senses, but to things which satisfy them all and can be tasted and eaten. It is a legendary world without a legend.

This need for the full enjoyment of things comes from his vision of the world, where man supersedes God, yet remains mortal. For Stevens we live in the world and die in the world, and this is the whole story. He believed this passionately, and consequently he had to become a stoic though by nature he was a hedonist. Living in the world we know, which batters daily against our hearts and senses, he affirmed a world of beauty and aesthetic enjoyment, an autonomous world of poetry: a stoical affirmation. The ultimate criticism of his poetry is that the miseries of the world were not misery to him, as Keats realised that they must be to a poet; they evoke in him only anger and scorn. He makes us feel that they should not be there, or that, being there, they are only of minor interest.

Yet when he is not conforming to an aesthetic pattern woven by himself Stevens is sometimes a wonderful poet. He is at his best in his first two books. *Harmonium* and *Ideas of Order*. After that the pattern becomes a copy of itself, endlessly repeated, an abstraction propagating abstractions. Perhaps the best idea of his powers can be had from an early poem—and the most widely known of all his poems. 'Sunday Morning' is a meditation on the traditional meaning of that day. In it the conflict between Stevens's sensuous imagination and his stoic intellect is movingly stated: in his later poetry it is merely resolved. The poem begins with the delight of the senses,

> Coffee and oranges in a sunny chair,
> And the green freedom of a cockatoo,

in which

> The holy hush of ancient sacrifice

is dissipated. A woman considers

> the dark
> Encroachment of that old catastrophe.

and asks

> Why should she give her bounty to the dead? . . .
> Shall she not find in comforts of the sun,
> In pungent fruit and bright, green wings, or else
> In any balm or beauty of the earth,
> Things to be cherished like the thought of heaven?

Yet she has to ask

> But in contentment I still feel
> The need of some imperishable bliss.

To which the poet's answer is:

> Death is the mother of beauty; hence from her,
> Alone, shall come fulfilment of our dreams
> And our desires.

Heaven is summoned, and dismissed:

> Is there no change of death in paradise?
> Does ripe fruit never fall? Or do the boughs
> Hang always heavy in that perfect sky?

The poem ends with an affirmation of the earth:

> We live in an old chaos of the sun,
> Or old dependency of day and night,
> Or island solitude, unsponsored, free.

In this poem Stevens gives a perfect and beautiful image of the world as he saw it, a world robbed of all transcendental meaning, and evokes a forlorn beauty which will move even those who deny his beliefs. The blank verse has an extraordinary sweetness and harmony. 'Sunday Morning' is the work of a very remarkable poet; it contains the essence of Stevens's poetry, though it does not represent its considerable variety. 'The Comedian as the Letter C', 'Le Monocle de mon Oncle', and 'Esthétique du Mal' are all remarkable in a quite different style.

If Stevens is not yet appreciated in England, it is because he is difficult in a different way from the difficult poets who are now generally accepted. He also wrote too much, and repeated himself tiresomely, until only his original argument remained, and feeling was almost forgotten. But he wrote more than a handful of poems which will not be forgotten.

III

FRENCH

MARCEL PROUST *The Guermantes Way* translated by C K Scott Moncrieff

Nation and Athenaeum XXXVIII, 3 October 1945, 20

These are volumes five and six of Mr Scott Moncrieff's remarkable translation of *A la Recherche du Temps Perdu*. They show no inferiority to the volumes which have already appeared; they are on the whole, indeed, more steadily excellent. To what quality Mr Scott Moncrieff owes his pre-eminence as a translator it is difficult to say. He has all the more obvious virtues of the translator: plasticity and adaptableness of mind; that secondary inventive faculty which can discover a great variety of ways in which one thing may be said (a power hardly ever possessed by the creative artist, and one which, if it were, would probably be inimical to him); the ability to fall into a given style as if one were born to it; a turn for impersonation not unlike that of an actor. All these qualities Mr Scott Moncrieff possesses; but what gives his work its peculiar excellence is an unusual penetration and intimacy of intuition, a discriminative sympathy such as is necessary, for example, in literary criticism, though it is seldom found there. One feels that Mr Scott Moncrieff might have been an excellent critic, if he had not chosen to be an excellent translator.

The Guermantes Way gives one a better idea than either *Swann's Way* or *Within a Budding Grove* of Proust's variety, range, profundity—of what the less timorous critics of other ages might have called his universality. It is this universality which impresses us most in reading him; he is the one writer of our age who has given us a picture of human life on a full and spacious scale; who, with the lack of embarrassment which reveals a master, has drawn all kinds of people, ordinary and abnormal, servants, the middle class, the intelligentsia, the various aristocracies; and who in doing this has made us understand how a great writer speaks, feels, thinks, and sees the world. He has the opulence, the wastefulness, which only in writers of a certain rank is supportable, because only in them is it unforced and natural. He speaks with authority as those do who know that their work is incontestable, even if a part here or a part there may justly be condemned on aesthetic grounds. This work is less a work of art, to adopt Arnold's verdict on *Anna Karenina,* than a slice of life. It has little arrangement in the ordinary sense; comedy, tragedy, psychological generalization appear at that point in the story when the author's mind happens to be interested in them, not at the point where they will have the maximum effect; and it is the duration of the attention of this mind which determines their length, the intensity of that attention which makes them exciting and dramatic. And how magnificent are the comedy, the tragedy, the psychology! What a feat of economy is the first introduction of M. de Charlus in *Within a Budding Grove*; what a triumph of minute and sustained portrayal is the dinner party at the Duchess de Guermantes'; what a *tour de force* of pure imaginative speculation the description in the first of the present two volumes of the difference which deafness makes to our visual apprehension of things: 'objects moved without sound seemed also to be moved without cause; deprived of all resonant quality, they show a spontaneous activity, seem to be alive'—and so on for several pages, until we seem to be initiated into the mystery of sound. It is this variety and profundity of apprehension which makes Proust a great writer. His meticulousness of observation is probably unique in literature, but it is always the reflection of an immense breadth of interest. In power of psychological generalisation he reminds us of the French aphorists of the seventeenth and eighteenth centuries; but he possesses also a dramatic power of a very high order. And, apart from these more traditional qualities, his intuitions of obscure states and changes of the soul are so subtle, so minute, so exact, and so nearly beyond what we are accustomed to think intuition can achieve, that, not knowing how they came to the mind, we are astonished by them as by something occult.

In their judgement of contemporaries most ages seem to be content with a writer who possesses one remarkable quality; and he who brings his single talent to perfection will be regarded as a great writer. But sometimes there bursts suddenly into this normal and orderly atmosphere a writer who has not merely one great quality, but half-a-dozen; a writer who seems to help himself to a faculty when ever he needs it, and who continues to astonish everybody because he says, feels, thinks, sees, understands, and imagines so much more than anybody else. Proust is a writer of this kind. He is not the equal of the greatest masters of the novel, of Dostoevsky and Tolstoy, but he is of the same order; he has the same apparent inexhaustibility and endowment. And he has also, like them, a certain uniqueness of utterance which, as it were, justifies itself, which we accept, and which we do not wish to be better or other than it is.

LOUIS-FERDINAND CÉLINE Journey to the End of the Night

Listener XII, 18 July 1934, 128

Céline's book has been praised by writers of established reputation; it has had an enormous circulation in France; and it has been discussed gravely in America. It is an astonishing performance; astonishing in its disillusionment, its frankness, and its thorough-going banality. There is no ignoring it, for in spite of its jauntiness it is sincere down to a point that is seldom reached in ephemeral fiction. But though it is arresting in such a singular degree, though one feels in reading it that this is what tens of thousands of men in post-War Europe must have felt without being able to express it, through lack of courage, or through inherent decency, or a mixture of the two, the book leaves an ephemeral impression. The substance is poor, except for a little pellet of bitter popular wisdom here and there, such as might be secreted by any man who has passed through hard experience. The style, which impresses one at first, is clever, slick and hard-boiled, and largely made up of clichés which are not customarily used by writers, and so give an effect of novelty. It is managed with considerable skill, and reminds one in turn of Mr Ernest Hemingway and Alfred Döblin, being less hard and exact than the former and less trashy than the latter. Céline's most salient virtue as a writer is that he says without embarrassment whatever comes into his mind. That, even now that frankness is a convention, is an unusual quality, and in itself it makes the book interesting. But the author's mind seems to be, apart from this, a commonplace one. His disillusionment is the disillusionment of an average sensual man gifted with a surprising facility of expression. An average sensual man, disillusioned, is no doubt potentially a figure of the most moving human interest; yet he would be more interesting as the hero of a novel than as its author. In *Journey to the End of the Night* he is both; this does not double the book's interest, however, but rather takes away from it, making the hero something of a ventriloquist's dummy. Still, Céline is a marvellous ventriloquist.

There is only one character in the novel, this dummy who gives utterance to all the author's thoughts. The other characters are mere smudges, though one or two of them, like Madelon, have an effective enough resemblance to well-known Bohemian types. The journey to the end of the night is the hero's alone, and the other figures are mere signposts on the way. The journey is an unfinished one, for though there are dark enough places in it, and the atmosphere throughout is dark, the vision of final darkness that Dostoevsky could conjure up for a moment now and then is quite beyond the author's scope. We first see Ferdinand Bardamu in the War, then in hospital, then in an outlying station on the French Congo, then in the United States, then in France again as a doctor. In all these places he finds himself in the position of an underdog. So society becomes his enemy, but more particularly the moral code which holds society together. To Bardamu, accordingly, morality is nothing more than a game with rules which are intended to trap him at every turn, and his technique of living consists in getting round these rules by means of a sort of honest, candid but invariably ineffective cheating. This cheating requires considerable courage, in many cases more courage than is needed to stick to the moral code. The cheating is justified in Bardamu's eyes by the fact that to him the moral code is a sham intended to fool and destroy him. Yet he has no illusions about his courage; for it is nothing more than the instinct of self-preservation, a means for keeping someone alive who sees no particular point in being alive. There could not be a more simple or banal conception of existence, and that probably accounts for the book's extraordinary popularity. Morality is a cheat, man an egoist, life a swindle: there is such a seductive absence of complexity about such an explanation of existence that when it is expressed in the language of the street and with complete candour it sounds almost convincing. Céline heightens one's feeling of his sincerity by a touch of sentimentality every now and then. Alcide, the rough-tongued French sergeant, spends six years in the inferno of a tropical colony so as to keep his little niece at a better-class convent school in Bordeaux.

> I didn't know what to say to him, I wasn't up to it, but he was so much a better man than me that I went red in the face . . . I did not dare say anything. I suddenly felt terribly unworthy to speak to him. . . . He was offering this little girl far away, tenderness enough to make a world anew, and no one would have known it . . .
>
> Suddenly he slept, with the candle burning. In the end I got up to study his features by its light. He slept like anybody might. He looked quite ordinary. It wouldn't be a bad idea if there were something to distinguish good men from bad.

That, though an unusually tender passage, is typical of the whole book, which, even at its most brutal or jaunty, aims at a sort of convulsive pathos. Robinson, Bardamu's disreputable friend, is blinded by a bomb which he was setting to kill an old woman. Bardamu tries to conceal from him that he is blind. One day he finds Robinson out of bed and standing at the open window.

> He had his arms sticking straight out of the window—into the open air. He could not see anything, of course, but he smelt the fresh air. Then he stretched out his arms farther into the darkness, as far as he could, as if to

> touch the other side of it. He didn't want to believe it was true—his own private darkness . . . I pushed him back into bed and I said a lot of things to try and console him, but now he wouldn't believe what I said. He was crying. He himself had come to the end of things. There wasn't anything you could tell him now. There is a moment when you are all alone by yourself and have come to the end of all that can happen to you. It's the end of the world. Unhappiness itself, your own misery, won't answer you now and you have to go back, among men, no matter which. One isn't difficult at moments like that, for even to weep you've got to get back to where everything starts, to where the others are.

That is as good as anything else in the book. It is the wisdom of a man who has suffered a great deal and come to what terms he could with life. But how uneven it is, and how sentimentally wordy! Within a few lines it ranges from the utter banality of 'There is a moment when you are all alone with yourself' to the really moving last sentence, which in the context actually gains by its maudlin naivety. The translation by John Marks, is full of spirit.

GEORGE DUHAMEL and HENRI de MONTHERLANT The Pasquier Chronicles; Pity for Women

Listener XVIII, 22 December 1937, 1394

The Pasquier Chronicles is made up of five novels, three of which have already appeared separately in English, while the last two now appear for the first time. These novels have a definite continuity, the continuity of the growth and development of the Pasquier family; and the whole may therefore be regarded as a single work. Regarded in this way, it is a purely traditional story, an old-fashioned novel. As far as form is concerned, it could have been written in the time of Galsworthy, of Tolstoy, of Dickens, even of Fielding. In sentiment it goes almost as far back, at least to Dickens, to the tradition of humanitarian pity which is associated with the romantic movement, and without which Dostoevsky would be unthinkable. *Pity for Women*, a more novel story, perhaps a more 'modern' one, whatever that term signifies, is quite without this special kind of pity (in spite of its title). Its sentiment, which is thoroughly romantic, is both exuberant and hard-boiled, like that of Stendhal and Byron: the sentiment of an exceptional man with a strong social sense (the pure romantic has very little social sense). Such writers take pleasure in being social personages, but of an exceptional kind: in the eyes of society the wrong kind. Society is an indispensable setting for them, or rather a foil; for to rail at society is one of their chief necessities. By doing so they make society look stupid, and the stupidity of society in turn adds lustre to them. They have a quicker grasp of the privileges presented by society than the mere society man, whom they despise. But their assumptions are much the same: it is in intelligence that they are different. They are writers of privilege: the proof, if needed, is that they always demand for their heroes a privileged position. This often makes them acute critics of privilege, for nothing sharpens a man's wits so much as competition. *The Pasquier Chronicles* tells us a great deal about life, but *Pity for Women* probably tells us more about society (that is about human relations in their general accepted form) simply because the hero always demands special treatment for himself, a fact which disposes a man to criticism.

The Pasquier Chronicles is one of the most remarkable novels that have been written in our time. It is remarkable, first, for its mere fidelity to truth, its unfailing naturalness, its unforced mixture of tragedy and comedy. Its nearest parallel in English is probably Galsworthy's *Forsyte Saga*, but there is a great difference between the two books. Both tell the story of a family in detail and at length, a story filled with the creaking of domestic life; but Galsworthy tells it as if he had once been a Forsyte himself and had never got over it, and Duhamel tells it with the complete human sympathy of a man who is much more deeply involved in life. The Pasquiers' quarrels are more violent and more vocal than those of the Forsytes; but when the Forsytes creak one can feel Galsworthy creaking along with them; we are never quite away from the upper middle class. What it is that gives Duhamel's story its sweetness, in spite of so much in it that is sordid and hateful, is hard to say; perhaps the belief that on some plane all the characters, even the most disgraceful, are justified in their existence; if not that, at least the power to see them from their own point of view, as human beings, not as members of this class or that. Duhamel's skill in characterisation comes from his pure interest in human nature; even his comedy owes very little to social conventions, the source of so much comedy. The members of the Pasquier family rise in the world; they begin in poverty and they end in moderate prosperity; Joseph becomes a very rich man, Cécile becomes a famous pianist; even Ferdinand, the mediocre member of the family, is quite well off. But the remarkable thing about them is their truth of type, not what society does with them: the fact that they become what their qualities destined them to become. They are all extraordinarily lifelike without being portraits; they grow and change, continually surprising us; they are so intimately revealed that they touch us by a sort of defencelessness. But they amuse us at the same time, perhaps because they are presented in a sort of undress; we know what they look like in their shirt sleeves, and when they put on their best clothes we recognise it as a likeable and necessary comedy.

Yet Duhamel allows them all a certain dignity: they have some justification. The continuous interest and liveliness of his characterisation is astonishing in such a long book: there is not a dull or a dead page, not a single insincere or conventional statement. The last book does not perhaps come up to the level of the earlier ones describing the youth of the Pasquiers, with their exquisite touches of poetry; but it gives the feeling that we can never have enough of them, and that they are inexhaustible. The translation by Miss Béatrice de Holthoir is natural and graceful throughout, a finely sustained feat of skill.

There is humanity in *Pity for Women* too, but it does not come from any obvious affection for mankind. The book is extremely brilliant, and it contains the most penetrating, the most perverse, the most heartless observations on life, on love, and on society in general. The theme of the story is the relations between a well-known French novelist, Pierre Costa, and the women who fall in love with him. Two of these are infatuated readers. The first is a mystical peasant girl, who finishes in a lunatic asylum. The other, a woman of thirty from a country town, makes a bold attack upon him, but has to admit defeat. The author states that he intends Costa as a 'rakehell' character, and he succeeds in making him thoroughly odious, though interesting. The disquieting thing is the absence of moral judgement; or rather the tendency to show Costa in a favourable light. And Costa is, from any standpoint but that of the author, a most disagreeable character. It is admiration that really makes him exciting:

> Some struggle against the endless limitations that control men's lives; not so Costa, and rather than allow them to cause him pain, he chose instead to worship them. For his whole existence was governed by this thought: when the universe offers us so much reason to be happy, only an imbecile would choose to suffer (suffering which has to be paid for in this life, since there is no repayment in the other). After suffering for years from seeing his country decline, he had suddenly decided to love that decline; and thus found an excellent means of ending his sufferings. For patriotism, not being innate, may get lost as easily as it is acquired. In the same way he had reacted towards social injustice, and, generally speaking, to the whole problem of evil in the world. 'If evil were a perpetual source of suffering to me, my whole existence would be a torture, and so sheer idiocy. Therefore, I must love even that'.

This passage is fairly representative, and gives an idea of the intellectually exciting quality of the book. Written with a different inflection, it might have come out of Dostoevsky. Costa himself, indeed, is a Dostoevskian figure described from the opposite pole. He is a fanatical yet business-like egoist:

> What had once been a charming feature of his character had now become a principle by which his life was regulated; to love (and dare) to the limit of his power, in everything its opposite. Thus, destiny whether it said yes

> or no, gave him equal satisfaction. Whatever happened he was always 'on velvet'; which was very pleasant for him and even satisfied his reason, which concluded that only dullards and mock philosophers could conceive of life merely as a struggle.

These passages, along with the fact that Costa is extremely intelligent and charming and coldly, even humorously, brutal, give a sufficient idea of him; what makes him remarkable is that the author has elevated him into a philosophical figure. His thought repeatedly touches fundamental human questions, brilliantly, profoundly, wittily. One cannot accept Costa as a character, he is more like a myth, with the illuminating power of a myth. The imaginative power and the wit of the book are superb. Few people will like it, but few will be able to resist reading it. The translation is excellent.

GEORGES SIMENON The Man Who Watched the Trains Go By

Listener XXVII, 15 October 1942, 507

To review novels in war time is extraordinarily difficult; the only thing one can imagine as more difficult being to write them. For the novel is a picture of life, and war makes life indefinably obsolete, dates it and turns it into a period piece; since by life we all mean 'ordinary' life, a state where we are concerned mainly with our personal affairs, where the business man draws his profits and the workman his wages (or tries in each case to increase them), when men and women fall in love for the first or the last time, marry, are happy or unhappy, bring up a family, are surprised how much the world has changed, fall out with their friends, relapse into comfortable resignation in a suburb, take up golf (the last resort), all without realising that life is a dangerous thing.

War makes all this unconvincing, and that may be the reason why novels seem to be off the mark and give the impression that they miss out something of obvious and primary importance. Simenon's book is a study of a homicidal maniac, a theme which would be regarded as serious enough, even unpleasant, in times of peace, but becomes merely odd in war time.

In *The Man who Watched the Trains go by* Simenon describes in detail the obsessions and hallucinations of a respectable Dutch bourgeois, Kees Popinga, who sees his comfortable existence smashed by fraud, grows sick of decency, leaves his family, and indulges on a grand scale all the impulses he had repressed for so long. Being thorough, he begins by raping and murdering a cabaret singer in Amsterdam, takes the train to Paris, does there whatever occurs to him, is sheltered by a gang of criminals who hope to get money out of him, betrays them to the police, rapes a prostitute and narrowly escapes murdering her, fights a shadowy melodramatic duel with the head of the French police, sends bragging letters to the newspapers, and in his megalomania sees all Paris as his helpless prey. Kees is not an attractive character, yet Simenon makes him a pathetic human being, explicable, forgivable, though not, it is implied, very interesting; merely a trite madman, a commonplace maniac. Kees' plans crash when an American pickpocket relieves him of all his money. His vanity forces him to attempt suicide; he writes a last letter to the newspapers announcing that he will shortly be far beyond the reach of the law, in an inaccessible place; then he strips himself naked, flings his clothes into the Seine, and lies down on a railway line, where the passing of the first train will make him an unrecognisable corpse. But the train pulls up; Kees is arrested, taken to the police station, recognised, sent back to Holland and put in an asylum.

This story brings to a point an impression gathered from Simenon's other books: that is, that he is a man who knows a great deal about human life but accepts no responsibility for his knowledge. He resembles Kipling in this, though probably in nothing else. He knows more than Kipling, and his knowledge is more out of the way; but he draws no conclusions; he does not seem to be interested; after telling all he has to tell (and that is a great deal) there comes a blank. Anything and everything turns for him into a story: homicidal mania suits him as well as plain violence or ordinary murder. As for his imaginative grasp of homicidal mania, one can only be astonished by it. We recognise that he is in his own way an expert on human experience, and like many experts has grown *blasé* so that the most extraordinary things seem trite to him—an excerpt from a thumbed case-book. At the same time, he has kept intact on a different level a great deal of kindliness, the kindliness of a professional man. After dealing with the case in hand in a purely scientific spirit he realises that the poor oaf is a human being after all—a fool, naturally, with no distinction, no poetry, no surprise even when he is a homicidal maniac, inept, fatuous, common, gross, but, for what that amounts to, human. This, and the excitement of the chase, is the only concession that Simenon makes to our metaphysical nature. He confronts us with a yawning blank. But before he comes to it he manages to tell us a number of surprising things about ourselves.

IV

GERMAN

Friedrich Hölderlin

The Scottish Nation I No 14, 11 September 1923, 6–7/15

It was in 1916 that for the first time a complete collection of Hölderlin's poems appeared. The poet had died seventy years before, and the period in which he had written was past for more than a century. During that time he had had an acknowledged place among the lesser German poets; but the discovery of the new poems by von Hellingrath changed at once his rank, and installed him in a position second only to Goethe's in the hierarchy of German poetry. He appeared now, by a happy chance, as not only the poet second in greatness to Goethe, but as the German poet most unlike Goethe, the poet who, in lacking most conspicuously the capacities which Goethe had, brought into German poetry a spirit and a vision which Goethe was prevented by the complexion of his genius from attaining. For Germany Hölderlin is in a sense the spiritual complement of Goethe, in a sense his spiritual antagonist, his salutory antithesis. Both seem to have felt during their lives an unspoken enmity. In Goethe's conversations there is, among encouraging comments on inferior writers, no mention at all of Hölderlin; and Hölderlin, in the long period of insanity which closed his life, pretended stubbornly, whenever the greatest of German writers was mentioned, that he did not know the name. Time has settled the quarrel; the genius of Hölderlin, discovered in its fullness only a few years ago, has to-day a greater influence on the German spirit than that of Goethe, and in the next decade it may well become still more powerful. That part of the German spirit which was incarnated in Hölderlin is coming into the consciousness of German culture, now that the influence of Goethe has fructified and been for the moment exhausted.

To try to define what the genius of a great poet signifies in a specific culture is always a perilous task, and most perilous of all when it appears to be successful. But there are one or two broad points of difference between Goethe and Hölderlin which make clearer the essential contrast between their spirits. Goethe was a many-sided genius, all of whose sides were not equally great. He was great, supremely great, as a lyric and dramatic poet; he was great also, on a definitely lower plane, as a repository of practical wisdom on life, as, on the whole, the most unembarrassed liver and observer of life that the world has given us in modern times. His greatness as a poet was the greatness of absolute freedom; his greatness as a practical philosopher was the outcome of his calm recognition of the limitations of existence. There was a third Goethe, and probably a fourth and a fifth; there was, prominently exhibited, at any rate, the 'eingebildet' Goethe, the hero of self-culture who created himself in his own image so indefatigably and with such self-sacrifice; and this Goethe, it will be generally acknowledge now, was certainly less great than the natural Goethe out of whom he was hewn, the mighty spirit who imagined the last act in the first part of *Faust*, and who wrote the lyrics and ballads. But whether we admire it or not, we must admit that this was one of the sides of Goethe. He was, as Arnold saw, a naturalist in the great sense, a man who before every phenomenon accepted or despised by the human spirit, asked imperturbably. 'But is it so? Is it so to ME?' He was, as Emerson perceived, a prince of culture, a man who incarnated, or, at any rate, heroically strove to incarnate the highest normal life of humanity up to his time. He was truly great perhaps only when he wrote pure poetry or concrete criticism of life. But with all his completeness, and indeed as a condition of it, he lacked strikingly that mystical strain which makes every literature in which it is found so much more satisfying to the eternal needs of humanity. He aspired to it, he essayed it; but when he essayed it he became at best didactic and at worst pedantic. Now Hölderlin is the chief mystical poet of Germany, as Goethe is its chief human poet. Goethe was greatest when he was pure artist; Hölderlin, when he was half-artist, half-prophet. To use very simple terms, Goethe was inspired by a vision of human life as it is eternally; whereas Hölderlin had his eyes fixed on the mystical goal towards which humanity is moving, and that chiefly inspired his genius. He was most truly himself when he described mankind not in its eternal normal state, but in its movement to a sanctified end. His landscapes are accordingly tremendous, and have the outline and the atmosphere of a gigantic dream; but their serenity is not that of rest, but of steady, celestial progress. He lived in this atmosphere, the atmosphere of humanity and of the gods, more permanently than any other modern poet except Blake. He lived with the gods, 'daring to bring the gods and men nearer together'. His problem was not, like Goethe's, to experience beautifully and normally the life given us by the earth, but to exist in a state of glory, in which the terrestrial and the celestial life were one, in which the terrestrial had become the celestial.

Even in his earliest poems he was haunted by the thought of the dual existence of the gods and of men. Why should they both exist, and why should there be an unbridgeable gulf between them? 'You wander up there in the light,' he says in one of the most beautiful of his earlier lyrics, the 'Schicksalslied', 'on soft lawns, spiritual beings. Fateless, like the sleeping child, breathe the heavenly ones. Chastely nourished in separate buds, the spirit blooms in them forever, and the spiritual eyes gaze in still, eternal clarity.' 'But to us,' he cries,

> But to us is given
> In no state to rest;

They vanish, they fall,
The suffering mortals,
Blindlings from one
Hour to another,
Like water from cliff
To cliff flung downward
Yearlong into the unknown below,

A profound sense of the irremediable division of life lies on all these early poems.

But in 1795, when he was in his twenty-fourth year, he became tutor in the household of a certain Gontard in Frankfort-on-Main, and there he came to know intimately his employer's wife, the Diotima of the poems. This seems to have been the turning point in his life. A youth still in appearance and in desire, with a face, as it is depicted in a portrait dated 1792, very noble and strangely feminine, of an extreme purity and gentleness, he seemed destined to suffer without release if he did not encounter someone with more strength and more calm than himself. Both strength and calm, so far as one can judge from Hölderlin's own words and from a fine relief showing a woman's face, serene, but a little masculine, Susette Gontard seems to have had. They fell passionately in love. 'My feeling for the beautiful,' Hölderlin writes a little after this time, 'is now beyond the touch of any disturbing thing. It is oriented forever on that Madonna-head. My mind goes to school to her, and my disrupted spirit is softened and calmed daily in her assured peace.' The phase of passionate love lasted for almost three years. In September, 1798, Hölderlin was ordered by Gontard to leave the house, and the next year and a half he spent in separation in the home of his friend and patron, Sinclair, at Homburg. But the strength he had gained in his companionship with Susette carried him over the years of grief. The happiness which he had experienced, the possibility, which he had proved, of a life of felicity on the earth, remained with him. In Sinclair's house his genius rose for the first time to its height; he saw the gods no longer as beings separated eternally from men; and he had that vision which inspired his greatest poems, of the return of celestial powers to the earth.

He was thenceforward a mystic; but he was a natural mystic, a poet who never turned away from the earth. His genius was inspired by three great human events which in their fullness, he believed, or rather thought he knew by the power of faith, were to bring Time to its final end, the 'Vergöttung der Welt'. The first of these was the mystical awakening of the soul in the immemorial forests of Asia; the second was the brief fruition of the godlike and the human in the culture of Greece: the third was Christ. Jesus was to Hölderlin the brother of Bacchus and Hercules, and like them a son of Heaven in a time of religious darkness; but He was greater than either. The inheritor of India and Greece was to be Germany, that Germany which Hölderlin loved with an affection in which there was nothing vulgar, and whose soul he found in its romantic landscapes and in the kindly life of its common people. In his poem, 'Germanien', the eagle, the messenger of the Highest, comes out of India, lights on Parnassus and on 'the sacrificial hills of Italy', flies over the Alps, and brings the heavenly gift to Germany. It was a sign perhaps of mere human limitation, a sign also, however, of the concreteness of Hölderlin's faith, that he sought to build Jerusalem in Germany, that is, in the midst of the life which he knew. Blake, a man of infinitely more realistic capacity, had before had the same vision, or made the same mistake, about England.

This grand vision of the destiny of humanity inspired the greatest poems of Hölderlin. It is contained in a collection of hymns, some written in free measures, some in hexameters more splendid in their music than those of Goethe; and constituting together a large body of poetry. That poetry is mystical; but there are few mystical poets who are more free than Hölderlin from any intrusion of theology, or who have less than him that subtlety which, however exquisitely it may be disguised in fancies, detracts from the pure poetic value of a work. His genius poured itself into tremendous visions and into thoughts which were simple and great: thoughts which move us not by their subtlety but by their elevation. He did not try to create in his poems an atmosphere of mystery, but to give everything an unearthly clarity; he lived not in the twilight which lies between the gods and humanity, but, at the moments of his highest inspiration, one might almost say, in the full light of both. He was in love with light, and no one has written more beautifully of its splendour and serenity, or of the ethereal clarity which it takes on in summer afternoons in his own land. Yet though he never strove after mystery, his poetry, like all the greatest romantic poetry does give a sense of high mystery, but it is achieved by sheer greatness of thought and style, and his poems have the mysteriousness not of twilight landscapes, but of great, rocky mountains lying in burning light.

He wrote about a score of long poems, but I have space in so short an essay to mention only one: 'Patmos', the finest, perhaps, in poetic beauty, and the most complete as an expression of his body of thought. 'Near is,' he begins. 'Near is and hard to grasp the god. But where danger is there arises the saviour also. In distance dwell the eagles, and fearless the sons of the mountains go over the abyss on light-built bridges . . . O give innocent water, wings give us, so that with unshaking hearts we may go up there and return back again.' Then follows a passage which is one of the glories of German poetry, but whose nobility is almost irrecoverably lost in translation:

So spake I, then led me,
Swifter than I could tell,
And far, whither I never
Thought to come, a genius

Out of my own house. Darkened
In twilight, where I went,
The shadowy forest
And the longing brooks
Of my home; never had I known these lands:
But swiftly, in new-risen splendour,
Mysterious
Through golden mist, bloomed,
Under the steps of the sun,
With a thousand fragrant peaks,
Asia up; and blinded I sought
One whom I knew, for strange to me
Were the broad lanes, where down
From Tmolus journeyed
The golden-hung Pactol;
And Taurus stood and Messogis,
And full of flowers the gardens,
A still fire; but in the light
Gleamed high the silvery snow;
And seal of deathless life,
On inaccessible walls
Ancient the ivy grew, and stood
On living pillars, cedars and laurels,
The solemn,
The god-built palaces.

I have been able to render hardly anything more here than the spacious, processional march of one of Hölderlin's sentences; a rhythm in which, despite the number of qualifying clauses, the movement is not retarded, but moves on with the serenity and breadth of a great emotion to which the poet has entirely given himself. But the splendour of the words it is impossible to convey, for Hölderlin, though not the greatest, is the most noble, the most unapproachable, of German poets. There follows on this passage an account of the poet's coming to Patmos, and an exquisite description of the friendship between Jesus and John, 'For all is good. Therefore He died', is Hölderlin's comment on the Crucifiction. But Christ disappeared from the earth; and Hölderlin interprets again, with that truth which he always showed in such things, the parable of the sower. There is a period between the sowing of the seed and its re-birth in the living grain, but this is a time of deprivation and not of evil; 'For the work of the gods is as our work.' The thing most hated by the gods, accordingly, is not silence, but the sound of false voices, and when that is heard on earth, mankind has for the time no significance. Then men do not act: 'Undying Fate acts, and its work goes on by itself and quickly comes to an end.' But when the heavenly destiny is about to commence again, then from the heavens 'a saving sign is given, and this is song, shining upon what is beneath, for nothing is common'. In such terms did Hölderlin conceive the task of the poet. The gods desire, he said, that of each a sacrifice should be made, 'and whosoever avoids the offering will never know the good and good will never be done by him'. He concludes with a prophecy of the second coming of Christ. Seeing that it has appeared once, the celestial Power which we call Christ must appear again in the course of time and deify all life.

Like Wordsworth, and with some striking differences, like his countryman, Nietzsche, Hölderlin was a mystic of the earth, of nature, and of man. He was concerned in his last poems with the gods only when they appeared on the earth, in history, and behind the forms of nature. He was no longer tortured by the dualism of a heavenly and a human life expressed so poignantly in his earlier poems; that was resolved for him in the end, he believed, in a form of being in which, while remaining human, he existed in a state of almost divine ecstasy. His task, as he accepted it, was, accordingly, 'to bring the gods and men nearer together.' This he regarded as a religious work, but where he differed from most of the religions which have fulfilled their mission in the world was in his belief that in order to exist as a seraphic being it was not necessary to deny the earth, but rather in a high sense to understand and be at one with it. He was a Pantheist, and his poems have no appeal to the weakness but only to the strength of mankind. They will attract perhaps no great number of men. But, however that may be, they have the power of ennobling those who live for a time in their atmosphere. That atmosphere is unlike anything else in German literature, and its nearest analogue is to be found in the music of Beethoven.

A great mystical poet, Hölderlin was also one of the masters of German poetic style. His sense of form, in a poetry which even at its greatest, even in Goethe, is distinguished chiefly by naturalness and spontaneity, was full-grown and sure. The masters of style, of style in the classical sense, in German poetry, are few. Outside Hölderlin there are only Platen, Hugo von Hofmannsthal, and Stefan George, but, fine as these were, Hölderlin was, as a stylist, greater than them all. At his best he wrote in the grand style, in a style noble and large, which in its processional movement gave the simplest words and thoughts the significance and mystery which things take on when they are set apart, in an atmosphere inaccessible to common men. Like Milton he was not only noble, but conscious of the nobility which his theme imposed upon him, and it is this which gave his verse its majestic movement, its conscious, processional advance. He was neither so sure nor so magnificent a master of the grand style as Milton: there are whole tracts of his verse where the manner maintains an incongruous dignity far above the weak inspiration of the moment; there are poems, again, in which the expression and the thought are alike prosaic. But at his best, and in his later poems he was almost continuously at his best, he wrote poetry which in elevation of utterance has not been equalled by any other German, and which has been surpassed by few except the very greatest poets.

His health was always frail, and he had to pay dearly for the exhausting visions which consumed him in the year and a half of his residence with Sinclair. In 1800 he returned once more to his life of drudgery, painfully tutoring the children of the well-to-do. He was for a while in Stuttgart, then in Hauptwyl, finally in Bordeaux. There he suddenly became insane, and hardly anything for a while was known of him. He seems to have started on foot on a bizarre and agonising pilgrimage across France to his own land. There is some record that, Heaven knows for what strange reason, he passed through Arles in the south of France. He arrived in Germany in the summer of 1804, ragged, filthy, and with his mind completely deranged. His friend, Sinclair, came once more to his help, and for a period less than a year he was well again, and his genius once more obeyed him. But in 1805, in spite of medical aid and the devotion of his friend, he relapsed, never to recover his faculties again. For more than three decades he lived a strange life, of which records remain, in the household of an intelligent joiner in a secluded German village; and when he died there he was an old man. The full half of his life was passed in irremediable darkness; and he himself seems to have had a premonition it would be so, for there is a poem written in the days when he felt insanity hovering over him, and entitled, significantly, 'The Half of Life'. 'Woe to me', he wrote,

> Woe to me, where do I take, when
> It is winter, the flowers, and where
> The sunshine
> And shadows of the earth?
> The walls stand
> Speechless and cold, in the wind
> Rattle the banners.

All his poetry was written before he was thirty-five. The sacrifice which he said the gods demanded from men was paid by him to the last drop.

Hans Carossa

Bookman (New York) LXXII, December 1930, 404–8

In December 1928 there appeared in Germany under the imprint of the Insel Verlag a beautifully produced little volume in honour of the fiftieth birthday of Hans Carossa. Among the twenty-five writers who collaborated in rendering him homage were Austria's two greatest poets, Hugo von Hofmannsthal and Rainer Maria Rilke, and several of

Germany's most gifted young writers, among them Paul Alverdes, whose small but exquisite masterpiece, *The Whistlers' Room*, has since been translated into English. At that time Carossa's name, I think it is safe to say, was virtually unknown either in England or America; and even now only the few who have happened to come across that strange book, *A Roumanian Diary*, published some time ago, will recognise it. That little volume had itself an ironical fate. It was caught in the spate of war books, and seems to have been allotted for review to experts who wished to see how Roumanian atrocities compared with Russian, or to generals who were resolved to uphold their own ideas on strategy against the author's. It was, however, a book bound to puzzle or exasperate the ordinary war reviewer; for, although the diary of a busy medical officer during the German campaign against Roumania, the most moving incident in it was the death of a cat. Besides, there was no glorification or impeachment of warfare, no noticeable symptom of patriotism or of pacifism: none of the usual and natural responses to the War.

There is indeed something enigmatical in all Carossa's books. He has a trick of unexpected emphasis, of passing over things which other writers would seize upon, and concentrating, yet never disproportionately, on some point which, but for his vigilance, would have been overlooked. These points are chosen with an unfathomable skill, by a faculty not so much of selection as of subconscious divination; and the light in which he sets them irradiates all the stretches of experience, whether terrible or merely dull, lying between, so that these never need to be described. Carossa's uniform method as a writer is to make some great alteration in our imaginative conception of life while ostensibly making only a minute one; and his art is an art almost entirely of implication. It is this, probably, that makes one feel in all his writings a sort of natural magic; a natural magic not fugitive and indefinable as in poetry, but constant and almost reasonable. Everything he touches is transmuted, yet never robbed of its diurnal reality; it becomes—one can only put it in this way—at once more ordinary and more strange.

Occupation with trifles, submission of experience to mysterious lights: these are often ways of escaping from problems too disagreeable for the writer to face; and a hasty reader might find Carossa evasive. But one has only to turn to a passage here and there in *A Roumanian Diary* to see how great is one's mistake. The following, for example:

> Like a swarm of hornets the shells dashed against the rocks, tearing the flesh from the limbs of the living and the dead. Sometimes German wounded called to us, sometimes Roumanian, who were now being mutilated for a second time by the fire of their comrades. Some of them suffered in silence; others twisted like wounded snakes. Through the zone of death we saw Germans lightly wounded descending the moun-

> tain, a few white and shaken, but others walking jauntily, dressed up as if for a fancy-dress ball in the gay-colored belts, jackets, and military decorations of their dead enemies. One had brought back a gramophone with him from the Roumanian lines; now an idea suddenly struck him, he placed it on a stone and set it going, the page in *Figaro* began to sing, and like the voice of a mad soul Mozart's music rose in a world of ruin.

Or again:

> Turning round I looked down in the face of a dying man of about thirty; his eyes were closed, his mouth terribly twisted with pain. His fingers still clutched fast the hem of my cloak. Through a gray cape which covered his breast a slight vapor was rising; R. threw it back; under his torn ribs his lungs and heart lay exposed, the heart beating sluggishly. A number of silver and copper medals of saints which he had been wearing on a black ribbon round his neck were driven deep into his flesh, some of them much bent. The man half opened his eyes; his lips moved. Simply for the sake of doing something I filled my morphia syringe, and then I saw that this was what he seemed to want; he pushed the cloak aside and tried to stretch out his arm to me in readiness. . . . After the injection he laid his head back against the birch almost in comfort, and closed his eyes, in whose deep sockets large snowflakes were already beginning to fall. We hurried on; it was almost an hour before we reached Hallesul.

How can one describe the spirit which breathes through these two scenes? It is a soft light that beats upon them; yet how definite is the detail, macabre in the gramophone-playing, horrible in the 'slight vapor' rising from the dying man's breast. There is a sentence in the same book which suggests better than any formula could Carossa's implicit attitude to his themes: 'The world, rough, raw and monstrous as it is—I live in it as in a thin and gaudily iridescent soap-bubble, holding my breath to keep it from bursting.' In his books every object is touched with the solicitous skill of a physician who knows the pressure which will maintain its true shape, or restore it, if it is lost, and who 'holds his breath' lest any too violent movement should injure or destroy it, whether it be 'raw and monstrous' or delicate. Every object is to him like a thing infinitely fragile and infinitely valuable, which must not even be handled too much, but rather placed in a not too urgent light. His style is a pure illuminating medium. It is clear as water; but it has an inner lustre like the limpid stream he found near the Roumanian front, which gave the common brown pebbles a gleam as of gold. He dips an object or an experience into that stream, and immediately it glows with all the hues which the customary light has dulled or worn away. His books paint a perpetual morning world where all things seem newly awakened, and have their first bloom upon them.

This quiet radiance plays with a particular magic round the scenes in his two little masterpieces, *Eine Kindheit* and *Verwandlungen einer Jugend*. There has probably been no books on childhood such as these since mystics like Traherne. By an inflection here and there, by the rhythm of the prose, sweet, tranquil and pure, they do indeed faintly but persistently recall Traherne. But the radiance which lies over them is less bright, and more diffused; it does not come directly from heaven, like Traherne's, but circuitously, through the hidden forces of the earth, which to the child are secretly bound with the heavenly ones. It is imminent in such things as a favourite splinter of granite, or a glass bead which the boy loves to swing against the window-pane; in all animals, in stones and trees, in houses, and especially in the house which is his home. To this world can be applied the words which Hofmannsthal applied to Carossa's work itself. 'Of Carossa's books,' he says, 'nay, of any chapter in them, one can speak as of some mysteriously operative substance such as radium from which a life-giving power goes out, only some of whose effects we know, and through which we feel that we are brought in contact with quite obscure realms; yet those powers work in silence, and are more akin to the powers in the growing seed or in the tree which heals itself than to those which come to being in the tempest.' Sometimes those forces appear in some dreadful guise, but then the child feels protective powers spontaneously arising to restore the balance, and heal the wound in the world which enfolds him. Take this curious passage, for example, from *Eine Kindheit*:

> All things, even the most terrible, when we encounter them, must take on a form consonant with our own nature; everyone has a profound knowledge of this, and because of it good men live in the world without fear. I had never been a nervous child, and though I had no desire to look on death, neither did I ever try to avoid it. With a feeling of solemn exaltation, while a shudder which brought tears to my eyes ran over me, I had seen in the mortuary the robed dead lying between their burning candles, and I had not thought of corruption. The feeling that the invisible God Who chose to manifest Himself in shadowy hints had here for once operated solemnly and immediately: this childish feeling with its grave terrors mastered me and allowed no trace of animal panic to rise. Strangely comforted I went my way, and everyone I met afterwards seemed to me very beautiful and good.

Here we see clearly the powers which make the bark of the tree heal itself, and the reciprocal working of the forms of the child's world.

To these forces the child resigns himself with an astonishing faith, which may be due simply to the fact that being three-parts potentiality, he has a deeper knowledge of all potential things than a grown man can have. Accordingly his affection goes out to all sorts of objects, making us feel that the life of children is indeed a kind of fabulous life. 'The presence of animals,' Carossa says in *Eine Kindheit*, 'always plunged me into a vacant, melancholy expectation such as I never felt among human beings. I wondered if other children felt the same thing, but I never discovered whether they did or not, and believed that I was the only one in the world to have this feeling. At such moments if thoughts of my father and mother, my lessons and prayers, came into my mind, I put them away as unendurably alien, as if under the spell of the animals I wanted to be nothing but an animal myself, and not to be drawn out of the innocent melancholy of animal life; until suddenly I would spring up in a kind of alarm and run home, glad to emerge again into the everyday life of mankind.'

Carossa's world of childhood has another main quality which all but the greatest writers on childhood have overlooked: it has an order far more immutable than that of the adult's world, an order in which all things seem to have rested on their stations forever. There like eternal patterns exist the figures, simple as an abstraction, immutable as the tables of a law, of father and mother, servant and teacher; figures which indeed seem all the more intensely real because they are incarnate symbols, because father and mother and teacher and servant are more than the general idea of a human being, and because through them the child guesses at the order of the world and resigns himself to it with greater security. That order is to him almost absolutely permanent; for the child has a sense of duration which not only runs back, like ours, into the past, but—as it has not still been undermined by doubt—forward into the future as well. In that world everything seems to have an additional dimension, and to exist in some space at right angles to Time; and it is here, and not in isolated passages, that Carossa reminds us of Traherne. As one watches the little boy in *Eine Kindheit* moving with such mysterious confidence and certainty in his world filled with beings greater than himself, one is reminded of the famous passage in which Traherne tells how, on 'a lowering and sad evening, being alone in the field, when all things were dead and quiet, a certain want and horror' fell upon him. He goes on to tell of the thoughts which came to comfort him, and some of these seem to take us into the very heart of Carossa's work. Among them were that he was 'concerned in all the world', that 'in the remotest borders the causes of peace' delighted him, that 'a remembrance of all the joys' he had from his birth ought always to be with him, and that 'the presence of Cities, Temples, and Kingdoms' ought to sustain him.

This is an almost complete key to Carossa's work. His intention, never explicit, is essentially to show that we are concerned in all the world and that distant and invisible things, 'the presence of Cities, Temples, and Kingdoms', sustain us, and, more particularly in his books on childhood, to remind us of all the joys we have had from our birth. There is, it can almost be said, no pain in his books, for pain has been transmuted in memory, or understood anew in relation to all that world in which we are concerned. In reading even his most trifling incidents we are conscious of the unshakable order of that world; and the movements of his figures there have something of the serenity of the motions of the stars. Trifling or erratic at first sight, we presently feel in them the thrill of an ethereal harmony, which comes from our divination that here all the things that have been torn from their stations have been se: back upon them again. This is Carossa's rare distinction as a writer: that he not merely describes things, but quietly, as if by an act of mystical legendemain, restores them to their places—where alone they are truly what they ought to be. This is why there is serenity in his descriptions even of pain. He does not soften it; he sees it as a mysterious and terrible force; but in the powers which rise to combat it he discerns the order of the world, and remembers that we all rest upon it. He has a constant sense that at every moment, no matter how terrible, the reconciling powers which hold the universe together are near us. His apprehension of those powers is in the last resort a mystical one; and like all mystics he finds significance in incidents and modes of experience which by the normal mind are accepted either as mysteries or commonplaces. But he differs from most mystics in always trying to provide a practical and everyday justification for his intuitions; for his perpetual object is completeness. It is therefore only in some of his rare dreams that we get a pure mystical vision, which he sets down without comment, and simply as part of the reality which he is trying to understand.

> I was a child again, and walking over stony mountains through a thunderstorm. I had a white scroll of paper in my hand, and did not lift my eyes from it. If I ask myself now what was on that white scroll, I must confess that it was blank, not a letter nor a sign on it; and yet I was enraptured by what I read there. Low rolling clouds rained upon it, lightning flashes flickered over it, the sky and the crags thundered, and from the distance the uncanny spirits of the dead called to me; but I read ineffably blissful words upon that blank paper, and was unmoved by the storm and the cries of the dead.

Even when he is describing the cries of the dying, Carossa seems to be reading on this scroll which is invisible to us of things which have lent to his utterance that peculiar purity, sweetness and serenity which are without a rival in modern German prose.

There has been a sort of literary agitation recently against books on childhood, an agitation justified partly, no doubt, by the mawkishness or irresponsibility of so much of that class of literature. It is assumed, and nine times out of ten perhaps rightly, that the writer is indirectly attempting to reassume the privileges of the child, and to be found charming by being found appealing. Yet it is obvious that there are as many ways of writing about the preoccupations of childhood as about those of adulthood; about sex, for example, to take the most salient of all, for its advent marks the end of the one stage and the beginning of the other. The saving virtue in any description of childhood and love, both so difficult to describe without excess of sentiment, is a sense of proportion, a just evaluation of the most subtle and yet insistent realities; and this virtue Carossa has in a high degree. For a writer who tries to set every object in its place in relation to the whole cannot overlook the fact that his main theme, childhood, has its right relation too; and it is impossible that he should treat it in the style, for example, of Mr A A Milne or Sir James Barrie. With Carossa the choice of childhood is indeed, one almost feels, a just incident of his method as a writer, which is, as I have said, to emphasise an overlooked factor, and to make a great alteration in our imaginative conception of life while ostensibly making only a small one. In describing the child growing up within its unit of the family, he insensibly evokes for us an image of humanity growing up within a unity far larger and more complex, yet still human. And, as he describes them, the virtues of this smaller economy are the same essentially as those of the greater. Childhood is not to him, as it is to Sir James Barrie, the period of irresponsibility; he is free from that almost universal illusion of the adult mind looking back on its first protected years. On the contrary he shows the child reasoning on cause and effect, guessing at and taking on responsibility almost as naturally as it plays and day-dreams, and recognising gradually that it is part of an economy.

This is one of the qualities which distinguish Carossa's descriptions of childhood from those of more conventional writers; another is his strong sense of continuity and tradition. Real integrity in a people consists in its truth to the deepest things in its experience from the time of its emergence; real integrity in an individual consists in the same thing. This is no doubt the true sense in which the child is father to the man; and this also is probably what makes us feel that the man who has quite erased his childhood is distorted from the pre-ordained human norm. In reading Carossa we divine that the truths which he expresses reach back through all his life; that they have the same continuously creative force as the traditions of a people. So although his subject matter is limited, he is more naturally and universally human than any other writer of his age. Nor is his humanity merely quietistic; the virtues he unobtrusively fortifies in us are active ones, and he fortifies them in the most natural way, by means of those 'life-giving powers' of which Hofmannsthal spoke, 'only some of whose effects we know', but all of which are salutary. He himself was for many years a busy doctor in the poor quarter of Munich, and an overworked medical officer during the War. And this fact may perhaps best explain his gnomic sentence, already quoted, about the 'rough, raw and monstrous' world which one must live in as in a soap-bubble, holding one's breath to keep it from bursting. In his daily life he saw no doubt enough of the rawness of the world; yet his vocation taught him that its health or sickness, its harmony or disharmony, depended upon an almost infinitesimal delicacy of balance, which a single erroneous movement could derange. Every sentence he wrote holds this double implication: of a world 'rough, raw and monstrous', and yet depending upon a balance of forces so sensitive that the mind can only guess at it. His two most characteristic books describe a few trifling incidents in the life of a boy; yet out of these he has constructed probably a more complete and proportioned image of the world than any other writer of his time.

Hermann Broch

The Modern Scot VII No 2, August 1932, 103-10

Hermann Broch's name is only beginning to be known in Austria and Germany; it is hardly known at all in this country. And that is easy to explain, for he has written only one book thus far. But that book is a masterpiece; it is, moreover, quite new in conception and method; and it resolves many of the problems with which the more advanced novelists, during those last two decades of experimentalism, have been struggling.

Literary criticism in the strict sense requires a collaboration between the reader and the critic; both must be acquainted with the subject of discussion; it must be present in both their minds before anything can be done. In this essay I shall be unable to prove any of my points; to show for example, as I could easily do if the subject were present, that Herr Broch's trilogy is a work of great beauty, and that its author is an exquisite artist, a psychologist of astonishing depth and originality, and a thinker of sweeping range. These qualities, which finally give his book its value and make it worthy of discussion, must therefore be taken in trust meanwhile, until the English translation has appeared. So this essay will have to be mostly informative and descriptive and confine itself to some account of the method and structure of the trilogy and the central body of ideas on which that structure rests.

The Sleepwalkers (*Die Schlafwandler*) is a trilogy, the separate volumes of which have appeared consecutively and at intervals in Germany. The first is entitled *Pasenow, or Romanticism*, and the action is laid in 1888; the second is *Esch, or Anarchy*, 1903; the third, *Huguenau, or Realism*, 1918. The action in each of the volumes is quite short, covering approximately about a year. Nor does the book resemble in other ways the ordinary trilogy, which is generally concerned with the history of successive generations of the same family, as, for instance, *The Forsyte Saga*. In *Pasenow* the action takes place partly on a large estate on the Polish border of Prussia and partly in Berlin, and it consists largely of the perplexities of Joachim von Pasenow, a romantic young officer of aristocratic family who sees the old traditions, the old security of life, losing their reality, and cannot come to terms with the new ways which insist on forcing themselves on his notice and determining his manner of looking at the world. The second volume, on the other hand, gives a picture of lower-middle class, working class and Bohemian life in the Cologne and Mannheim of 1903, with a glimpse of the socialist and trade union movement which was becoming powerful then. Only two of the characters in *Pasenow* come into this volume, and they have already assumed a rather legendary appearance: Edouard von Bertrand, a former friend of Joachim's, who deserted his class to go into business, and is now a very rich man, and Ruzena, Joachim's mistress, who has fallen on evil days (she appears only for a few minutes). Esch, the hero of this volume, is an incarnation both of the confusion of the age and of its frantic and yet muddle-headed desire to put things right and achieve a new order. The old security to which Joachim von Pasenow clung so desperately is no longer effectively in existence; Esch does not know where he stands; even the most respectable and solidly established things turn out, when he looks at them, to be unstable or unjust or corrupt: confusion everywhere. With the third volume we are in 1918, the last year of the war. The scene is the little Rhineland town of Kur-Trier. Now appears the man who in Herr Broch's eyes is the typical representative of our age; Huguenau, the realistic business man without prejudices, without morality, without a sense of values, and with no traditions save those of his specialised occupation. The old security has now almost completely vanished; even Esch's struggles to find some trace of a just and reasonable order in the world have lost their reality, have deteriorated into a despairing battle with shadows; and nothing much remains but the naked and almost meaningless actuality, in dealing with which Huguenau, the man without prejudices, is alone perfectly at home. In this volume, where all the implications immanent in the first two volumes are resolved, Joachim von Pasenow and August Esch appear; the heroes of the three books are thrown together in the petty daily commerce of a small provincial town. But no satisfactory solution of their relation to one another is possible, and it is violently ended in the few days of the German Revolution, when Esch is killed and Joachim von Pasenow's car is wrecked by the mob and he himself loses his wits. Huguenau remains triumphant.

This is a bald account of the structure of the trilogy. But in spite of the skill that is obvious in that structure, for instance, the changing of the social setting from the first to the second and from the second to the third volume, giving one a feeling of witnessing the development not merely of a family but of a civilisation and at the point in each case where that development can be most clearly seen in operation, what I have said thus far about the structure of the book tells one very little about it, for that structure merely repeats the lines of a second structure, a structure of imaginative thought to which all the action has a strict relation, and which itself amounts to a philosophy of history. To make clear the relation of this philosophical structure to the action of which the trilogy consists I shall draw upon the best known illustration I can find. The formal structure of *The Divine Comedy* is clear, logical and satisfying in itself. But we know that implicit in it is the structure of medieval theological thought, and that without the existence, the support, of the edifice of medieval thought, it could not have been what it is. In his book on Dante Mr T S Eliot has made admirably clear that to enjoy *The Divine Comedy* as a poem it is not essential that we should accept its body of ideas, though it is necessary that we should understand them. The same is true of Herr Broch's trilogy. It can be enjoyed, but not enjoyed rightly, if one ignores altogether the philosophical conception informing it and giving it shape; but its full significance can be seized only if one understands that conception, which is not an afterthought or a moral tacked on to the story, but is immanent in the action and determines the development.

As there is no other modern novel of which, so far as I know, this is true, it will be advisable to make a distinction before going on to outline Herr Broch's underlying conception. His trilogy, for example, is not a propagandist work; he does not use fiction as a means for making certain views prevail against certain other views, as Mr Shaw does in his plays and Mr Wells does in his novels. Nor are his ideas introduced in the form of philosophical dialogues on matters in general, such as the dialogues which Mr Aldous Huxley writes with so much intelligence and skill. The vice of such dialogues in a novel is that they are rarely in character; the thoughts put in the various interlocutors' mouths could be exchanged without making any essential difference. There are no dialogues of that kind in *The Sleepwalker*; the characters do not talk to amuse, or enlighten, or persuade us; they talk about their own concerns and in a style that fits their natures. Herr Broch's thought is implicit not in what they say but in the destinies he gives them and the world in which he sets them; it is silent for the most part, until in the last volume he gives it explicit and formed expression in a philosophical essay consisting of nine chapters appearing at intervals throughout the book. When these chapters come at last they have the effect of a crystallisation towards which all the preceding action has been making; they are the legitimate expression of the logical content of the work, a content which has throughout been immanent in the action, and could only in this way and at this point be given a final intellectual formulation. The book both starts from the works up to the ideas embodied in this philosophical essay, and so before going further, it is necessary to deal briefly with them.

The chapters in which they are developed are given the separate heading of 'Disintegration of Values'. Leaving out all the proofs and qualifications, Herr Broch's thesis is briefly this: that ever since the dissolution of the medieval synthesis a disintegration of values has been going on which today is almost worked out. This process could not have been avoided, and cannot be stopped until it has reached its conclusion; and it was rendered necessary by the bankruptcy of medieval logic itself, by the fact that medieval theological thought, a closed deductive system, could not resolve its own antinomies, and so had to allow reason to start anew from the fact of the empirically given world, or rather from the multitude of facts presented by that world. But the world of medieval thought rested in God; all knowledge, all value, all experience, were given their place in the medieval hierarchy solely with reference to God as the ultimate Reality; and all thought ended in Him. When the medieval synthesis was dissolved the Christian God was no longer left enthroned as the finite-infinite, heavenly-earthly bourne of all human aspiration and thought: man's goal was now projected into the infinite, and there no longer remained any ultimate symbol in which all human values converged and were bound together, any meaning that was more binding than the meaning of each value individually. As these values, however, could no longer find a final common point at which to meet and to rest they had to run on parallel to each other, driven on by their own immanent logic, until each became autonomous, each one pressing forward to break its own record. So military technique becomes an end in itself, business an end in itself, art an end in itself, getting rich an end in itself, even revolution becomes an activity in itself: each governed by its own laws, each regardless of its neighbouring values, and each reaching its *reductio ad absurdum* in a state where only a business man can understand business and only a painter can tell what is the intention of a picture. This process is what Herr Broch means by the 'Disintegration of Values', and the state I have just described is, according to his analysis, the state of the modern world. The logic which informs these parallel and autonomous value-systems is characterised by a complete ruthlessness, by what Herr Broch calls 'an almost metaphysical lack of consideration for consequences'; and the end towards which it is making is a world in which the old ties that bound men together are destroyed and where understanding is impossible, so fatally are men entangled in separate value-systems that ignore each other and cannot comprehend each other. It is a state in which the isolation of the individual grows more and more intense and the value of human life progressively contracts until all that it covers is an occupation or a *métier*. This is the process that is described in the three volumes of *The Sleepwalkers*.

But though *The Sleepwalkers* ends with the consummation of this process, though the author pursues his analysis of the disintegration of our time to the bitter end, his book is not an invitation to despair but far rather a confession of faith. The process of disintegration is, as he sees it, a necessary and painful liquidation of the medieval bankruptcy; but when it is consummated the Platonic idea is fated to return, the community of men bound together by one aim, united by one faith, must necessarily return, because the very laws of human reason, the needs of the human soul, make it inevitable. Throughout the book these two perceptions run parallel: the perception of the historical process through which civilisation is passing, and the perception of the everlasting human need for salvation.

This is a very bald summary of a historical and philosophical essay filled with the most subtle and exact thought. My purpose, however, is merely to give a sufficient outline of it to show the conception from which the trilogy derives its structure: for the whole book follows, or rather imaginatively incarnates, this conception of the disintegration of values. It does this so thoroughly, indeed, that each of the three volumes, recording different moments in the intensifying process, has a separate form of its own. In the first volume the ostensible plot is simple, and consists merely in the solution in action of various perplexities in the hero's mind, these being symbolised by his relation to his friend Bertrand, which he never understands, and his feelings towards his mistress Ruzena and the girl Elisabeth whom his family wish him to marry, which he also does not understand. But the dying tradition to which he clings has still sufficient power to step in and round off the plot neatly: for he marries Elisabeth. This volume is a miracle of delicate suggestion, of suggestion so subtle and fine that it produces an impression of magic. In *Esch*, the second volume, human relations are not so simple as they are in *Pasenow,* in his struggle to establish order in his world the hero involves himself in all sorts of confusion and absurdity, and although in the struggle he does achieve something, not what he desires, but still something, he becomes a comic figure, a figure portrayed with a rarefied humour not unlike that of Franz Kafka. It would be difficult to say what the plot is, for cause and effect in this book work in a peculiar and wholly idiosyncratic way; but the method is still suggestion, used here to open up sudden abysses beneath the action and to show us states of mind never before, I think, explored by any novelist, states of mind in which the seeds of the future seem to be growing in darkness. The action in this book may be called deliberately arbitrary; it is irrational, but irrational in a particular, methodical way, with an irrationality which resembles the reasoning of a child, and indeed Esch, confronted with the anarchy round him and resolved to set it right, is very like a child. In the third volume, *Huguenau*, there is hardly any action at all; the lives of the characters run in the main parallel to one another, converging only now and then, unfruitfully or disastrously; and a catastrophic event from outside, the outbreak of the German revolution, is needed to unite for a moment their disparate destinies.

In all these three volumes there is felt by all the characters a dim perception of two things: that the world is becoming a more and more homeless place, more and more insensible to their desires, their deepest needs; and that a way of salvation must be found. A consciousness of the dehumanisation of the world, and of the need for salvation: these are the two motives which run through the lives of the characters in *The Sleepwalkers*, the two motives which recur again and again in countless metamorphoses throughout the trilogy. One of these motives is rounded off in the essay on 'Disintegration of Values' in the third book. The other is given its final expression in the same volume, in a curious section, also dispersed throughout the text in recurrent chapters, entitled 'Story of a Salvation Army Girl in Berlin'. It is a separate story, with no attempt at realism of presentation, cutting across the parallel strands of the narrative. It is altogether outside the narrative in a world of its own, it is indeed almost outside the book, as one imagines Herr Broch intended it to be. Part of it is written in sonnet sequences, part in prose. In these poems the aspiration for salvation and the sense of spiritual loss, felt by the characters in this and the preceding books, are raised to a different plane, where they serve as a counter-theme to the theme of disintegration. It will be seen that the pattern of the book is extremely complicated, but it is an ordered and deliberate complication, the complication of a musical composition which results in a harmony.

From this account one may gain some impression of the extraordinary formal elaboration and harmonious balance of this astonishing book. I can give no idea of the profundity and exactitude of the author's psychology, for one must cite examples, one must extract scenes or whole characters, and the book is so closely knit that such a thing is almost impossible. Herr Broch's psychology may be called deductive as against the inductive psychology, for example, of Proust. Proust began with certain sensations or feelings and followed them as far as they would take him; and in the end by this means we learn that he did achieve a metaphysic of his own, as the last volume of his colossal work shows. Herr Broch starts from an extremely comprehensive, profound and exact knowledge of the human heart and mind, from certain universal emotions and thoughts which all human beings must feel and think, rather than from what one particular character will feel or think. But, as they are felt and thought by the various figures in this trilogy, these emotions and thoughts take on subtle individual modifications, and are pursued, on the opposite route from that of Proust, to their most secret and almost invisible manifestations. Herr Broch is certainly a very great psychologist, and at his best the effect he produces on one's mind is that of pure illumination. He lays bare desires so secret that only by the road he has pursued could he have reached them, desires more secret than could ever have been discovered by a writer like Proust who started from the given concrete data of sensation, and the limits of whose exploration were determined by that fact. It is as if Herr Broch were taking us within the mind itself and from there were showing us horizons of which we have only dreamed before.

This, I think, is the essential thing to be said about his trilogy. As for the subtlety and harmony of his style, I can convey no idea of that, nor of the consummate skill with which he presents a scene or suggests an atmosphere, nor of the exquisite finish which he has given to all the separate parts of a balanced and majestic whole. But I have tried at least to show that he has made a new contribution to the modern imagination and, incidentally, to the modern novel, widening the scope of both. The nature of that contribution cannot be considered until the book itself is available.

THOMAS MANN The Tales of Jacob, translated by H T Lowe-Porter

Listener XI, 13 June 1934, 1020

Thomas Mann is one of the most variously gifted of contemporary writers. He is a master of prose; he is also a philosophical observer of life and history, and a scholar of formidable erudition, which he carries easily. In his latest book, *Joseph and His Brethren*, a trilogy of which *The Tales of Jacob* forms the first part, he has chosen one of the greatest of stories as his theme. He has treated it exactly in the way that an imaginative writer of the present day, one feels, should treat it. He has not tried to be naive or archaic; instead he has embroidered the short Bible story with all the wealth of knowledge and experience that has gathered since its original telling. This has at first a somewhat disconcerting effect, both on the reader and the simple two-dimensional characters, who look apprehensive, almost startled, when they suddenly find themselves part of a world so much vaster than the one they once imagined they moved in. But Herr Mann's skill is such that these fears visibly subside even in this first volume. Jacob becomes a consciously historical figure, and indeed enjoys himself in the role; and one feels that Joseph, who is conceived as a much more complex character, will as he develops have even more of the historical sense than his father. For the essential difference between the original story and this retelling of it is that the first is completely without the historical sense and that the second is drenched through and through in it, so that not even the characters escape. The historical sense is a modern thing; it can be a powerful spur to imagination, but is, I think, fatal to imagination at its highest reaches, for it can never get away from time. Herr Mann has spread a huge expanse of time round Jacob and his sons, where before there was only a thin transparent strip. He has deepened time behind them, evoking a sense of countless civilisations that rose, flourished and died before they appeared; and in his mind is a constant awareness of the historical development since. Here he is truly impressive; his learning is vast and his imagination is equal to it. But the significance of the original story, a story so simple and unchangeable that it seems to be set against eternity, has been lost; everything has become richer, but by the accretion of perishable substance, by the shoring up of time upon time. This was clearly Herr Mann's aim, and there is probably no writer living who could have carried it out with such brilliant success. He has tried to make of the story of Jacob and his sons a universal human story by enriching it with all the overtones of time. The question is whether that is a way in which the human story can be made universal in a work of imagination. It is the way of history, and it presupposes that human life is historical not only in its development but also in its essence. That is a very debatable view, which cannot be dealt with in a parenthesis; but it is held by many people, and it has a very considerable influence in contemporary literature. *The Tales of Jacob* is a historical novel in this radical sense; it takes its inspiration not from the period with which it deals merely, but from a universal conception of history. That being so, it is a remarkable work. Probably in no novel written during the last few years are so many interesting and illuminating things said, or such wide prospects opened to the mind. The one quality which it necessarily lacks is the absolute significance of the original timeless story.

Perhaps the most exciting part of this first volume is the 'Prelude', in which Herr Mann fills in the vast background to his story. We see Jacob's ancestors losing themselves in the mists of pre-history; Abraham, his reputed grandfather, becoming a shadowy figure mingling into others still more shadowy, until we are left with nothing more than a myth which perpetually repeats itself in flesh and blood. After this the actual introduction of Joseph comes as an anti-climax, and only the author's immense skill succeeds in allaying our doubts. Jacob does become an actual figure in the present volume; Joseph is nothing more than an unconvincing sketch, but in the next two volumes one feels sure that the author will manage to bring him to life, or at least to historical life. The way in which digression is woven into the narrative is admirable; the one becomes just as much an organic part of the book as the other. A serious fault is the edifying tone which Herr Mann insists on assuming. It becomes burdensome at times, and is occasionally marred by facetiousness. This comes out even in simple descriptions such as that of Rachel at her first meeting with Jacob:

> As she looked, the nostrils—perhaps too thick—of her little nose seemed to dilate drolly, and her upper lip, which stuck out somewhat beyond the lower, to shape with it in the corners of her mouth, all by itself and with no tension of the muscles, that lovely thing a tranquil smile.

Herr Mann gives this moralising turn to many other things besides tranquil smiles, and the effect is always one of slight complacency.

GOETHE Essay on Faust

New English Weekly VII, 26 September 1935, 391-2

''Tis a disagreeable canting tale of Seduction, which has nothing to do with the Spirit of Faustus—Curiosity. Was the dark secret to be explored to end in the seducing of a weak girl, which might have been accomplished by earthly agency? When Marlowe gives his Faustus a mistress, he flies him at Helen, flower of Greece, to be sure, and not at Miss Betsy, or Miss Sally Thoughtless.' This was Charles Lamb writing to William Harrison Ainsworth after reading Hayward's translation of Goethe's *Faust*; clearly he was disappointed after the magnificient poetry in Marlowe's play. And in a sense it may be said that Goethe's *Faust*, both in the first and the second part, is a deflation of Marlowe's. Lamb says that the spirit of Faustus is curiosity; it would be truer to say that, as Marlowe conceived him, Faustus was the first modern aesthete, seeking to realise in life the possibilities given to him by his imagination. These possibilities were not possibilities of good or of truth, but exclusively of beauty, and the pleasures which it produced. To experience these pleasures, infinitely desirable in themselves, Faustus had to make a definite pact with evil; he had in other words to act for the rest of his life as if the good and the true did not exist; and this at last turned the world for him into a vacuum filled only with his beautiful imaginings.

I do repent; and yet I do despair.

The penalty which Marlowe's Faustus pays for this turning away from reality, this corporeal escape into the world of imagination, is damnation:

> My God, my God, look not so fierce on me!
> Adders and serpents, let me breathe a while!
> Ugly hell, gape not! come not, Lucifer!
> I'll burn my books!—Ah, Mephistophilis!

Nevertheless, except for the marvellous last scene, the whole poem is a glorification of an aesthetic attitude which, with many modifications, has been often held since, by writers such as Rochester, Byron, Stendhal and Nietzsche, down to Oscar Wilde and M. André Gide. It represents a whole tradition of literature.

One of the most interesting things about Goethe's *Faust* is the way in which during the long course of its composition, which occupied almost his whole life as a writer, this attitude was transformed. His early choice of *Faust* as a theme, and his great admiration for Stendhal and Byron (excessive in the latter case) show that he was deeply attracted by it. The first *Faust*, like Marlowe's, was the work of a young man, a fact which we often forget because we know that Goethe lived to extreme old age. As a play it shows incomparably greater range and variety of power than Marlowe's; and the last act is probably the greatest piece of dramatic poetry since Shakespeare. But it was in his knowledge of all the factors that were involved in the theme that young Goethe showed himself most of all superior to Marlowe. The spirit of his *Faust* was curiosity at first:

> Habe nun, ach! Philosophie,
> Juristerei und Medizin,
> Und leider auch Theologie
> Durchaus studiert, mit heissem Bemühn.

But he turned from curiosity, and his turning from curiosity was a turning to experience, and experience was Gretchen, not Helen: that is, it brought not only pleasure and the exercise of power, but responsibility as well. If Faust had 'flown at' Helen instead of at a simple German girl, as Lamb wished him to do, he could never have felt remorse, and could never have known either what he had actually done. He wanted to realise in life the dreams of his imagination as Marlowe's Faust did; but Goethe shows what actually happens when such dreams are realised: he shows that their realisation creates a whole series of problems that at first seemed to have nothing to do with them, immediately confronting Faust with the values he had ignored. He is pricked with remorse for the consequences of his actions; he learns as a moral being, in other words learns how to act well in this world; and all because he flew at Gretchen instead of Helen. Marlowe's Faust is merely terrified at his own damnation; nothing that he has experienced can be of use to him in this world or in the next:

> I do repent; and yet I do despair.

The theme of Faust occupied Goethe's mind all his life, and the long second part was completed only a short time before his death; its disjointed and rambling shape indeed shows that it was a task laid down and taken up too often. It is, nevertheless, an endlessly interesting poem, with episodes of the most ethereal strangeness and beauty; and it is especially fascinating as a demonstration of the growth of Faust in Goethe's mind. He began with Marlowe's Faust, that is the aesthete resolved to realise in experience the dreams of his imagination. In the first part of the poem he had already transformed Faust into a moral being. In the second part he puts Faust through a course of exercises in the moral virtues and in the understanding of human relations. Faust becomes for a time what we would call a social reformer, and reaches the goal of his earthly life when he sees before him, as the end of all his striving, an unenslaved society:

Ja! diesem Sinne bin ich ganz ergeben,
Das ist der Weisheit letzter Schluss:
Nur der verdient sich Freiheit wie das Leben,
Der täglich sie erobern muss.
Und so verbringt, umrungen von Gefahr,
Hier Kindheit, Mann und Greis sein tüchtig Jahr.

At this point, in earthly achievement, he dies. But then the greatest passage in the whole second part follows, raising the drama to another plane, after this, which seemed the final one. Mephistopheles steps forward:

Mephistopheles:
Ihm sättigt keine Lust, ihm gnügt kein Glück,
So buhlt er fort nach wechselnden Gestalten;
Den letzten, schlechten, leeren Augenblick,
Der Arme wünscht ihn fest zu halten.
Der mir so kräftig widerstand,
Die Zeit wird Herr, der Greis hier liegt im Sand.
Die Uhr steht still—
Chor: Steht still! Sie schweight wie Mitternacht.
Der Zeiger fällt.
Mephistopheles: Er fällt,es ist vollbracht.
Choir: Es ist vorbei.
Mephistopheles: Vorbei! ein dummes Wort.
Warum vorbei?
Vorbei und reines Nicht, vollkommnes Einerlei!
Was soll uns denn das ew'ge Schaffen!
Geschaffenes zu nichts hinwegzuraffen!
'Da ist's vorbei!' Was ist daran zu lesen?
Es ist so gut, als wär' es nicht gewesen,
Und treibt sich doch im Kreis, als wenn es wäre.

That is to say, the moment which to Faust had been the supreme moment of his life is also perfectly empty, and gone as soon as it is seized. His earthly achievement is perfect in human terms, and yet it is immediately 'past, a stupid word', 'as good as if it had never been'. After Faust's death comes the chorus of angels, ending in the Chorus mysticus:

Alles Vergängliche
Ist nur ein Gleichnis;
Das Unzulängliche,
Hier wird's Ereignis.

Faust is shown passing through experience to moral consciousness, exercising that consciousness as, if it is real, it must be exercised, for the bringing about of a good society; but, at the same time, all that he has achieved is 'as good as if it had never been', a parable, a symbol, a *Gleichnis*; and even then 'past, a stupid word'. Starting with only one value, like Marlowe, Goethe incarnates in the figure of Faust all the others, one after another, up to the supreme value of religion. Without the final metamorphosis—Faust's death and translation to heaven—the poem would have no meaning. If Goethe had ended with Faust's vision of a free society, the ending would strike us as fatuous. This point is not interesting in itself, but it is interesting at present; for a great deal of contemporary poetry ends in a vision of a free society; and the reason why this does not always seems to be fatuous is because it is never dramatically stated: we do not see it as the supreme utterance of a human character who will die. As soon as we think of the total destiny of any human being such an utterance becomes stupid. Any reflection on the completely efficacious nature of human action or on the transitoriness of human existence is in danger at present of being called 'defeatism', and the last few scenes in the second part of Faust could easily be called that. Yet it is these scenes that give the poem its final significance, and that is a reflection which, it seems to me, is particularly required at present.

RAINER MARIA RILKE The Duino Elegies with translations by J B Leishman and Stephen Spender

Scotsman, 12 June 1939, 15

The Duino Elegies make up one of the most extraordinary poems of the present century. It is a very difficult poem, both in its ideas and its style, and the ideas require some explanation even after the difficulty of the style has been overcome. However, to call the style difficult may easily be misleading; it is never a knotted or contorted style; what is disconcerting in it is rather an extreme naturalness and immediacy which come from a continuous concentration on the object of thought, a concentration such as the reader can hardly sustain. It is a rapid style: if we could detach it from its meaning, we should see that its main quality was a magnificient ease. Most of the poem was written in a few days: 'There was a nameless storm, a hurricane, in my mind.' Rilke wrote to his friend Princess Marie von Thurn und Taxis-Hohenlohe.

The Commentary

The difficulty is due to this extreme concentration, which is not congested but impetuous, so that one feels that if one could follow everything that is said with equal concentration it would be perfectly clear. But even then the poem would need a commentary, for Rilke's ideas and images are bound to seem peculiar until one knows the meaning he attached to them. By merely reading the poem it is easy to get a sense of its passionate exaltation. But to grasp it as a whole one needs an English rendering to compare it with, and an informed commentary. Mr Leishman and Mr Spender have provided us with this. The translation follows with astonishing success the movement and idiom of the original, and it will give any English reader unacquainted with German an impression of the quality of Rilke's poetry: a very difficult feat. The commentary does perfectly what it has to do; it would be impossible to exaggerate its helpfulness. There is a reproduction of a picture by Picasso, which is referred to in one of the elegies: there are extracts from letters in which Rilke explains his ideas. Everythng has been done to present to the best advantage one of the greatest poems of our time, and this is therefore a book of quite unusual importance.

Human Imperfection

The Duino Elegies is a religious poem, and its prevailing note is one of lamentation over imperfection. The temper of this lamentation can perhaps be best understood from some words which Rilke jotted down on the writing-pad containing the last two elegies written:

> Art cannot be helpful through our trying to help and especially concerning ourselves with the distresses of others, but in so far as we bear our own distresses more passionately, give, now and then, a perhaps clearer meaning to endurance, and develop for ourselves the means of expressing the suffering within us and its conquest more precisely and clearly than is possible to those who have to apply their powers to something else.

Rilke sets man with his divided aims and finite achievement against the Angels, who have 'nothing to do with the Angels of the Christian heaven (rather with the angelic figures of Islam).' For the Angel will and accomplishment are equal, and life and death are one realm: 'There is *neither a here nor a beyond; but only the great unity,* in which the "angels", those beings that surpass us, are at home.' The poem is an attempt to 'express the suffering within us and its conquest'; it is therefore more than a lament, and rises to a religious affirmation of suffering and of death, which is 'our reverted, our unilluminated, *side of life*'.

Rilke's idea of a unity including both life and death is a difficult one, and equally difficult his idea that man's task is to make the visible invisible, transforming the world of objects into an image in the mind. The Angel is the being who has completed this act of transformation, and in him space is therefore 'included'. In the poem Rilke tries to see our world, 'no longer from the human point of view, but as it is within the angel'. At the same time he feels it as a human being who has not yet achieved the transformation, who is not equally at home in the kingdom of life and of death, and the note struck in the first line:

> Who, if I cried, would hear me among the angelic orders?

sounds again and again throughout the poem.

Rilke's Philosophy

But if the angelic orders will not listen to him, to whom can he look for help in the human world? Here too Rilke's thought is highly personal. 'Not angels, not men,' he decides at first, but then turns with a faint hope to the 'great lovers', to those who died young, and to the heroes: a curious selection of saviours. Extracted from the poem like this, Rilke's philosophy indeed is so personal and so curious that it seems the idiosyncrasy of a great mind, of a childish one too; it is as if a child, from some deep source of knowledge, were creating a god and a theology of his own. To understand the poem one must know that theology, but separated from the poem it seems to mean very little: the strange thing is that, incorporated there, it means so much. For the poetry of the Duino Elegies is great religious poetry—greatest perhaps when its note is one of lamentation, but great too when it expresses the hopes which Rilke associated with his highly personal beliefs. We can feel the spiritual realities with which he deals through, or in spite of, the idiosyncratic forms he gives them; we can feel particularly the power of his searching imagination, working at intense heat, and making, in defiance of his own injunction, the invisible visible: for that is the effect which the poem produces. It is shown, for instance, in the last two lines of this passage, brilliantly rendered by the translators, lines very characteristic of Rilke:

> There remains, perhaps,
> some tree on a slope, to be looked at day after day,
> there remains for us yesterday's walk and the cupboard-love loyalty
> of a habit that liked us and stayed and never gave notice.

Mastery of Language

Rilke's mastery of language was extarordinary; he used it as a painter uses colours; as if it were fluid and he could mix it to produce any effect he wanted; his mastery sometimes actually gives an impression of slickness, though more often of wit, as in his description of the church.

as clean
and disenchanted and shut as the Post on a Sunday

To render such a poem must have been inconceivably difficult, and the translators have done it brilliantly.

Thomas Mann Lotte in Weimar

Listener XXIV, 28 November 1940, 782

Lotte in Weimar is, compared with *Buddenbrooks* or *The Magic Mountain* or *Joseph and His Brethren*, a trifle, and at the same time one of the most perfect works that Dr Mann has ever produced. It is a trifle of 135,000 words; light in movement and yet bearing a massive weight of experience and reflection. Its lightness is not a lightness of texture, but comes from the perfect balance with which every aspect of an extremely difficult situation is suggested or stated. Lotte, the heroine of *The Sorrows of Werther*, now Frau Kestner, a widow with a large family, pays a visit to her sister in Weimar forty-four years after her last meeting with Goethe, and in her heart hopes that she will meet the great man again. As soon as it becomes known that she is *the* Lotte, crowds gather in front of her hotel, the hotel porter, who has a literary turn of mind, gloats adoringly over her, a bustling English-woman bursts into her room and insists on sketching her, Dr Reimer, an envious admirer of Goethe, appears to pay his modified compliments; Fräulein Schopenhauer, sister of the future philosopher, comes to tell a long and painful story and make an appeal, and at last August, Goethe's unhappy son, arrives with an invitation to lunch. All this takes up more than half of the book, and is an indirect description of the old Goethe, showing him through the eyes of those who know him best. Then in a chapter of semi-monologue Dr Mann tries to recreate the hidden, secret Goethe thinking his thoughts as he lies in bed and his manservant Carl dresses his hair. The luncheon comes—an acute disappointment for Lotte; Goethe plays the great man to his sycophantic admirers, and shows hardly a sign of human warmth to herself. She is tormented by the sense that beneath their homage and admiration they are consumed by frustrated envy:

> She seemed to see a spectral vision: a scene with many roofs, towers with little bells, and in the street beneath, a train of people, repulsively sly and senile, in pigtails and sugar-loaf hats and coloured jackets; they hopped first on one foot and then on the other, then liftted a shrunken long-nailed

> finger and in chirping voices pronounced words that were, utterly, fatally, and direfully, the truth.

Goethe had just said jestingly that the Chinese were the real democrats, who held that 'the great man is a national misfortune'. Lotte was afraid

> lest the too loud laughter round the board might be hiding an evil something that threatened in a reckless moment to burst forth: somebody might spring up, overturn the table, and scream out: 'The Chinese are right!'

Lotte's uneasiness at the lunch is perfectly crystallised in that vivid little image. She leaves without having her scruples allayed. Then at the last moment, as she is returning from the theatre in Goethe's carriage, she finds the great man waiting for her, and he seeks forgiveness. This eloquent little scene is Dr Mann's atonement to Goethe for a portrait which wavers between irony and satire.

The treatment of this incalculably difficult theme is throughout a miracle of balance and lightness. Goethe, as Dr Mann presents him, is not a prepossessing figure, being sometimes repellent, sometimes ridiculous, sometimes smug; but a sense of his greatness remains. Yet surely no man so great in genius ever had such a vulgar philosophy, if it is expressed in Faust's famous resolve to die on the day on which he said to the passing moment: '*Verweile doch, du bist so schön.*' Dr Mann gives effect in his portrait to that particular vulgarity, the vulgarity of a climber, which made Goethe such a favourite during the pushing, competitive nineteenth century. The thought that Goethe refused to rest in even the most beautiful moment gave the diligent business man the feeling that he was obeying a moral law when he went on tirelessly expanding his business, no matter how big it was. The unnatural moral uplift of the Victorian age can almost be deduced from this famous sentiment; Goethe was the poet of the climber; what he really cared for in people was ability. He is much hated now in Nazi Germany because he sided with Napoleon against the Germans and was in his Olympian way one of the Fifth Columnists of his time. But Dr Mann's attitude to him, which is one of respectful deference tinged with amusement, is far more deadly. It can afford to be deadly, for in spite of his horrible complacency, Goethe was a great poet. This book is, among other things, an exquisite piece of criticism, in which the balance of Goethe's qualities are brought out with infinitely more delicacy and justice than a short review could indicate; but it is first of all a work of art.

HANS CAROSSA The Year of Sweet Allusions

Observer, 1 July 1951, 7

Except for some poetry, and a novel called *Doctor Gion*, all Hans Carossa's work has been autobiographical. Two small volumes, the first about his childhood, the second about his early youth, appeared in English in the early thirties. The present volume continues the story and records the happenings of a year towards the end of last century, when the author, who is a doctor and the son of a doctor, left a little provincial town in Bavaria to study medicine in Munich. Like his other books, it is filled with radiance and charm and a sort of rightness, partly instinctive, partly reflective, which enables him to set down every incident, every situation, in its own essential shape.

This curious perfection comes from an acceptance of things, unusual in our time, so that one has the feeling that everything is in its place. Yet how they came to be there, so surprisingly in a time of displacement, Herr Carossa does not divulge. He certainly has no abstract scheme into which he fits them; indeed, he interferes with them as little as possible and is anxious that they should be allowed to exist and speak for themselves. Yet there, almost without his connivance one would say, everything is, in its own shape, painful or pleasurable, accepted spontaneously; objects evoking serious thought or simple delight.

Between the thought that things should be as they are and delight in their originality and shapeliness, we are held as we read in a sort of dreamlike suspension, a poetic mood. Yet everything is prosaically set down, each incident treated with a solicitous care as if it were an object of priceless value, not on any account to be injured or damaged. This is perhaps why all Hans Carossa's books give us the feeling that we are the better after reading them. Without appearing to do so, he has a curative effect on us. Hofmannsthal said of them that they resembled some medicinal substance that brought sweetness and health to the mind.

The incidents in the book are quite orinary. Herr Carossa describes his youth passed in an age when in Germany, and in other countries, the young were being exhorted to break through the traditional bonds, act freely and become 'Emperors of Life'. The very atmosphere of the age is evoked though with a touch of humour. Carossa shows us the figures thrown up by that wave of absurd enthusiasm and the extravagant things they did. There is a very funny description of a poetry reading given to a large uncritical audience in Munich by the German poet Richard Dehmel. Two working-class women behind the author are busily discussing measles, most of the audience cannot understand the poems that are being read; at last they burst out laughing, and Dehmel, with great dignity, retires. It is a typical incident.

But the descriptions of more ordinary things, of holidays in the country and the enigmatic experiences of youth, show best of all the mysterious power of Carossa's art. He is never emphatic; the effect of mystery seems to be achieved by a complete avoidance of emphasis, as if he were concerned simply to preserve intact in every object its own strangeness. All this is the result of a perfect art. It is high time the two earlier autobiographies were republished. Along with the present one they would give at last an adequate idea of the rare genius of this writer.

HEINRICH HEINE Heinrich Heine by B Fairley

Observer, 2 January 1955, 9

I wonder if Heine has still an enchantment for the young in Germany, after its recent history. Like many people I once felt it, and later on told myself that I had got over it. Now, reading Professor Fairley's fascinating book, I found that it was still there, but whether it was real or false I could hardly tell. That is the riddle which Heine presents. He is too good or too bad to be true.

Professor Fairley sets out in this book to show that Heine's miscellaneous works are consistent with themselves and present a coherent imaginative picture. It will be invaluable to those who are attracted by Heine, those who are repelled, and those—I fancy they are the majority—who are simultaneously attracted and repelled. The book is for readers who know German; the quotations from Heine's verse are in the original, as they had to be for Professor Fairley's purpose. Students of German literature will find his diagnosis of Heine's imaginative world intensely interesting.

What he has done is to bring out and tabulate the ruling images in Heine's poetry and prose, and to read from them the peculiar character of Heine's vision of life. These central images are 'song within song' (I shall return to it again), music and dance, chorus and procession, theatre and ceremony, carnival and costume, and animal fable: all of them, that is to say, except for song and fable, essentially theatrical. They recur persistently in Heine's work, and are used for all sorts of purposes; to tell a classical or medieval or modern story, or to describe heaven or hell. Professor Fairley points out 'how normal and intelligible' these images are:

> In point of intelligibility it is enough to remind ourselves of the frequency with which they occur in common speech. Song, dance, tune, stage, chorus, mask—how often we use them, and use them as images. We dance attendance, we face the music, we play the fool, we drop the mask.

And he finds that animal images are still common in ordinary speech:

> We use our horse sense, we act the giddy goat, we take the lion's share.

But do people actually talk, except in public speeches, about dancing attendance, or facing the music, or taking the lion's share? If we encounter these images in print we recognise them as clichés. Think of someone who uses them all the time, and you will have a grotesque but recognisable picture of Heine. A case could be made out for the thesis that Heine's world of imagination, as Professor Fairley charts it, was really a sort of *grand cliché*, a substitute for the real thing. The cliché can deal with the various worries, disappointments, sorrows of life, including the long agony of Heine's last illness. It covers everything, but at a remove. Heine could not escape from it; at the same time he saw through it; that is what Matthew Arnold called his 'mockery', and that remains his riddle. We still ask whether he was profound, or whether he was not even shallow, as Nietzsche complained about someone else.

There seems no doubt that he used these properties—and no other poet deals so largely in properties—with a full sense of their effectiveness. He was lavish with nightingales and lilies, and enlisted the lotus to give his verse a new look. They did their work, and they still contrive to do it, though we feel there are too many of them gathered in their over-heated summer. The lilies chime, the lotus gazes amorously at the moon, the pine tree in the far north dreams of the southern palm. It is not the world of romantic poetry, but a world of romantic properties, true neither to poetry nor to life. He saw through it, and his irony could reduce it to its true level.

Professor Fairley notes that:

> Heine's most conspicuous success—the greatest hit possibly in the history of lyrical poetry—was scored in the one phase of his verse where his richer nature was suppressed.

Heine's conspicuous success was in the songs, the 'Lieder'. The song form, Professor Fairley holds, 'was too slight to release his images freely', so that 'he was in large measure reduced to the song image itself'. But it seems to me that the songs are so simple and beautiful because in them he was released from dance, stage, chorus, carnival, mask, and all the paraphernalia of the *grand cliché*. The song in itself is simple and universal, and it came so spontaneously to Heine that it was beyond the reach of his irony: at least when he did not insist on appearing as a stage lover. Professor Fairley notes finely that *Die Lorelei* 'is a song about a song or about a subject of a song'. On what he calls 'song within song' he is wonderfully illuminating, as when he points out that in one of the early poems Heine

> dreams a dream of a fairy-tale, a 'Märchen', and in the 'Märchen' there is a song, and in the song there is a girl.

The true enchantment of Heine is in such things as these. His songs have a deeper reality than his later sophisticated verse, the simultaneous reality of past and present, dream and ordinary life; at their best they achieve the simple immemorial depth of folk-song, singing to itself. Here Heine is truly great.

Though I disagree with Professor Fairley's conclusions about Heine, I have nothing but gratitude for his book. I can think of no other book which illuminates Heine's imaginative world so clearly, and brings out so much in his poetry that was unguessed at before. And simply as an inquiry it is fascinating.

THOMAS MANN Buddenbrooks: The Decline of a Family and *The Last Years: A Memoir of My Father* by Erika Mann

New Statesman, 18 April 1958, 536

Thomas Mann was twenty-six when *Buddenbrooks* appeared. It was recognised almost at once as a masterpiece, and it remains his most perfect work: he had not yet acquired the flaws which make his later novels interesting and exasperating. He had the strange fortune to reach perfection at the start; a sort of innocence which had to be lost, or rather discarded, so that he might undertake a lifelong inquisition into the nature of experience itself. *Buddenbrooks* is like a clear and luminous mirror, and the mirror is managed with extraordinary skill, held at the exact distance where it can reflect most clearly the figures which pass across it, and show us the young growing up, the old passing away, and the inevitable gradual calm decline and fall of the Buddenbrook family. This gives the story a plastic beauty and that stillness which seems to belong to time once it is past; and this is what distinguishes it from the crowd of family chronicles which became popular twenty years later. These were mostly a matter of popular history rather than of imaginative invention; they showed the generations being changed from without by general events and temporary ideas or fashions. But *Buddenbrooks* is a true family tragedy, and the Buddenbrooks are brought down by the qualities, good and bad, which they have inherited and cannot any longer transmit. Changes in the general history of Europe touch them now and then, but distantly, and their fate is decided by heredity and the dispositions, spiritual and physical, with which it has endowed them: tradition, pride, mercantile honour, public responsibility on the one hand, and on the other the thinning of their blood, bad teeth, and a fascination with the arts. Thomas Mann was brought up in a similar mercantile family and left it to become a writer. The book is like a final recollection and goodbye, quite without bitterness, rather with delight at discovering the ways in which things had happened in a family so well known, where the virtues of the fathers were visited on the children for three generations.

Time is a continuous presence in the story; we are conscious of it almost as much as of the characters, for it is the element that reveals them, almost that shapes them. They are dipped in time and lifted out again at this or that point in their lives, and we see that they have become themselves in a new way, as if they had undergone a lustration. They are changed, yet are more than ever themselves. These moments may occur in childhood and foreshadow the course of a life. At dinner one evening the queer little boy Christian Buddenbrook

> turns pale and puts back on his plate the peach into which he has just bitten. His round, deepset eyes, above his too-large nose, have opened wider.
>
> 'I will never eat another peach,' he says.
>
> 'Why not, Christian? What nonsense! What's the matter?'
>
> 'Suppose I accidentally—suppose I swallowed the stone, and it stuck in my throat, so I couldn't breathe, and I jumped up, strangling horribly—and all of you jump up—ugh! . . .' and he suddenly gives a short groan, full of horror and affright, starts up in his chair, and acts as if he were trying to escape.

His mother rises in agitation, thinking that he has really swallowed the stone. But Christian gradually becomes calmer and says: 'I only mean, suppose I actually had swallowed it'. Meanwhile,

> The Consul has been pale with fright, but he recovers and begins to scold. Old Johann bangs his fist on the table and forbids any more of those practical jokes. But Christian, for a long, long time, eats no more peaches.

The demon of imagination has frightened the Buddenbrooks for a moment. Christian grows up a playboy, an eccentric, a failure at every occupation he tries, a black sheep, a valetudinarian, a sick man ruined morally and physically by the strange thoughts that enter his mind. He is a farcical music-hall image of the artist, and an embarrassment to the family. Still he is only a younger brother and so he can be dealt with. But when the infection of art spreads, when it overtakes the sole remaining heir of the Buddenbrook business, a beautiful, physically degenerate boy and a born musician, the end comes quickly. The boy's father winds up the business and dies soon after. The day of the good house is over. A poisoned strain, announced in Christian and plainly confirmed in Hanno, the heir to the business, has destroyed the Buddenbrooks. It is a strain, Thomas Mann implies, necessary for the production of art.

That is how the story ends. There is no theorising. Christian and Hanno are simply left for our consideration. Yet the problem of life and art, and of the relation of disease to artistic creation, occupied Mann in almost all his other novels. In *Tonio Kröger*, a fine short story, he describes the alienation of the artist from ordinary life. *Death in Venice*, a Walpurgis Night of disease, perversion and art, is curiously stilted and unconvincing. Yet Mann was still only at the threshold of his preoccupation. Years later he built in *The Magic Mountain* a colossal metropolis of disease. In the great sanatorium, which is more like a nurse of disease than of the sick, we can smell and taste and feel a deadly enhancement of life. The senses and the intellect are sharpened and inflamed in that air; Naphtha and Settembrini carry on an endless dialogue on dictatorship and democracy which would have bored them in the first month if their health had been sound. The book is exhausting because we feel the author is resolved to exhaust his theme and uphold disease against the dull gross health of the ordinary world. The theme was never exhausted. In *Doctor Faustus*, one of his greatest novels, he elaborately traces the connection between disease and genius. Adrian Leverkühn, a musician at a loss, achieves freedom and greatness, symbolically by a pact with the devil, and actually by the after-effects of syphilis. Because of this, his music cuts him off from the ordinary life of people, as Tonio Kröger had been cut off from the life he described in his novels. In return, his music becomes a source of pleasure to the very people from whom he is alienated.

It is curious how the productiveness of disease continued to fascinate Mann. His second-last novel, written when he was almost eighty, described the rejuvenation of a middle-aged woman, the ghostly restoration of her youth by a disease which presently killed her. We are made to feel that a similar cause produces the exhilaration from which art springs. Tonio Kröger in the early story sees the artist as a sick man:

> He looked back on the years that had passed. He thought of the dreamy adventures of the senses, nerves, and mind in which he had been involved; saw himself eaten up with intellect and introspection, ravaged and paralysed by insight, half worn out by the fevers and frosts of

> creation, helpless and in anguish of conscience between two extremes, flung to and fro between austerity and lust; *raffiné*, impoverished, exhausted by frigid and artificially heightened ecstasies; erring, forsaken, martyred, and ill—and sobbed with nostalgia and remorse.

Tonio describes a sickness; in *Doctor Faustus* the sickness becomes a disease. Adrian Leverkühn's music, which is 'life-enhancing', is rooted in disease; so that there must be a word to be said for disease. The idea that 'the artist' is a neurotic type, that he takes to art because he is of no use for anything else, has become quite common. Analytical psychology makes it easy to frame such generalisations. Mann came to his conclusions about art and disease from his own experience; and the conclusions were determined by that something morbid in his genius which comes out so clearly in *The Magic Mountain* and *Doctor Faustus*. But he describes an experience; he does not elaborate a theory.

And in *Joseph and His Brothers*, perhaps his greatest book, he presents quite a different portrait of the artist. Joseph is the born favourite, and exists in a special dimension of time, where ordinary things and ordinary people—his brothers for instance—are different from what they appear to others. Whatever they may do to him, they cannot touch him. He has the vanity of innocence and in his dreams he dreams of his own glory, and sees his brothers bowing down before him, and the moon and the eleven stars making obeisance to him. When he tells his brothers of his dreams he is surprised that they are offended. He is strangely fortunate, and good fortune is part of his character. He stands outside the human spectacle, but without the sense of desertion which afflicted Tonio Kröger. He is filled with the conviction that everyone must love him, and therefore that he cannot come to harm. His life is a dream of the truth; it saves him, but it saves Egypt as well, and his father Jacob and his eleven brothers.

In his old age Thomas Mann became a representative public figure. How seriously he took his public responsibilities one can learn from his daughter's touching tribute to him; he took them with all the seriousness of a traditional Buddenbrook. It may be that his consciousness of his position imparted a not quite authentic solemnity to some of his later pronouncements; when one knows the whole world is listening, one's speech insensibly becomes simple, decent and bourgeois. Mann could never philosophise without becoming heavily solemn. Yet the last years of his life produced his one great Rabelaisian fragment, the *Confession of Felix Krull, Confidence Man*, indeed a triumphant exit for the artist.

V

GENERAL

'Plots' *Synopses of English Literature* by Nora Sholto-Douglas

Nation and Athenaeum XXXIX, 11 September 1926, 615

The intention of this volume is modest and utilitarian. 'These stories,' Miss Sholto-Douglas begins, 'each giving in the briefest possible form the gist of a classical novel, are intended to supply the want of the many people who have no time to read the originals in their entirety, and to whet the appetites of those who have leisure to enjoy in their completeness the pearls of literature dealt with.' It is no doubt salutary that 'those who have the leisure to enjoy in their completeness the pearls of literature' should have their appetites whetted; I sincerely hope Miss Sholto-Douglas has done so; but one doubts whether 'the want of the many people who have no time to read the originals in their entirety' can ever be supplied; they must be left, with sincere regret, to their fate. As a sufficient test of the author's capacity to supply that want, one turns naturally to her synopsis of *Tristram Shandy*. In eleven pages she does her best; nobody, perhaps, could do more; but, in spite of this, one is not conscious that any want has been supplied. On the other hand, Miss Sholto-Douglas's whetting is more successful. But she whets indiscriminately. From 1551 to 1810 she synopsises fiction of a fairly high standard—*The Scottish Chiefs* by Mrs Porter excepted—but 'after 1810 novels were written in ever-increasing numbers'. 'Part II, therefore,' the author says, 'deals with a selection of novels of literary merit which are not as well known to the general public as they deserve to be.' Among these are *Life in London*, by Pierce Egan, *Handy Andy*, by Samuel Lover, *Valentine Vox* by Henry Cockton, and *The Snowstorm*, by Mrs Gore. Do these deserve to be well known? Is not Miss Sholto-Douglas leading the many who have no time, etc, into strange regions? Is she not whetting appetites which would be more profitably left in their original leisure? Should those who will read Mr Arlen in any case be exhorted to read Henry Cockton? Should those who have no time to read Scott be encouraged to read *The Scottish Chiefs*? Miss Sholto-Douglas's book will not serve, one feels, the purpose with which it sets out, nor, one feels still more strongly, would it have a salutary effect if it did serve that purpose.

Nevertheless, it is interesting to have presented in little the plots of a number of representative English novels. The problem of the plot is psychologically a very important one. A certain framework with figures, events, scenes, and a central action, arises in the writer's mind. Without this framework he can do nothing; with it, if he is a great writer, he will do what at the time he most desires to do. If he is not quite a great writer, if his sincerity is incomplete, there will be a break, an imperfection in the plot, which he will have to bridge by improvisation. He will have to bring in a makeshift of some kind, as Charlotte Brontë does in *Jane Eyre* to unite Rochester and her heroine, and this makeshift will be a palpable revelation of a failure in inner sincerity. When Richardson was writing *Clarissa Harlowe*, 'pressure was brought to bear on him,' to quote Miss Sholto-Douglas, 'to induce him to make Lovelace repent and Clarissa relent and forgive him. Many ladies on their knees passionately besought the author to spare her, Colley Cibber seconding them and vowing that "he should no longer believe Providence or eternal wisdom or goodness governed the world, if merit and innocence and beauty were to be destroyed". But Richardson was inexorable.'

And Richardson was inexorable because it was important for him that he should remain faithful to the drama as it was given him, to the chart of his unconscious, as, after the discoveries of psycho-analysis, we might say now. It is this that gives his plot a second reality behind the first obvious reality which we find in the plots of Fielding and Smollett. In the great English prose fiction which approaches the condition of poetry, the plot is not merely the framework of a picture of life; it has a meaning in itself which we cannot decipher, but which we accept. We are conscious of this meaning in *Wuthering Heights, Moby Dick,* and certain of Mr Hardy's Wessex Novels. We are conscious of it in the great poetic tragedies of the Elizabethan age. The characters in works of this kind live in two worlds simultaneously; they are figures in a pattern, strangely significant, which comes, complete and unanalysable, out of the writer's subconscious mind; they are at the same time human characters, resembling, but also more rich and more remote than, the characters in novels in the purely English tradition of fiction, those of Fielding, Smollett, Thackeray, and Trollope.

It is perhaps only of works such as the first of these, and of the epic and the poetic tragedy, that we should say that they have a plot. The construction of *Tom Jones* has been much praised; but we can detach it and think of it by itself; it is not involved with the whole meaning of the novel as the plots of *Wuthering Heights* and *Moby Dick* are. It is external, reasonable, congruous, but in itself it has no significance. In *Tom Jones* everything happens at the right moment; every encounter is beautifully timed; but we do not feel an action developing inevitably, but rather a wise and skilful hand arranging the events, and partly, at any rate, for the reader's entertainment. The difference between the happenings in *Tom Jones* and those in *Wuthering Heights* or *The Return of the Native* is that we feel the first, from our experience of life, would have happened, whereas we feel that the second must have happened. It is, to use very hackneyed terms, but the best I can find, the difference between the literature of vision, which, when it is true, we feel to be absolute, and the literature of observation, which, when it is most true, we feel to be relative. Vision creates the pattern, and all the writer's experiences find their places and their values in it. Observation accumulates a mass of material, and has aftewards to construct a pattern, more strict or more loose, as a form for his experience. The form may be as closely woven as Fielding's, or as easy as Sterne's; it will not much matter, for what the writer is trying to communicate is his knowledge of life and his ideas about life, not an imaginative vision whose plot, whose articulation, is given absolutely, because created, by its content.

Looking through Miss Sholto-Douglas's synopses of English novels, one realises that the organic, the truly poetic, plot is very rare. Yet, after according the great masters of the English novel the homage they deserve, after acknowledging the vast and rich province which they have added to English literature, we must recognise that it is this kind of plot that gives the novel what Mr Clive Bell has called 'significant form', and makes it pure art. The real impulse behind every valuable modification of the form of the novel in the last two decades has been the impulse to make it a more and more pure art form. We are not satisfied with the type of novel whose great master is Fielding, and which retained its essential characteristics until the end of Victoria's reign; there is far too much unresolved matter in it, and it is a necessity that this should be resolved. The generation before ours, represented by Mr Bennett and Mr Galsworthy, got rid of a proportion of this encumbering matter; but the novel was not transformed, it was only lightened a little. The real attempt to solve the problem of the novel, to make it completely an art form, is to be seen in works such as *Ulysses* and *Mrs Dalloway*, works which have no plot in the conventional sense, but which do have, though in both cases incompletely, a plot in the more essential, poetic sense. The task of these writers,the original vision of life being given, has been to make everything 'aesthetic' (I use the most generally comprehensible term); to give every incident, every impression, not merely the everyday reality which Mr Galsworthy and Mr Bennett would give them, but the reality of forms in the world of art. To do this truly is not to leave anything that is essential out of the novel as we know it; it is rather to resolve elements in it which, because they have not been resolved, have not been completely real. The plot has rarely been resolved in this way in English prose fiction, and that is a sign that a number of important questions have not been answered.

'The Contemporary Novel'

European Quarterly I No 2, August 1934, 70-76

To write about the contemporary novel presents two main difficulties. In a time of rapid change it is very hard to tell in the first place what is contemporary, and in the second, what is the novel. There is the additional difficulty that every age seems to contain a whole conglomeration, a whole jumble of ages, all of which regard themselves, no matter how modestly they may disclaim it, as the authentic one. Is Mr Priestley the real representative of our age, or Mrs Woolf, or Mr Huxley, or Mr James Joyce, or Mr Hemingway, or Mr Faulkner? To ask the question is to be disconcertingly conscious that all these writers, the advanced no less than the conservative, have already, in a few years, become almost historical figures. It is nearly twelve years since *Ulysses* appeared, a book which was greeted variously as the end of the novel, and as the beginning of a new prose literature. *Ulysses*, with all its genius, has done extraordinarily little to fructify or to influence prose fiction; and by now it has more or less fallen into the past. The same is true of the novels of Mrs Woolf and Mr Huxley, both of whom a few years ago stood in the forefront. Is this their fault or the fault of circumstances over which neither they nor anybody had control? Is their supersession due to some defect in their gifts or to the increasing rate of change in the civilised world, which will not allow anything new to remain valid for more than a few years?

The most original work in prose fiction during the last twenty years has been influenced by a factor which in the novel before then was almost unknown: the historical sense. By this I mean not merely a peculiarly clear awareness of the uniqueness of one's own period as a stage in a more general development, but also an ever-present knowledge that all civilisations have only a relative validity, that they are, even in periods of apparent stability, in perpetual change, and that, considered all together, they make up at best only a fluctuating and imperfect entirety. To see in this way is to see everything, not as a form or a category, but as a development; and so the novel itself sometime in the beginning of the century became a development, something that was not to be accepted as an obvious and satisfying form, but was on the contrary to be 'carried further'. So what interested the novelist of Mr Joyce's and Mrs Woolf's generation was the stage which the novel had reached, and how it could be developed. The learned novelist appeared, the novelist who knew all about the ancestry, beginnings and proliferation of the novel, and

Ulysses is, among other things a sort of résumé and summing up of the history of prose fiction. A somewhat similar achievement appeared in poetry about the same time: Mr Eliot's *The Waste Land*. Almost all the most original work in fiction during the last twenty years—except perhaps the most original of all—has been decisively conditioned by the historical sense. The novel has ceased to be an accepted category as it was to Dickens and Thackeray, even to Bennett and Galsworthy, and become a changing organism. In other words it is no longer an absolute convention, but a process, a relative thing.

But the historical sense, if one carries it to its conclusion, sees not merely this or that but everything as a development, a secular development which does, it is true, imply certain universal principles impressive in themselves, but yet insensibly so insists on the differences between one age and another that it tends to see less clearly the permanent categories that rule all human life than they were seen in former times. We are all far more clearly aware than our fathers were that time changes everything: not only ourselves in our progress to death (the sixteenth and seventeenth centuries had a far deeper sense of that than we have), but the world around us, our physical and intellectual environment, the ordinary customs and prejudices that give direction to our existence. Time has become the problem of the modern novelist; it is the theme of Proust, of Thomas Mann in *The Magic Mountain,* of Mr Joyce in *The Portrait of the Artist as a Young Man* and *Ulysses*, of Mrs Woolf in *To the Lighthouse* and *The Waves*, of Hermann Broch in *The Sleepwalkers*. It may describe the development of a single character, like *A Portrait of the Artist as a Young Man* or that of modern civilisation, like *The Sleepwalkers*. But the insistence is on change rather than on what is changeless, on potentiality rather than on finality. If this kind of novel is executed by a writer of great philosophical as well as imaginative powers something may be produced which transcends its category, as *The Sleepwalkers* does. *The Sleepwalkers* is saturated perhaps more thoroughly in the historical sense than any other modern novel, but by its intellectual and moral passion it rises above the contemporary, and in a new way shows us human life as an eternal category, perpetually changing and perpetually returning to itself. It is a resolution of the time novel such as is not likely to be achieved again for some time, for it is rarely that Hermann Broch's union of philosophical and imaginative power is found in a novelist.

The Sleepwalkers, therefore, is not typical of the time novel, one of whose characteristic signs is this very stopping short of a resolution. Its immediate ancestor was the period novel, the best example of which was Arnold Bennett's *The Old Wives' Tale*, a book which has been imitated a score of times and is still being imitated. What makes *The Old Wives' Tale* impressive is really a profound sense of the passing of time which is as old as story-telling itself and can be found in the tale of King David in the Bible. But it also showed very clearly a sense of period; it described a world changing and the stages in that change; and in doing that it gave a new theme to the novelists, who seized upon it eagerly, for they too were living in a rapidly changing world and consequently saw human existence in the same way that Bennett did, though they had not been conscious of it before. The next step was an inevitable one. In the period novel the generations had indicated the stages in the mutations of time; in its successor these stages were concertinaed and became stages in the development of the characters, so that every character became a series of changes, each of them, including the last, relative and inconclusive. *A Portrait of the Artist as a Young Man*, one of the best examples of the time novel, describes the main character, Stephen Dedalus, as passing through a number of mutations from childhood to manhood; but Stephen himself is never there actually; he is always becoming, and he is still becoming when the book ends, though the author tries to give a decisive turn to the last stage to which he brings him. Most novels of development end in this way, showing the hero experiencing a more than usually deep illumination or coming to a more than usually firm resolve; but one has only to reflect that these states too are mere stages to feel that such a conclusion to a book is as purely relative as the rest. M. Ramon Fernandez has said finely that the imagination works in a continuous present; and the time novel, the novel which describes life as a series of stages, never achieves that present. Its characters are perpetually on the threshold of it; a single step more and they would plant their feet in it; but they cannot take that step, the moment of realisation is continuously postponed; for time is a development, an invisible moving line between the past and the future, and never a state, a present.

There is another consequence of this conception of personality as a series of stages: that it insensibly analyses the personality into a succession of states in which it is lost. This process is carried to its extreme limit in *Ulysses*, where the personality is reduced to mere floating sensations, idle or serious thought associations, a stream of consciousness that flows for something less than twenty-four hours, and like a tap is left flowing. *Ulysses* is an extraordinarily powerful work of imagination, and in taking it as the most striking example of a literary process carried to its extreme conclusion I do not wish to impugn its genius, which I sincerely admire. It is in itself far more than the carrying of a process to its conclusion: it is an attempt to break through by the use of the historical sense into another kind of present, complex and many-faceted, a sort of synthetic present of which the actual present is only the last echo. But whatever its actual achievement, it destroys the traditional organic absoluteness of the present and of human character and fate, which can be felt not only in novels of tragedy like *Wuthering Heights* or *Le Père Goriot*, but in the novel itself at its most normal as a convention that has lasted for two hundred years. The abundance and complexity of the relations

Ulysses piles up is unexampled, and seems designed to fill a bottomless gap that no powers, however ingenious, can fill; so that it remains, in spite of this, in the realm of the relative, like all novels inspired by the historical sense, which is the characteristic modern one. Such works must by their nature stop short of that feeling of the simple organic reality of the present which used to be the obvious and expected mark of any work of imagination.

All perhaps that this amounts to is that the novel, like everything else in our modern world, has become part of a problem apparently moving to its resolution, but not yet resolved. The historical sense is a modern mode of thought and feeling; it cannot be simply washed away, even if that were desirable, which it obviously is not; but on the other hand its effect on the work of the novelist has been to make his picture of life merely relative and therefore less significant than the work of the older novelists, simple and naive in comparison as that was. Our feeling for time has grown, our feeling for the timeless dwindled.

We know on the one hand that history is a vast process of change, and on the other that the world is changing round us and that it will not be the same world in ten or twenty years' time. This knowledge is urgent and importunate; it necessarily colours all our images of existence; the future has become almost a palpable part of our lives, like the past, and it is no longer a source of comfort, a channel for all our hopes, as it was thirty years ago in the heyday of Mr Shaw, but a matter demanding real and anxious consideration like the present. From this scheme, past, present and future, there is no outlet, and yet in its totality it does not make up a satisfactory entity, for it is nothing but a process of change in which the present is swallowed up in the past and the future, in a simultaneous state of 'having been' and 'about to be'.

The feeling for the present seems to depend upon a feeling for eternity. The historical sense as it exists and operates is inimical to a feeling for eternity, and indeed acts as a dissolvent of it. Yet we can neither escape from it nor wish with a good conscience to do so. It is there, a capacity of great potentiality which we cannot but use. Nevertheless it is obviously insufficient, obviously conducts us, if we employ it primarily, to a conception of life which has neither shape nor solidity nor meaning. The characteristically modern novel is the novel in which it is employed primarily, and that, it seems to me, is the reason why the modern novel is so tentative, and why it so quickly goes out of fashion. The feeling for eternity has an obvious connection with the sense of form and the capacity to produce it; the feeling for time has obviously a connection with the sense of change and flux. The feeling for eternity and for time are both natural to man, and in the man of imagination they operate simultaneously. Accordingly the novel of the last twenty years may be roughly described as the result of a disastrously exclusive consciousness of time. This, I know, is an extreme simplification of a very complex problem, and countless qualifications would have to be made in order to establish it. Yet, roughly, I think, it is true.

Side by side with this time novel there has appeared something which is its direct opposite, something that many people would not consent to accept as coming within the scope of the novel at all. In the novel of which I have been speaking all is time; in such stories as Franz Kafka's *The Castle* there is no sense of historical time at all. The whole action takes place in a timeless world, and the eternal categories of providence and fate are the only determining ones. Between these two poles, where everything is relative on the one hand and absolute on the other, there is nothing of much vitality in the contemporary novel. Kafka's work may thus, from the purely historical point of view, be regarded as an absolute protest against the philosophy of flux that is implicit in the time novel, and as such as something newer than it. It reinstates the changeless present with the force almost of a discovery, and although its effect has been small till now, one feels that is is bound to grow.

'The Confusion of Modern Criticism'

Scotsman, 3 January 1935, 11

If anyone were to take a representative selection of poetry reviews written fifteen or twenty years ago and compare it with the poetry criticism generally written today, he would find a very great difference between the two. Except in ages when a critical intelligence of the first rank appears, such as Coleridge, the critics of any time tend to give emphasis to one element in literature, and judge contemporary work by reference to it solely. Coleridge himself was not a complete exception to this rule; he could not be just to Pope, just as nowadays we cannot be just to Tennyson; but the criterion by which he judged poetry, that is the imagination, was so comprehensive, and his grasp of it was so profound, that, apart from his criticism of the poets of the eighteenth century, we still feel his judgements on poetry to be as true and penetrating as when he first made them.

The criticism of poetry fifteen or twenty years ago was concerned hardly at all with imagination and a great deal with technique: the main reason for this being that many technical experiments were at that time going on in poetry, some of which, indeed, have been of very considerable value, adding to the poet's possible means of expression. But since then a quite new kind of criticism has appeared, which has nothing to do with poetry at all, and judges it by standards which are outside it. The question which this particular kind of criticism asks is not whether the poem is a good poem, well written, and showing imaginative power, but rather whether it expresses an affirmative, and generally a revolutionary, attitude to life, voicing the desire of the poet to get things done, to build bridges, make flying records, organise communal factories, or exterminate the bourgeoisie. It asks, in other words, whether poetry tends to induce 'action' or leads to 'defeatism'.

Now such criticism is quite unlike the criticism I mentioned at first, and I think unlike any intelligent criticism that has ever appeared in the past. Uninstructed lovers of poetry in the Victorian age, when everything had to be moral, regarded poetry in somewhat the same way, though from a different angle. To them 'The Psalm of Life' was good poetry because there was not the faintest trace of defeatism in it. They demanded that morality, by which they meant the morality of the Victorian age, should invariably be vindicated, no matter how much imaginative truth might suffer in the process (imaginative truth was not a virtue very highly rated by the Victorians); and what strange results this sometimes led to is shown by Mr Hugh Kingsmill in his book on Matthew Arnold, where he very acutely and amusingly analyses the relations between King Arthur and Guinevere, as described by Tennyson in 'Idylls of the King', showing how the poet made them conform to the prejudices of his time.

Moral Effect on Reader

The action of great poetry upon us is, of course, moral in the highest degree: that has been axiomatically understood by every good critic, and was often laid down by Coleridge, perhaps the greatest of them all. But, on the other hand the action of poetry upon us has nothing to do with its conscious message: with the fact that it expresses an 'activist' or a 'defeatist' attitude to life (one must employ this jargon to clear up the point, since it has been employed so generally to confuse it). Almost every poet is at different moments of his life 'activist' and 'defeatist', since he is no more exempt than other human beings from hope and dejection. But we cannot judge, for instance, the poetic merit of the two well-known poems of Shelley which begin respectively:

> Best and brightest, come away,
> Fairer far than this fair day,
> Which, like thee to those in sorrow
> Comes to bid a sweet good-morrow
> To the rough year just awake
> In its cradle on the brake.

O World! O Life! O Time!
On whose last steps I climb,
  Trembling at that where I had stood
    before;
When will return the glory of your prime?
  No more—O never more!

—we cannot judge the poetic merit of these two poems by the fact that the first is affirmative and activist, and the second despairing and defeatist. Nor can we judge by such standards their moral effect on the reader. For after reading these poems we do not jump up at once and beg the best and brightest to come away, or go about for the rest of the week groaning, 'O World! O Life! O Time!' Yet the activist critics assume that the reading of poetry has some such consequence, and the activist poets seem to agree with the assumption, so persistently do they strike themselves, or rather the reader, on the chest. To cheer people, to encourage them to join the local Labour party, take a cold bath every morning, and practice Swedish drill, is no doubt a salutary thing. The evil comes in when this is conceived as the highest task of poetry, and when poetry is praised in as far as it produces these results, and blamed in as far as it fails to produce them, or does not try to produce them.

Critics and Karl Marx

This kind of poetry and criticism, in other words, implies a conception of poetry which is so simple and shallow that it has an appearance of originality. Almost all simple and shallow conceptions of literature have the support of a philosophy, and are very often, indeed, made possible only because they have that support. The philosophy which makes possible the latest kind of criticism is that associated with the name of Karl Marx. This philosophy, applied uncritically, gives very often a quite new significance to things, the meaning of which has been for a long time settled by tradition. Marx himself was not responsible for this kind of criticism: in literature he was quite orthodox, and a great admirer of Shakespeare; but once a philosophy has got out of its creator's hands it can be applied to anything. Consequently the modern critic who praises a poem because it breathes action and condemns another because it oozes defeatism has a different conception of poetry altogether from the accepted one, and is not speaking of poetry, but of an ideal of poetry in his mind. But at the same time he is dealing with actual poetry, or what pretends to be actual poetry; and the confusion which arises from this situation is beyond all clearing up.

Another contributory and honourable cause of the rise of this kind of criticism is the feeling that society is in a bad way and must be put right. Society can be put right only by political action; and if one is perfectly sincere in desiring to put it right the obvious thing is to throw oneself into political action of some kind. Instead of doing this, however, the majority of the younger generation write political criticism, which biases criticism., or political poetry, which dilutes and enfeebles poetry. The error in all this lies in demanding of poetry that it should have an effect different from the effect it is capable of producing. In demanding this, criticism encourages an error. Such criticism is intellectually feeble, it is true, but it is increasing, and it has a considerable influence. More attention should be directed upon it.

'Deep in Joyce'
Dublins's Joyce by Hugh Kenner

Observer, 17 June 1956, 11

Criticism, especially in America, is becoming more and more like a mining operation. The critic soon leaves behind the outward contour of the book or the poem he is considering, and presently forgets it, he is so busy exploring the underground corridors and galleries. The book is everywhere around him, yet it cannot be seen. The common reader, if he is susceptible, is tempted to enter the labyrinth himself; and reading has become one of the dangerous occupations, especially for students at certain English and American universities.

I fancy that no critic should quite forget his first thoughts about a book. His second thoughts are certain to come, and they may last for a good long time. But when he comes to his twentieth or thirtieth thoughts, he is in danger of forgetting the book itself and what it was written for, and occupying himself with thoughts inspired by other thoughts about it. He discovers 'symbolisms' of a more and more ingenious remoteness, and becomes involved in them. The critic who is led into these subtleties has not swallowed the book: the book has swallowed him. You might think that his struggle with the symbolism would help the common reader to understand the book more clearly; but it is hard to say, for one can easily follow the symbolism of an imaginative work and completely miss its meaning. For if you do not see it in proportion and in plain daylight you have no means of judging it.

My first thought on Mr Kenner's difficult and interesting book—and first thoughts are all that a reviewer can afford—is that it would have been more illuminating had it been written at an earlier stage. As it is, he is quite unusually intelligent, and he has a critical discrimination rare among New Critics. On the profound influence of Ibsen on Joyce he has new and valuable things to say. On the resemblance between

Sherlock Holmes the detective and Stephen Dedalus the aesthete he is both amusing and pointed. He shows, I think for the first time, how deeply Joyce's early volume of poetry, *Chamber Music*, was coloured by the genteel romantic Irish songs once so elegiacally sung in Dublin drawing-rooms. He is best of all on Joyce's use of Dublin speech, where 'every phase of thought and action has a received analogue or bookish correspondence'. Joyce got over this by 'double writing', a sort of parody; 'his attention focused on the invisible point of coincidence betweeen half-living people and half-real literature, opera, oratory, and music.'

Mr Kenner deals with these important aspects of Joyce in such a way that future critics will have to take note of him. It is when he sets out to track down Joyce's symbolism that he loses all measure. Everyone knows the opening page of *Ulysses* where Buck Mulligan comes from the stairhead of the tower bearing a bowl of lather on which a mirror and a razor lie crossed, and wearing a yellow dressing-gown 'ungirdled', and intoning: 'Introibo ad altare Dei'. The scene is easily, comically symbolic. This is how Mr Kenner deals with it:

> Mulligan stands at the head of his altar steps, atop the tower, with a vacancy for an altar. The narcissist mirror and the slaughterer's razor make a bitter cross on his chalice; the razor introduces the theme, later to receive enormous amplification, of the priest as butcher. . . . His yellow dress-gown is a gold chasuble, 'ungirdled' because the priest's cincture symbolises unMulliganian chastity; it is sustained by air instead of by a server.

It is easy to read into a passage what is not there, simply by reading too much. Buck Mulligan wanted to shave, and to shave you need a mirror and a razor. Mr Kenner ignores the situation and deals only with the words, and not very good comedy turns to deadly earnest. I quote this as a single instance of what happens frequently when Mr Kenner is dealing with symbolism. *Ulysses* has certainly a symbolical plan; Joyce himself insisted upon that. But to give the symbolism its due weight, to distinguish between the passages where it is lightly or comically indicated and those where it is seriously meant is not easy, and this is where Mr Kenner fails, and fails through his method, not his intelligence.

Ulysses is a remarkable work, both for its genius and for the fact that, in spite of its magnificent dialogue, there is hardly any real intimacy between the characters, except now and then on the biological level. This warm blarney enveloping an inward coldness characterises Dublin life, according to Mr Kenner: paralysis and death are the term in which he repeatedly describes it. But I feel myself that the coldness came from Joyce himself, the detached artist; the *Portrait of the Artist as a Young Man* gives ample reason for thinking so.

Yet in spite of faults of emphasis, this remains an excellent book, and should be read by all who read Joyce.

NOTES

The main purpose of the notes is to list treatments of the authors in other notable essays and reviews by Muir not included in this selection.

Abbreviations: ***L*** The Listener; ***N and A*** The Nation and the Athenaeum; ***O*** The Observer; **R** Review.

Aiken. **R** of *Blue Voyage* in ***N and A,*** XLI (18 Jan 1927) 373.

Auden. **R** of *New Year Letter* in *Horizon* IV, No. 2 (Aug 1941) 139–43.

Bates, Ralph. **R** of *Lean Men* in ***L,*** XII (19 Sept 1934) 506.

Bennett. **R** of *The Woman who Stole Everything* in ***N and A,*** XLI (16 July 1927) 519–20.

Broch. The Muirs translated Broch's *The Sleepwalkers* (1932) and *The Unknown Quantity* (1935). Willa Muir translated his 'A Passing Cloud' in *Modern Scot* IV (1934) 304–12. In turn Broch translated Muir's poem 'The Threefold Place' (originally 'Transmutation') in *Die Literarische Welt* VIII (2 Sept 1932) 5. See P H Gaskill 'Hermann Broch as a Translator of Edwin Muir' in *New German Studies* IV (Summer 1978) 101–15.

Broch was pleased with this essay, and wrote that 'you express most correctly the structure and intention of *The Sleepwalkers*'.

Carossa. Under the pseudonym 'Agnes Neill Scott' Willa Muir translated Carossa's *A Roumanian Diary* (1929), *A Childhood* (1930), *Boyhood and Youth* (1931) and *Doctor Gion* (1933).

Cary. **R** of *The African Witch* in ***L,*** XV (13 May 1936) 938; of *The Horse's Mouth* in ***L,*** XXXII (5 Oct 1944) 386.

Compton-Burnett. **R** of *More Women than Men* in ***L,*** X (23 Aug 1933) 294; of *Daughters and Sons* in ***L,*** XVII (31 Mar 1937) 622; of *A Family and a Fortune* in ***L,*** XXI (2 Mar 1939) 489; of *Parents and Children* in ***L,*** XXV (5 June 1941) 815; of *Elders and Betters* in ***L,*** XXXI (10 Feb 1944) 166; of *A Father and his Fate* in ***O*** (11 Aug 1957) 13.

Eliot. **R** of *After Strange Gods* in *Spectator* (9 Mar 1934) 378–9; of *The Family Reunion* in *Spectator* (23 Mar 1939) 6; of *Little Gidding* in *New Statesman and Nation,* XXV (20 Feb 1943) 128; essay in *Transition.*

Faulkner. **R** of *As I Lay Dying* in ***L,*** XIV (16 Oct 1935) 681; of *The Wild Palms* in ***L,*** XXI (30 Mar 1939) 701.

Ford. **R** of *A Man Could Stand Up* in ***N and A,*** XL (23 Oct 1926) 116; of *Last Post* in ***N and A,*** XLII (18 Feb 1928) 752.

Forster. **R** of *The Eternal Moment* in ***N and A,*** XLIII (12 May 1928) 184.

Gibbon. **R** of *Cloude Howe* in ***L,*** X (9 Aug 1933) 222; 'An Appreciation' in *Scottish Standard* I (Mar 1935) 23–4 and in *Uncollected Scottish Criticism.*

Goethe. **R** of *Letters of Goethe* in *New Statesman and Nation,* LIII (27 Apr 1957) 545–6. See P H Gaskill 'Edwin Muir and Goethe' in *Publications of the English Goethe Society* XLVIII (1978) 22–51.

Green. **R** of *Party Going* in ***L***, XXII (12 Oct 1939) 734.

Greene. **R** of *It's A Battlefield* in ***L***, XI (21 Feb 1934) 340; of *The Confidential Agent* in ***L***, XXII (28 Sept 1939) 638.

Gunn. **R** of *The Serpent* in *Scots Magazine*, No. 34 (Aug 1943) 382–4 and in *Uncollected Scottish Criticism*.

Hemingway. **R** of *Fiesta* in ***N and A***, XLI (2 July 1927) 450/452; of *Winner Takes Nothing* in ***L***, XI (21 Feb 1934) 340; of *To Have and Have Not* in ***L***, XVIII (27 Oct 1937) 925.

Hölderlin. The essay in this selection is a slightly expanded version of an essay first published in the American *Freeman* VIII (1 Aug 1923) 488–90. See also 'Friedrich Hölderlin' in *The Adelphi* 3 (May 1926) 799–807; two essays in *Essays on Literature and Society*, Muir's poem 'Hölderlin's Journey'; and three essays by P H Gaskill—'Edwin Muir as Critic of Hölderlin' in *Forum for Modern Language Studies* XIV No. 4 (Oct 1978) 345–64; 'Edwin Muir's Friend in Hellerau: Iwar von Lucken' in *German Life and Letters* New Series XXXII No. 2 (Jan 1929) 135–47; and 'Hölderlin and the Poetry of Edwin Muir' in *Forum for Modern Language Studies* XVI No. 1 (Jan 1980) 12–32.

Hutchinson. **R** of *The Unforgotten Prisoner* in ***L***, X (20 Dec 1933) 968; of *The Fire and the Wood* in ***L***, XXIII (27 June 1940) 1211.

Huxley. **R** of *Two or Three Graces* in ***N and A***, XXXIX (12 June 1926) 284; of *After Many a Summer* in ***L***, XXII (26 Oct 1939) 833; essay in *Transition*.

Joyce. **R** of *Finnegan's Wake* in ***L***, XXI (11 May 1939) 1013; essay in *Transition*.

Kipling. **R** of *Debits and Credits* in ***N and A***, XL (9 Oct 1926) 28/30.

Lavin. The two other 'good stories' referred to are *Daylight on Saturday* by J B Priestley, and *Corporal Jack* by David Scott.

Lawrence. **R** of *The Boy in the Bush* in ***N and A***, XXXV (20 Sept 1924) 752; of Frieda Lawrence, *Not I, But the Wind* in *Scotsman* (14 Feb 1935) 13; essay in *Transition*.

Mann. **R** of *The Magic Mountain* in ***N and A***, XLI (2 July 1927) 452; of *Joseph in Egypt* in ***L***, XIX (25 May 1938) 1146; of *Joseph the Provider* in ***L***, XXXIV (9 Aug 1945) 162.

Maugham. **R** of *The Casuarina Tree* in ***N and A***, XL (9 Oct 1926) 28; of *Up at a Villa* in ***L***, XXV (5 June 1941) 815.

Myers. **R** of *The Root and the Flower* in ***L***, XIII (13 Mar 1935) 468; of *Strange Glory* in ***L***, XV (8 Apr 1936) 690. The 'Mr Waugh' referred to is presumably Alex Waugh.

Powys, J. C. **R** of *The Pleasures of Literature* in *Scotsman* (28 Nov 1938) 13.

Powys, T. F. **R** of *Mr Tasker's Gods* in ***N and A***, XXXVI (7 Mar 1925) 780; of *Mockery Gap* in ***N and A***, XXXVII (26 Sept 1925) 767.

Pritchett. 'Mr Bates's novel' is H E Bates *The Poacher*.

Reid. **R** of *The Retreat* in ***L***, XV (8 Apr 1936) 696; of *Peter Waring* in ***L***, XVIII (22 Sept 1937) 1164.

Riding. **R** of *A Trojan Ending* in ***L***, XVII (28 Apr 1987) 832; of *Lives of Wives* in ***L***, XXII (28 Sep 1939) 638.

Rilke. **R** of *Poems 1906 to 1926* in ***O***. (3 Nov 1957) 15.

Simenon. **R** of *Maigret Sits it Out* in ***L***, XXV (19 June 1941) 887; of *Havoc by Accident* in ***L***, XXIX (25 Feb 1943) 250.

Stead. **R** of *Beauties and Faeries* in ***L***, XV (13 May 1936) 938.

Upward. The other three books mentioned are Tilsley's *I'd Hate to be Dead*, Beckett's *Murphy* and M S Johnson's *The Mountain Speaks*.

Walpole. **R** of *The Old Ladies* in ***N and A***, XXXVI (25 Oct 1924) 154; of *John Cornelius* in ***L***, XVIII (22 Sept 1937) 637; of *The Joyful Delaneys* in ***L***, XX (18 Aug 1938) 357.

Waugh. **R** of *A Handful of Dust* in ***L,*** XII (19 Sept 1934) 506; of *Work Suspended* in ***L,*** XXIX (4 Feb 1943) 154.

Woolf. **R** of *To the Lighthouse* in ***N and A,*** XLI (2 July 1927) 450; of *The Years* in ***L,*** XVII (31 Mar 1937) 622; of *A Haunted House* in ***L,*** XXXI (2 Mar 1944) 250; essay in *Transition*.

INDEX